e Due

J. C. to I. J.

Xmas 1914.

PAUL

AND THE

REVOLT AGAINST HIM

PAUL

AND THE

REVOLT AGAINST HIM

BY

WILLIAM CLEAVER WILKINSON

Author of " Some New Literary Valuations "; " Modern Masters of Pulpit
Discourse "; " Daniel Webster : a Vindication, with Other Historical
Essays "; " The Epic of Saul "; " The Epic of Paul ";
" The Epic of Moses "; etc., etc.

———

PHILADELPHIA

THE GRIFFITH & ROWLAND PRESS

BOSTON   CHICAGO   ST. LOUIS
TORONTO, CAN.

A living and life-giving soul! A source
   And origin, exhaustless like the sea,
   Of impact, impulse, movement, energy!
A radiant centre throbbing thick with force,
In pulses of momentum sped their course
   Wherever, down the lines of history,
   Thought has been moulding human destiny!

A glorious voice, unchangeable to hoarse,
   Or mute, but ever ringing loud and clear
Its one great message in the ears of men:
   "Christ Jesus risen, ascended, from His sphere
Above all height, beyond all finite ken,
   Bending to sway a sovereign sceptre here,
And one day to return to earth again!"

PREFACE

MANY readers will remember the story told of some advocate of renown—probably it was Rufus Choate—that after he had addressed a jury in an important case (which, of course, if it was Choate, he won), a friend of his who had listened to his argument rallied him by saying: " Do you know, Mr. Choate, there was one point in your address to the jury that you went over not less than six times?" "Yes, I know that very well," was the reply; "I got six men of the jury the first time I made that point. The rest, all but one man, fell in one after another, as I went on; but to get the twelfth man I had to go over that point, as you noted, up to six times—but on the sixth I got him."

I fear there may be among my readers some so firmly set against the contention of my book—the contention, namely, for Paul as *authoritative* teacher of Christian doctrine—that I shall fail to win them over at last; but, as they will find, if they continue to read, it will not be for lack of the sixth repetition! I do not apologize, but I show that I am aware of the repetitions that occur of certain topics, under varying forms of expression, and answering to different aspects observed from different points of view. Without these repetitions, I could not satisfy myself that I was emulating that trait of Paul which one hostile German critic, with choice of word very happy for his unfriendly purpose, calls

" importunacy " (possibly the felicity is the translator's), but which I should call unquenchable earnestness; so I close my prefatory word by quoting a characteristic importunate utterance of Paul's—which I beg readers to take from me as, with all due respect and with sincere modesty, addressed to them:

" To write the same things to you, to me indeed is not grievous, but for you it is safe."

CONTENTS

PAUL, AND THE REVOLT
AGAINST HIM

CHAPTER I

PAUL THE MAN

THE individual attitude of the present writer is confessedly that of hero-worshiper toward Paul. Paul's
personality has always been exquisitely, irresistibly, at-
tractive to him. That attitude of his will plainly enough
appear throughout the following pages.

The true main motive, however, of the book is not
hero-worship, worthy as, in this case, that motive would
be. Much less is the main motive pure love of historic
truth with desire to vindicate it in the teeth of prevailing
error. That also would be a good motive, and a sufficient.
Both the two motives thus mentioned are indeed present
and active here, but they are subordinated to the main
motive, which is other, deeper, higher.

The main motive is concern for the cause of Christ
Jesus, my Lord, with compelling sense of responsibility
to do my part, humble though it be, toward the rescue
of brother souls whom I see involved in danger through
the prevalence of fatal error around them.

I was asked the other day by a friend of mine what
I thought would be the final effect on the future fortune
of Christianity in the world, if " Paulinism," as he called
the system of Christology and theology imposed by Paul
on the acceptance of the Christian church of nineteen
centuries past, should come to be discredited and discarded. The friend who asked me this question had

committed himself in print to the support of the crusade of revolt against Paul which has occasioned the production and publication of this book. Circumstances prevented my answering his question at the moment, but my friend, if he does me the honor to read what is herein set down, will find the answer that I should have returned had the occasion permitted.

What the man was (or *is,* I feel like saying, Paul is so living still!), what the man himself was against whom the warfare is now waged, that, of course, is a matter of prime importance to the argument of this book. Let us accordingly follow the order of treatment suggested in the title of the volume, and begin, as that title begins, with Paul the Man. Afterward, in due course, we will take up the question of the revolt against him.

Obviously Paul was first of all and most of all a preacher. It is almost startling to think that really Paul was little else than just a preacher! His apostolic office was fulfilled mainly by preaching. He always preached, whether expressing himself by tongue or by pen. Let not the reader then be surprised to find himself confronted at the outset with the figure of a preacher in Paul the Man.

The purpose of this opening chapter is to make a study, somewhat in the spirit of the living present, of this illustrious preacher of apostolic times.

I. THE PARADOX OF PAUL

In entering on this task, we are undoubtedly first struck, and most strongly struck, with the puissant and pungent personality of the man with whom we have to deal. If we recall Phillips Brooks's formula to express the value of the individual preacher, " Truth plus personality," we feel at once that in the case of Paul, however great might be the truth entrusted to the man to deliver, the man himself that delivered the truth would

inevitably be a force, a moment, demanding to be taken
very seriously into account. Beyond question, such a
man as he was would have made himself profoundly felt,
whatever might have been the cause that he espoused.
Indeed Paul did make himself thus felt, first on one
side, and then on the other, of the same cause. The
demonstration therefore is perfect that his final enormous influence, both living and posthumous, is due to
something besides the mere fact that he had the good
fortune to choose the winning side in a cause of supreme
historic importance. If he had chosen in that cause the
side which was destined eventually to lose, Paul would
yet probably have lived in history, alongside of Julian the
Apostate—full peer of that redoubtable opposer of Christianity, though gifted with incalculably less outward advantage than the latter enjoyed for making his efforts in
opposition effective.

The second thing to strike us, in our present study, is
the absoluteness with which this great personality submitted itself, prostrated itself, only not annihilated itself,
before the character, the will, the authority, of another.
Paul at the feet of Jesus is certainly one of the most
striking spectacles to be seen in history. Rightly regarded, that spectacle is argument to the degree of
demonstration for the truth of supernatural Christianity.
There is absolutely no way of accounting for the conversion of Saul the Pharisee into Paul the Christian apostle,
no way of accounting for the continuous subsequent
paradox of a man naturally so high and haughty in
temper as he was, maintaining that historic attitude of
Paul's, the attitude of adoration and of adoring obedience before Jesus—no way, but to suppose the New Testament story of Jesus' resurrection and ascension literally
true. That supposition accounts for it completely; and,
I repeat it, nothing else that man can imagine will. A
lordly personality captive—captive to an unseen Lord;
such is the aspect in which we are compelled to con-

template Paul, when we study him as preacher of the gospel of Jesus Christ.

For, in the preacher that Paul became, both of these two contrasted, yet perfectly reconciled, characters, the native lordliness and the acquired lowliness, are conspicuously evident; as they were also both conspicuously influential in making him become such a preacher. But especially will the prolonged final attitude, on his part, of subjection to Jesus, of rapt and transcendent hero-worshiping devotion to the Ideal Man confessed by him the Son of God with power, be found an important element in the intellectual and spiritual phenomenon presented to us in the preacher Paul. In speaking thus, I make indeed an extravagant understatement. That attitude of prostration before Jesus Christ is the one central controlling fact and force of the apostle Paul's evangelism. The conception exemplified in it of the normal relation in which Christ stands to all human souls as their rightful absolute Sovereign and Lord, gave to Paul the great master principle, the universal regulative law, of his preaching. This will duly appear in its proper place as we proceed with the analysis of our subject.

But we have not yet fully indicated the amazing nature of the spectacle exhibited to history in the apostle Paul's subject and obedient relation to Jesus Christ. Not only was this self-prostrating hero-worshiper himself, as we have seen, a man of supremely ascendant and dominating spirit—a man, in fact, such, in naturally self-asserting will, as to leave it little likely that he would be mastered by any one; he was also full of the pride of conscious genius and conscious high attainment. That is the next thing to strike us in the character of Paul. He was a man of genius, of genius accomplished by sedulous self-culture; and he was haughtily conscious of himself as such. True it is, many among Paul's intellectual acquisitions were of a sort to seem to us Westerns and moderns of comparatively little value. True also, his exercised skill in dialectics was affected with what we may, without disrespect, call a rabbinical quality that makes both its processes and its subsidiary results often almost null to an intelligence cultivated under our own very different conditions. But these considerations, justly weighed, only make more remarkable the solid wisdom that displays itself throughout Paul's utterances, no matter what may be their obsolete forms of expression, as well as the consummate art with which, in his speech, reason wielded logical weapons now, among us at least, no longer in use. Besides the Hebraic culture of which Paul was a master unsurpassed, he had enjoyed, we have hints for believing, a discipline also in Greek literature and philosophy. At any rate, the impression is immediate and overwhelming, that we encounter in Paul a mind of the first order in original gift, and a mind adequately furnished and trained to do its work without waste of power and to the most fruitful effect.

Keeping in our thought these latter additional traits found in Paul, namely, his genius and his culture, with his pride in them both, let us call up again that paradox already spoken of in his character and career—the attitude which on a memorable occasion he suddenly assumed, and which afterward he steadily maintained, of absolute subjection, body, soul, and spirit, to the will of another. We have not yet felt the full proper effect of that paradox. When to the Roman Christians he introduced himself by letter in the words, " Paul, a bond-servant [slave] of Jesus Christ," it was only one outright express confession on Paul's part of the relation to Jesus in which he habitually, even if sometimes tacitly, stood before his hearers in preaching.

Shall we imagine a parallel, to make a little more appreciable the full meaning of this? But it will not be easy to imagine a parallel even approximately adequate. It is somewhat as if, a few years ago, the apostle and high priest of culture and refinement in English letters had staggered his admirers and disciples by writing himself down before the world, " Matthew Arnold, slave of Joe Smith " (the founder of Mormonism). Joe Smith is not more a scorning to the Brahman caste in contemporary culture, than was Jesus of Nazareth to Paul's fellow Pharisees in his time. But Matthew Arnold was neither in gifts nor in reputation a match for what Paul was in relation to his Jewish contemporaries. Imagine then this, as written, or dictated, by Goethe himself, " Goethe, slave of Joe Smith," and you have a suggestion of the paradox it was for Paul to announce himself a " slave of Jesus Christ." But a suggestion only ; for in this second proposed parallel, as also in the first, a very essential element of sufficiency is wanting. Paul was a born man of affairs, a born leader and lord of his fellows. If a modern Julius Cæsar, superadding to the culture and genius of Matthew Arnold or of Goethe the commanding and organizing force of the founder of the Roman Empire, at the crisis and culmination of his self-aggrandizing career, were to scandalize his followers by announcing himself some fine morning " a bond-servant of Joe Smith," that would come nearer providing us the parallel we seek.

I have insisted thus on this point for a reason which will presently appear. But first let us dispose of a question which will naturally have suggested itself. What basis have we, either in contemporary description or in authentic original remains from the preacher's own lips or his hand, on which to found an estimate, at the same time trustworthy and complete enough to be useful, of Paul's preaching, its character and style? Well, it must be confessed that data are not so abundant as were to be wished. But neither, on the other hand, are the data existing so scanty as might at first blush be supposed. True, there is not extant a single fully reported formal sermon of Paul's. But there are sketches and fragments of several, so given as to throw a light clear and full beyond what was naturally to have been looked for, on the probable habitual matter and manner of the preacher. Besides this, we have very clear and satisfactory indication, from a competent reporter, of the line of thought and treatment followed by Paul in discourse on a signal occasion. I refer to the address before Felix and Drusilla. In this case, the narrative describes additionally the effect produced on the chief hearer. Such also is the fact with reference to two other incidents of Paul's oratoric experience, his address on Mars Hill, in Athens, and his speech to the mob from the stairs at the Castle Antonia in Jerusalem—while here also are supplied abstracts or sketches of what Paul said.

If it be objected, ' These are not instances of regular sermons from Paul '; that may be admitted; but one address at least was probably as formal and regular a sermon as it was Paul's usual practice to preach to miscellaneous audiences. Paul, like Jesus, took occasions as he found them, or as they were forced upon him, and preached accordingly; often doubtless with interruption —of question, of challenge, or of dissent—from his hearers. This would be in keeping with the well-known somewhat tumultuary temper and habit of Eastern public assemblies, even those of a comparatively ceremonious character; much more, of those casually, perhaps excitedly, brought together. Such public speaking as that, so called out, is of the most real and living kind in the world; and of all public speaking the kind most likely to furnish fruitful lessons in the art of eloquence. If now we add a reminder of that touching and beautiful address of Paul to the Ephesian elders, readers will see that we are by no means without the material for a fairly full and various examination and study of Paul's characteristics as preacher. Beyond all this, Paul's Epistles are virtual sermons, often best understood when studied as such. And then—what was perhaps least to have been expected, and what also perhaps is least likely to have been duly considered by the ordinary reader of the New Testament—those Epistles contain not only hints, but explicit statements, of the highest value for our purpose in understanding aright and intimately the true matter, method, spirit, and aim of this greatest of merely human preachers.

2. PAUL'S MASTER-THOUGHT

Let us go at once to an inestimably valuable statement of the kind now indicated. Paul had one master-thought and feeling—thought fused in feeling, let us call it—which was ascendant and dominant in his preaching, as it was also in his life. That thought and feeling, that passion of both mind and heart, nay, of conscience and of will no less—for the whole being of Paul was one flame herein— what else was it, what else could it be, but consuming zeal to have the lordship of Christ universally acknowledged by men? The apostle's own personal experience made it impossible that this should not be so. And the evidence of the fact that it was so he has waterlined ineffaceably into the tissue and fabric of his writing. But we are not left to such mere inference, however overwhelmingly strong. Paul has put it into express record and testimony. He says of himself as preacher, " We [I] preach . . . Christ Jesus as Lord."

One is not to read these words without attaching to them their own just and definite meaning. They mean precisely what they say. Paul in them was fixing, in permanent, unchangeable phrase, a statement from which all generations following might know, first, what it was that he preached—it was Christ Jesus; and second, how he preached Christ Jesus—it was as Lord. Not, observe, as Saviour; not as Teacher; not as Example; much less, as Friend, as Brother. Paul preached Christ Jesus as Lord.

We have thus at once reached what is most central and most regulative in the principle and practice of

Paul as preacher—the fact, the threefold fact, first, that he preached a person; second, that that person was Christ; and third, that the aspect or relation in which he preached Christ was the aspect or relation of lordship to men. But are we not staking too much upon a single text? Let us see. When, at Philippi, the frightened and penitent jailer cried out his question, " What must I do to be saved? " how did Paul reply? " Believe on the Lord Jesus." Consider what that reply imports. It requires faith. Yes. It requires faith in a person. Yes. That person is Jesus Christ. Yes. Faith in Jesus Christ as—what? Saviour? No. The jailer's inquiry indeed was for the conditions of salvation. Yes, but the reply did not direct him, in terms, to a Saviour. It directed him to a Lord. " Take Jesus Christ for your Lord, and you will be saved "—that is what in effect it said. Jesus Christ is a Saviour to any man that takes him for Lord.

As thus to sinners repenting, so likewise to Christians, Paul preached forever obedience to Christ. In showing this to be true, I may safely ignore the critical objections that have been raised against the authentic Pauline authorship of the Epistle to the Colossians, and treat that Epistle here as being, what I believe it is indeed, the issue of the one mind and heart known to us in all the tide of time that could have produced such writing, namely, the apostle Paul. Take this, then, as Paul's master direction to Christians for the conduct of life: " Whatsoever ye do, do heartily as to the Lord; . . for ye serve the Lord Christ." I do not forget that this particular instruction was directed especially to the slaves among the Colossian Christians. It was Paul's noble decree of emancipation for those unhappy bondmen. They were to escape servitude to their perhaps cruel masters, by feeling themselves bound in transcendent obligation to a quite different Lord, the same Lord that he himself acknowledged when he wrote those words, or dictated them, " Paul, a slave of Jesus Christ." What exquisite adaptedness of teaching on

Paul's part was thus exemplified! The apostle and they were fellow slaves, bound alike to serve the Lord Christ!

Obedience to Christ as to a Lord having supreme right to command—that is the keynote to Paul's effort, whether for unbelievers or for believers, whether with tongue or with pen. Indeed he expressly describes his mission in the world as having that idea for its comprehensive end and aim. "We [I]," he says, in writing to the Roman Christians, "have received grace and apostleship for obedience to the faith among all nations." Even that "faith," of which Paul has so much to say, is conceived and presented by him as an act, or a state, of obedience to Christ. In the midst of a fervid discussion of the subject of righteousness by faith, Paul speaks of *obeying* the gospel as a thing in his mind equivalent to believing—nay, identical with that. Observe this Pauline consecution of thought: "Not all *obeyed* the gospel. For Esaias saith, Who hath *believed* our report?"

We have discovered the chief thing characteristic of Paul's preaching, when we have fully seen that the omnipresent object of it all was to get Christ obeyed. But we need to understand obedience to Christ in the profound, the all-inclusive, sense in which Paul understood it. It was with Paul no mere outward conformity to specific moral, much less to any ceremonial, command. In Paul's view, there was nothing in all the being of the man that was not bound to the obedience of Christ. To that obedience was to be brought captive every thought. When a preacher has seized this idea, when he has then let this idea seize him and master him, that preacher has gone the farthest that any one step could carry him toward becoming such a preacher as Paul was.

3. PAUL AS TRUSTEE AND STEWARD OF REVELATION FROM CHRIST

After the attitude on Paul's part already now ascertained, of absolute obedience to Christ, next to strike us is a trait in him of even greater importance to distinguish his individual quality among preachers, namely, his sense of peculiar, incommunicable relation to Christ as recipient and trustee of immediate revelation from him. This sense on his part is a note that keys all his communications, as preacher and teacher, to his fellow men. It is impossible for the attentive student to ignore the characteristic in Paul that I thus point out. It is a trait different from mere ardor of conviction. It is a trait different from natural positiveness, self-assertion, spirit of domination. These latter traits also marked Paul as preacher and teacher. But over and above these, supporting these while qualifying them, was an authentic, unmistakable, sense on Paul's part of being recipient and trustee of special, supernatural revelation from Jesus Christ. This would be clear enough from the general tenor of Paul's utterance; but he has put the matter into express and emphatic statement—statement so express, so emphatic, as to warrant us in saying that language is not capable of asserting such a claim, if Paul has not asserted this claim for himself. To the Galatians he wrote: " The gospel which was preached by me is not according to man; for I also did not receive it from man, nor was I taught it, but I received it through revelation of Jesus Christ." There follows a solemn attestation, nay, an *oath* sworn by him to the truth of his words on this point: " Now as to the things which I write to you, behold, before God, I lie not." If Paul was a sane man, and also not a conscious perjured liar, he preached and taught under the influence of direct supernatural communication as to what he preached and taught, received immediately from Jesus Christ himself. The watchword current now, " Back to Christ! " when it is used—as it is sometimes, perhaps most commonly, used—for the comparative discrediting of Paul, as a source of Christian doctrine, has the effect, if not the purpose, of disloyalty both to Paul and to Christ. If Paul was a sane man, and if he told the truth, then there is no good sense in calling us back from him to the Evangelists, for our information as to what Christ's gospel is. Paul is as good a reporter as is Matthew, for instance. If there is any discrimination between them to be made, Paul is even a better reporter than Matthew. He was a finer intelligence, and he was more thoroughly trained. He had as much sympathy with his Master. He reported apparently with less interval of time than did Matthew after the receiving of the thing to be reported. What point is there in favor of Matthew to place him superior to Paul as representative of Christ through tongue or pen? That is, always provided Paul was neither insane nor mendacious. "Back to Christ!"? Yes, but to Christ as Paul represented Christ, not less than to Christ as Christ was represented by the Evangelists. Unless Paul's prodigious and beneficent influence on history was exerted by a lunatic or a liar, we are shut up to admit, what stares us in the face from every page of Paul's writing, that he worked his work as one supernaturally communicated with by the risen and ascended Christ. This is a brand broad and deep on all we have from the brain of Paul.

4. PAUL AS DEPUTY OF CHRIST

Another conspicuous characteristic in Paul as preacher is the tone of authority with which he speaks. This tone of authority is no bold mere assumption on his part; and nowhere is it for a moment felt to be such. So far from being an assumption, an arrogation, prompted by pride or by consciousness of superiority or of worth, it is always the sign in him, the unmistakable sign, of a sense which he has—a sense which has him, say rather—of an investiture put upon him that he may in no wise rid himself of. He could not divest himself of it if he would. It is a trust received from God. He is helplessly the steward of it. But of course I do not mean that his stewardship is against his own will. His will joyfully consents, but his will consents humbly. He wonders and adores that he should have been thus chosen. He expressly recognizes that it is a " grace," as well as an " apostleship," that he has received. But he never lets his sense of the grace overcome his sense of the apostleship.

The extraordinary accent of authority coupled with humility, thus found in Paul, is vitally related to that in the man which was first to attract our attention in the present paper, namely, his attitude of absolute obedience to Christ. In truth, the exercise of authority on his part is less in spite of his humility than because of his humility. It is an essential part of obedience with him. He could not obey Christ without using authority; for he is bidden use it. Hence the nigh unparalleled example that Paul gives us of authority without wavering but equally without assumption. It is really mere steadiness of obedience. There is no self-assertion in it, no egotism. In form, Paul does indeed now and again assert himself. But, in spirit, there is still no self-assertion; for it is Christ in him, or it is he in Christ, that speaks, and the speaking is for Christ and not for Paul. With perfect simplicity, in absolute sincerity, indignantly, he asks in self-effacement, " Was Paul crucified for you? "

Of course the authority that Paul thus purely exerts relates itself not only to his spirit of obedience toward Christ, but also to the consciousness that he inalienably has of being in a peculiar relation to Christ as recipient and trustee of immediate revelation from him. This latter relation to Christ Paul claimed for himself with definition and with emphasis such, that if his claim of it had been false, the false claim itself—that alone— would inevitably and justly have defeated his influence on the world. That his influence, in quality as in quantity, was not defeated is, wisely considered, proof approaching the point of demonstration, that his claim of peculiar authority supernaturally bestowed was a true claim.

We have considered two capital characteristics of Paul as preacher, such in their nature that they cannot be presented for emulation on the part of the preachers of to-day. No one now can speak—and speak with a sane consciousness like the sane consciousness which Paul had—of speaking by direct, unmediated communication of truth from Christ; and no one now can speak in the exercise of such authority as was Paul's.

5. PAUL AS A BELIEVER

But Paul's absolute obedience to Christ may be emulated; as also may be emulated Paul's absolute fidelity to the idea of making obedience to Christ from all men the comprehensive object of preaching. And I have now to bring forward another trait of Paul as preacher, in which he may well be emulated. Paul preached in a tone of intense personal conviction. It might seem that Paul's sense of peculiar relation to Christ as Christ's oracle, should have rendered faith, on his part—faith rising to the degree of intense personal conviction—a matter of course, a matter, as it were, of necessity. But such was not the case. That this is true is shown by Paul's own confession. He says, " We [I] also believe and therefore also we speak." This is the language, not of authority, nor of present overcoming consciousness divinely impressed upon the user of the language, that he is the inspired and infallible organ of revelation from God; it is the language of faith, of personal conviction. Of the same character is the language of that magnificent climax, ending the eighth chapter of Romans, which, by sheer virtue of its unsurpassable eloquence—an eloquence that indeed transgresses the bounds of mere eloquence and passes into the realm of sublime poetry—has become one of the most familiar commonplaces of literature: " For I am *persuaded* that neither death, nor life, nor angels, nor principalities, nor things present, nor things to come, nor powers, nor height, nor depth, nor any other creature, shall be able to separate us from the love of God, which is in Christ Jesus our Lord." The triumphant, the soaring, quality of the faith that thus expresses itself, must not blind us to the fact, that it is faith, true human faith, not an easy acceptance on Paul's part of peculiar divine inspiration. Let us make no mistake. Paul, we must suppose, had as much opportunity, and as much need, of exercising faith, as has any ordinary Christian. He had to have faith in order to receive from Christ the communication that Christ wished to impart. Paul's faith was the ever-open receptacle for the treasures of truth of which he thus became steward. He preached, therefore, with faith, with conviction, vivid and vivific, and not simply as a possessed, and, so to speak, involuntary, mouthpiece for the Spirit of God.

6. PAUL AS A DYNAMIC

Born of his conviction was that inextinguishable zeal which was a further characteristic of Paul as preacher. Paul's zeal was as tinder to his energy. The two together engendered an incomparable locomotive force lodged in him—like the enclosed and enkindled powder that bears the rocket on its aspiring parabola into the upper air. There was never another such unresting embodiment, as was Paul, of disinterested zeal in propagandism enlisted on behalf of an apparently hopeless cause. When just consideration is given to all the conditions of Paul's case, his single-handedness, his nakedness of apparent weapon against such a conspiracy of hostile powers, his poverty in material resources of whatever kind, his physical ill-health and weakness, the arrests and imprisonments to which he was subject, the indignities, the cruelties, he suffered—when these things are duly considered, and over against them is placed the enormous, the yet unexhausted, the apparently inexhaustible, success that he achieved, making the world and making history new, I confidently submit that no parallel to Paul can be found

among men. I thus speak, counting out of calculation for
the moment the supernatural coefficient that multiplied
the results of Paul's activity. I am far from ignoring
that supernatural coefficient. But, remembering it well
and according to it much, I still reckon Paul's personal
achievement, quality and quantity both considered, something that surpasses what can fairly be credited to any
other individual human force working in history. Alexander the Great, Julius Cæsar, Napoleon Bonaparte, are
not worthy to be named in the comparison. And it was
the extraordinary, the amazing, *vis viva,* pure energy set
on fire of zeal, in Paul, that—exceptional Divine assistance being for the moment left out of the account—
should perhaps mainly be esteemed the secret of his
power. Such a heart-beat of force, forever equal, and a
little more than equal, to its need, as throbs in Paul, like
the pulse of a great ocean steamer's engine making her
whole bulk tremble! It might seem that the energy thus
attributed to Paul belonged to the man, rather than to the
preacher. But the man and the preacher are always in-
separable. And what differences preachers one from
another, with respect to the total volume of influence
that they finally exert, is, I am persuaded, as much as
any one thing, the original endowment of *energy* which
they put into their work. Paul's prodigious energy as a
man was not only an indispensable, but a very important,
element in his power as a preacher.

7. PAUL AS A THINKER

I have already alluded to the advantage belonging to
Paul in the possession of an intellect thoroughly trained
and furnished for the work that it had to do. Paul had
thought long and deeply ; and the quality that only long and
deep thought can give to a man's intellectual product, is
everywhere recognizable in Paul's writing. We are quite
warranted in assuming that the character of his preaching
corresponded. It was a thinker, not a mere homilist, that

so easily struck out that fine generalization with its illumining comment, which surprises and delights us as we read the thirteenth chapter of Romans: " He that loveth his neighbor hath fulfilled the law. For this, Thou shalt not commit adultery, Thou shalt not kill, Thou shalt not steal, Thou shalt not covet, and if there be any other commandment, it is summed up in this word, namely, Thou shalt love thy neighbor as thyself. Love worketh no ill to his neighbor: love therefore is the fulfilment of the law." Luminous general observations open vistas and prospects into wide realms of truth, at frequent intervals throughout Paul's writings. But what need of particular instances to illustrate Paul's intellectual height and breadth, and the richness and ripeness of his thought? It suffices to remember that one of the very greatest intellectual, as well as spiritual, achievements in history, I mean the erection of Christianity, out of Judaic narrowness and sterility, into a world-wide religion fit for all time, was due, by eminence, to the sympathetic comprehension by Paul, as a thinker, of his Divine Master's thought and purpose for the rescue and elevation of mankind.

8. PAUL AS MAN OF AFFAIRS

But, not less, Paul the thinker was also Paul the man of affairs. There is no closet atmosphere about his writing; and still more impossible was it that there should be any such atmosphere about his preaching. He knew *men,* as one who was himself a fellow man; not simply *man,* as being a philosopher. He lived and thought and felt and spoke in a world of concrete realities. Hence the omnipresent pertinency, the practical adaptedness, of his teaching. He had instant infallible sagacity of the situation, the need. " Making a difference "—his own words of advice to the young preacher—might be taken as the maxim and motto on which he himself practised.

Out of this indescribable realness, livingness, in Paul,

B

sprang his instinct and habit of availing himself of opportunity. It was a perfectly conscious aim with him to be, in the best sense of that ambiguous word, an alert opportunist. He said of himself that he became all things to all men in order that he might by all means save some. "Redeeming the opportunity" (that is, making thrifty use of the passing occasion's particular chance), a combination of words having, where it occurs, the force of a precept, is another expression from Paul's pen indicative of the value he set on the idea of matching the moment with just that moment's fit word.

Of close kin to the trait in Paul's preaching last named, yet distinguishable from that, and worthy of separate note, was his habit of dealing, as Christ also dealt, with individual souls, not less—perhaps more—than with masses of men. This might seem to be a pastoral, rather than a homiletic, habit; and such no doubt it predominantly was. But no preacher who is also a pastor, as was Paul, can fail to have his preaching profoundly affected by the pastoral quality; and that quality is, discriminating attention to individual souls. Paul emphatically testifies to the particularity of his concern for those to whom he brought the gospel. This testimony is marked with repetition, as well as with emphasis, of statement; and it is very instructive. To the Ephesian elders meeting him at Miletus, Paul said: "Ye know . . . how . . . I . . . have taught you publicly and from house to house. . . I ceased not to warn every one night and day." To the Colossians, he wrote: "Whom [that is, Christ] we preach, warning every man and teaching every man, that we may present every man perfect in Christ Jesus." Nothing could exceed the individualizing spirit of such faithfulness in preaching as Paul thus describes, claiming it to be the habit of his own apostleship. To the Thessalonians: "Ye know how we exhorted and comforted and charged every one of you, as a father does his children." Paul then did not deal with men as it were by wholesale merely; he aimed his lasso at individual hearts and consciences. To change the figure, his discourse was like a net, flung over his hearers, that captured them one by one, each, so to speak, in a separate mesh specially prepared for him and specifically aimed at him. How completely that instinct, and that cultivated habit, in Paul, of which I shall speak presently, I mean his quality of gentleman, saved this intent individualizing of his hearers from degenerating into offensive personality, the signal example of his address before Felix well shows. Here Paul gave to a cruelly unjust, a grossly licentious, Roman ruler a discourse on righteousness, on self-control, on impending judgment. He was faithful enough to make his guilty hearer tremble; but at the same time gentlemanlike enough not to affront him.

It need hardly be said that naturally such preaching as that thus described had for its object practical results immediately to follow. I have just now arrested my writing to take, by rapid perusal of the narrative, a fresh impression of the character of the history recorded in the Acts, in that part of the history which is concerned with the activities of Paul. There is nothing more striking about it than the intense livingness that throbs in it and the abounding fruitfulness of the apostle's labors. He went like a reaper through a field white to the harvest. He appears everywhere in the act of gathering sheaves. If he struck a region or a class of people that yielded no return of fruit to his labors, he went elsewhere. He was not satisfied unless he saw of the travail of his soul. This spirit of desire in him tended irresistibly to its own fulfilment. It will always do so in every preacher's case. It was by virtue of his quality as man of affairs—a quality now displaying itself in the spiritual sphere—that Paul was preacher and pastor such as I have described.

Ancient eloquence in general seems not to have indulged, so much as modern eloquence (especially perhaps among English-speakers) tends to indulge, in quest of illustration to enliven and enlighten discourse. Paul, accordingly, judged by current standards, could not be said to abound in illustrations; and he was far enough from being the master in this kind that Jesus was. Still he did illustrate strikingly, and this, as in contrast with all the other New Testament writers and speakers, deserves to be especially noted of Paul. Witness his consummate analogy adduced in setting forth the truth concerning the fact of the resurrection. Witness again his analogy of the human body with its various parts to the church of Christ, whole and one, yet made up of individual members. Then too, his vivid imagery drawn from the equipment and discipline of the Roman soldier.

9. PAUL AS A GENTLEMAN

A man with *savoir-vivre* so abundant, tact so swift and so versatile, as were Paul's, could of course not be wanting in the social accomplishment of good manners. But Paul had a courtesy that went much deeper, and was therefore, much surer, than good manners. He was a gentleman to the very heart of him. To be sure, it is from Peter—from whom less perhaps than from Paul, was to have been expected such an instruction—that we have the precept " Be courteous." The school of Christ proved to Peter, as it proves to all who are willing learners in it, an admirable school of good manners. But Paul, in his more wide-sweeping way, says the same thing, and more, when he says, " Render to all their dues," which is the very definition of politeness. And Paul, under all circumstances, exemplified in his own conduct what he thus taught. Once indeed he was provoked into a form of disrespect toward a Jewish ruler who had outraged him beyond endurance. But how quick, how perfect, how consummately high-bred, the self-recovery, and the amends that he made! The moment's lapse—if lapse it ought to be called, that fine indignation against insult and wrong—served but the purpose of

bringing out into stronger relief the exquisite self-control
which was Paul's habit, and which is the basis of courtesy.
Paul had so much unavoidable occasion to challenge men's
passions and to cross men's prejudices, that it was
immense gain to him not to affront anybody needlessly.
The present writer, during a period of his life in which it
was a part of his duty to advise young preachers, proposed to them as a maxim of wise pulpit discourse the
following: "Yield to your audience in every respect
save that one respect in which it is your present object to
get your audience to yield to you." Paul exemplified this
precept in his practice.

I shall seem to have been describing a negative rather
than a positive quality in thus attributing to Paul the grace
of high breeding. In fact, however, Paul sought the good
will of those with whom he was dealing—self-evidently
always seeking it for their advantage and not for his
own—by a positive practice of his, proper to him as a
well-bred man, which deserves separate mention. He was
a generous bestower of praise—not indeed an undiscrim-
inating, but a generous, bestower. The generous measure with which he bestowed commendation might indeed
sometimes almost have made Paul seem to be a flatterer;
but he always praised with such exquisite delicate tact
as could be born only of innermost truth and sincerity.
And then, besides, commendation from him had a certain
peculiar character of its own, fitted to make the persons
commended feel, less that they deserved it, than that
they should be glad to deserve it better; and this all the
more because they likewise felt perforce that the commendation was bestowed to that very end—not merely
for the sake of giving them pleasure, much less for the
sake of winning their favor. Preachers may learn from
Paul a fruitful lesson both in the practical value of praise,
and in the holy art of bestowing praise. Note the infinite
grace and delicacy with which, for instance, in the following, from the Epistle to the Romans, the didactic

earnestness, the magisterial superiority, of the apostle is modulated into the urbanity and complaisance of the fellow disciple and the peer. Who could resist the sweet seduction of praise so almost unobservably insinuated? Who could fail to be inspired by it and uplifted? "For I long to see you, that I may impart unto you some spiritual gift, to the end ye may be established; that is [and now as if the writer would change his tone and put himself alongside of those to whom he was writing, in a relationship of equal reciprocal helpfulness playing back and forth between him and them], that I may be comforted together with you by the mutual faith both of you and me."

What a note of pathetically joyful appeal by praise is sounded in this rhythmical verse from the heart of Paul, in his Epistle to the Philippians: "Therefore, my brethren, beloved and longed for, my joy and crown, so stand fast in the Lord, my dearly beloved"! There is no praise equal to the praise which consists in an outburst of affectionate exclamation like that.

Was there a danger near—the danger of conceding too much, of being over-complaisant, even of seeming subservient? Paul avoided this danger; still, not so as to escape the charge from his enemies of loving the favor of men—in short, of being a trimmer. He was aware of being thus accused, and when, on one capital occasion, he felt obliged to use sharper language than he liked ever to do to his Christian brethren, he alluded to the false accusation. "Do I now please men?" he asked, with a moment's indignant, but not ungentle, sarcasm. Immediately recovering his more natural tone, of candor and earnestness, he appealed to his life, to his apostleship, to his relation of bond-slave to Christ, for his vindication against the charge. If my object had been to please men, he said, I certainly should not have gone about to accomplish my object by making myself a bond-servant of Christ. *That* was not *then* the road to popularity!

Such was Paul's sensitive fondness for deferring to others, for being complaisant, that, when he had imperative need to use sternness, he found it easier to do so in letters than in face-to-face contact with men. This habit of soft-heartedness in him sometimes prompted those who opposed Paul to seek their ends by making, to the persons concerned, a certain representation about the Apostle which has been strangely misunderstood by many readers of the New Testament, even by many New Testament commentators. Thus Paul's opponents told the Christians of Corinth that however stern he might be in his letters, they need have no apprehension of his being seriously severe when he should actually be present among them. He makes great demonstration beforehand, they said, of what he will do when he comes; but he does not carry out his threats. His letters are formidable; but his behavior when he is personally present does not at all correspond. As the passage is translated, "His letters are weighty and powerful, but his bodily presence is weak and his speech contemptible." Paul himself cites this language, to assure the Corinthians that, if need continue, he will in truth show himself when he comes all that is warned and threatened in his letters. The phrase "bodily presence," which the context proves to mean only presence in the body, as distinguished from absence, has misled students to find here an allusion to Paul's personal appearance and to his style of elocution—both which ideas are remote from the thought of the passage. Of Paul's physical appearance we really know nothing, and nothing of his style of elocution—one remarkable trait of the latter excepted, a trait to be noted hereafter in its proper place and order. We certainly have no reason to think that Paul's physical equipment for oratory was in any respect despicable; though had this been the case, it would only increase the wonder of his apostolic achievement.

In a subsequent chapter of this book certain names

will occur of rationalizing German critics of Paul, to
whom I accord sincere praise for their candor, their
scholarship, and their thoroughgoing mastery of their
subject. Among these names that of Weinel is eminent.
Yet even Weinel makes the mistake that I have alluded
to, in interpreting the passage in Paul's Epistle about the
contrast between his " letters " and his " bodily presence."
The point is of no great importance, but it is curious,
as it is instructive, to note that while Weinel breaks freely
with tradition and is fresh, independent, individual, in
his treatment of Paul's Epistles as " sources," where
they can be made to subserve his purpose of destroying
the great apostle's *authority,* he contentedly falls in with
the utterly ungrounded, unwarranted, traditional misunderstanding of the passage just now in question, making
it refer to Paul's personal appearance—" a man who
seemed at first sight insignificant and ugly!" are
Weinel's words. By the way, Weinel in this connection
carelessly treats what Paul quotes from his enemies
against himself, as if it was Paul in his own person that
said it; " he emphasizes," Weinel says, " that he himself
was no trained orator." Carelessly again, Weinel says:
" His adversaries *tell him* scoffingly his letters are weighty
and strong, but his bodily presence is weak and his speech
contemptible "—whereas it is not " him " that they tell,
but others, viz., Paul's Corinthian disciples.

10. PAUL AS PROPHET

I mean " prophet " in the Old Testament Hebrew sense
of the word. Having spoken so strongly—not too
strongly—of Paul's instinct, and habit, and skill, of ad-
justing himself to occasion and need, I must now not
fail to speak as strongly—and too strongly I could not
speak—of his eventual unswerving fidelity, both in word
and in deed, to his convictions of truth and of duty.
Nobody could flame hotter than he in denouncing in-
iquity; nobody could use language more towering, more

overawing, in vindication of what was vital to the doctrine of Christ. "Though we or an angel from heaven should preach unto you any gospel other than that which we have preached unto you, let him be anathema"—so he wrote to the Galatians. He dictated the letter. One can imagine the inspired man dilating his form and his stature, and raising his hands in commination to heaven, as, pacing his room, he poured out those burning words. Then, lest the very passion of those words should, by raising a suspicion of hyperbole, partly defeat their purpose, hear him immediately repeat them: "As we have said before, so say I now again: If any man preacheth unto you any gospel other than that which ye received, let him be anathema"—as if to give notice that not one jot was to be abated from the fulness of the meaning of that which he had thus so startlingly protested. I have no need to cite anything in illustration of Paul's power and his will in invective; but that branding imprecation of his upon Elymas, the sorcerer at Paphos in Cyprus, springs to my mind, "O full of all guile and all villainy, thou son of the devil, thou enemy of all righteousness," etc.—words so fierce in their energy that, as one reads them even now in translation, they almost seem capable themselves of working by their own unaided virtue the blinding effect that followed them—yet how carefully weighed, how restrained withal, they seem, as if "half his power he put not forth"!

But Paul greatly preferred to use gentleness; and his gentleness has always a certain fine enhancement of effect, due to a sense inspired all the time that the user of it had weapons at command that he might employ to compel, or to punish, where he could not persuade. What eloquence there is in an appeal like the following: "Now I Paul myself beseech you by the meekness and gentleness of Christ"! "I Paul myself beseech"! Paul seems conscious of something paradoxical in what he is saying, or rather in the attitude he here assumes. That a man like him, a man so sensitively alive to the just demands of his own character—that he, Paul himself, should appear in the posture and act of one "beseeching"! And then, as if to say, It is not I, the natural Paul; I "beseech you by the meekness and gentleness of Christ"! How exquisite, how inimitable, how like Paul—Paul alone, of all men!

II. PAUL AS AN ETHICIST

Strangely enough, Paul's popular reputation is perhaps chiefly that of one who by eminence and by preference was a logician. This is due probably to the disproportionate and distorting use which the systematic theologians have made of Paul's writings. He does indeed reason in them—after the manner natural to a man of his race, and his time, and his mental training. But Matthew Arnold, sadly as he failed in criticizing Paul, was quite right in insisting that such writing as the Apostle's was not dogma, but literature. As already suggested, Paul *preached* in his Epistles; he did not construct a theological system in them. Still, there was the substance and there was the effect of argumentation in Paul's representations of the gospel. In other words, there was an intellectual basis to his discourse. If Paul had not been so gravely misrepresented as predominantly logical in his mental make-up and method, I should have felt it necessary to say, with the emphasis which just proportion seemed to me to require, that an important element of his preaching was the appeal in it to reason and judgment. As it is, I need only mention the undoubted fact, and try to abate the estimate generally prevailing of its relative importance in a true appreciation of Paul. He was indeed a doctrinal preacher. But he was still more ethical than doctrinal. His doctrine was for the sake of conduct. His epistolary sermons will, in important instances, be found to hinge their whole inculcation on some connective word or phrase that turns the discourse from doctrinal exposition to insistence on right behavior. Thus, in the Epistle to the Ephesians, after three chapters of lofty doctrine, the pivotal word "therefore" carries over the discourse to inculcation of practice corresponding to the doctrine. "I, therefore, the prisoner of the Lord, exhort you to walk worthy of the calling with which ye were called." The motive everywhere is love to Christ, born of Christ's love to men. It is Christ's atoning love, his love shown in sacrifice of himself, his vicarious love. "Who loved me, and gave himself up for me," is the sort of language that Paul characteristically used. To the Ephesian elders he spoke of the "Church of God" as purchased by God with his own blood. Such language makes Paul's ethical teaching differ by the whole heaven from the ethical teaching of those who treat Jesus as a mere Teacher, and not as a suffering Saviour. It is noticeable that even when Paul seems most purely theological, when, for example, he is setting forth his master doctrine of justification by faith, he expresses himself in language determined by his favorite principle of obedience. Thus he speaks of persons not "submitting" themselves to the righteousness of God. He conceived of the doctrine practically. Saving faith was an act and attitude of obedience.

12. PAUL AS A MAN OF SENTIMENT

I am led naturally now to the naming of a further trait of first importance in Paul's preaching—a trait which has indeed already been shown, as could not but be the case, in occasional glimpses throughout these pages, but which has been purposely reserved, for full and fit signalization, to the conclusion of the present chapter. No one whose attention has been held to read what has herein previously been said and implied about Paul's just intellectual rank among men, will commit the mistake of imagining that I underestimate his gifts of mind, when I say, as I do say, that after all it was Paul's heart, almost more than his brain, that made him the preacher that he was. If we may judge from the documents in evidence, his was the greatest and the tenderest heart—by far the greatest and the tenderest heart—that beat in the breast of any one of the apostles of Christ. It was Paul's power of love and of all lovely emotions, quite as much as it was his intelligence, that enabled him so sympathetically, beyond all peers of his own time, or of any time since, to take up the thought and feeling of his Lord.

It is not too much to say that the " mind " of Christ—that is, the peculiar doctrine and spirit of Christ—is exhibited in Paul with such a fulness of varied application to life, that the rich and beautiful representations of the four Evangelists would be incalculably less effective than they are, if they were without that inspired apostolic commentary to interpret and apply them. Christ chose with marvelous wisdom, when he chose Paul to be his apostle to the Gentiles. We dishonor Christ when we seek to honor him by disparaging Paul in comparison with the Evangelists. We could scarcely better afford to dispense with Paul's Epistles, than we could afford to dispense with the Gospels. And, rightly read, those Epistles present Paul to us as a great magnetic heart, charged full from Christ with power to move a mighty brain, to sway an imperious will, to subdue an importunate conscience—in short, to swing a whole majestic manhood, unswerving through a lifetime, along an orbit of joyful, harmonious obedience to a Master loved and adored as at once human and Divine. Yes, let us not fear to say it—for it is the truth—Paul was markedly an emotional preacher.

This we know, not only from contemporary narrative, but from Paul's own abundant confession, nay, profession and testimony. For this great man was emotional to the degree of frequent, if not habitual, capitulation to tears in his preaching. Such meaning seems unmistakably implied in this from his address of farewell to the Ephesian elders: " Watch, and remember that by the space of three years I ceased not to warn every one night and day with tears." That is one only of two allusions made by him, in the course of the same address, to his own tears. Even in writing his letters—and therefore without the incitement to emotion furnished by the presence of a sympathetic and responsive audience—Paul, he himself tells us, had fits of weeping. He repeatedly appeals to his tears in witness of his love, his longing, and his earnestness. To the Corinthians, in his second letter, he said: " Out of much affliction and anguish of heart [this refers to a previous occasion that had required severity from him] I wrote unto you with many tears." Then, as if not thus to excite in them a painful sympathy for himself, he adds, with an inimitable delicacy characteristic of Paul alone: " Not that ye should be grieved, but that ye might know the love which I have more abundantly unto you." Once more, in his letter to the Christians of Philippi, he writes: " Many walk, of whom I have told you often, and now tell you even weeping, that they are the enemies of the cross of Christ."

Of course, due allowance is to be made for the naturally more demonstrative impulse and habit of the East, as contrasted with the phlegm and self-repression of our race. But the difference is not all a difference of race and of climate. Paul is the only one of the apostles of whom such emotional outbreaks appear to have been characteristic. Peter indeed, on one memorable occasion, " wept bitterly "; but that, so far as the record enables us to judge, was a solitary exception for Peter; and it appears a case without parallel in the experience of any other apostle, save Paul. In truth, Peter's case does not, even for that one exceptional occasion of his weeping, constitute any parallel to Paul's case. Peter " wept bitterly," for the tears he shed—noble, affectionate tears though they were—were also, in part, tears of remorse and of shame. Paul's tears were altruistic, vicarious, sacrificial; he wept sweetly rather than " bitterly."

Now I am quite ready to admit that Paul's readiness to shed tears might justly be reckoned not very significant—if indeed it were not rather even to be reckoned significant of weakness on his part—except for a certain highly important interpretative fact which must be taken into account in connection. That fact is this: Paul habitually spoke and wrote under an influence of emotion in his heart such that tears were not unfrequently the inevitable expression of it. Paul's tears were not the easy outflow of a shallow sensibility. They marked the culmination and climax of a great elemental passion in his soul—a tenth wave, so to speak, of the sea in storm. Whatever Paul thought he thought passionately, whatever he believed he believed passionately; in short, he was passionate in whatever he did.

I cannot be misunderstood to mean that Paul was a creature of unreasoning impulse, or that he was blindly impetuous and heady in a frenzy of zeal. On the contrary, no man was more considerate than he. But he moved, when he did move, with his whole heart. The entire man was engaged. Still, no word less intense than "passionate" would adequately express the fervor of the movement in which, with Paul, both heart and brain were perpetually astir. Not that he could justly be described as lacking in capacity of repose. But his repose he found in the absolute unobstructedness of uniform advance toward a goal. It was a peace like the peace of God, which is reconciled, we know, with incessant activity. "My Father worketh hitherto," Jesus said. It was Paul who taught: "Let the peace of God ["Christ" rather, instead of "God," should perhaps be the reading] rule in your hearts." That teaching was out of a spirit in the teacher that had itself realized the peace recommended. Passion reconciled with peace, was Paul's experience. His love of Christ was a passion. His love of his fellow Jews was a passion. His love of all men was a passion. He adored passionately. Witness the fountain-jets of doxology that every now and then, unexpectedly, in the midst of his Epistles, burst like the vent of an artesian well out of the levels of quasi-logical discussion. It was a passionate heart adoring, that forced them forth. Nobody reads Paul aright, who does not feel the oceanic ground-swell of emotion that continually heaves underneath the words. And in his preaching, beyond doubt, the passion was manifold more than it could be in his writing. No cold-hearted logician, like what Calvin seems, was Paul. And then the infinite, all-loving condescensions with which this great man stooped to the state of the lowly about him! How he ministered to the slave! How he toiled with his hands for his own support while he preached! " These hands," he eloquently called the Ephesian elders to witness, " have ministered to my necessities, *and* to those that were with me." (I could not refrain from italicizing that conjunction—lest some reader should partly miss the implication it introduces.) His love was no cloistered, seclusive, serene sentiment supported by mystic contemplation. It was a hard-working, practical, ministrant affection.

When I think of this man with his magnificent gifts, devoted, all of them, laboriously devoted, to the self-sacrificing service of his fellow men in lifelong absolute, adoring obedience to the crucified Nazarene, recognized by him as the Son of God with power; when I think of his claims to be recipient and trustee of unmediated revelation straight from Christ himself—claims that must be acknowledged as valid, unless they were either a wild hallucination or a monstrous lie; when I think of all this, and then hear men crying, " Back to Christ from Paul! " I feel like replying to them: ' Nay, but back from the Paul of your false conception to the real Paul of the Acts and the Epistles; and, through this Paul, nearer and ever nearer to that Christ whom he, more perfectly than any other of the sons of men, knew and loved and represented in word and in deed! '

13. PAUL AS AT ONCE A BUSINESS MAN AND A MYSTIC

Two more characteristics, paradoxically united in the apostle Paul as preacher, must still be taken into account before our analysis of his extraordinary personality and genius can be considered even approximately complete. Paul was at once a master of administrative detail—that is, a practical business man—and a mystic.

In claiming thus for Paul that he possessed qualifications of a thorough business man, I have not in mind that large capacity of organization belonging to him, which gave him success in establishing churches and in maintaining effective oversight of them through suitable subordinate agents selected and directed by himself. This gift and skill of his I have already adverted to, in speaking of him as an accomplished man of affairs. But Paul, to such organific power of statesmanship, superadded a certain other talent—a talent far humbler indeed, yet most useful, namely, the sagacity to perceive what was needed in the way of means and methods for the carrying out of designs projected. What other man than Paul could preach, as Paul could preach, the duty of almsgiving, by ennobling appeals to motives the highest, the deepest, the most elemental? The climax of such appeals from Paul was finely characteristic of the man that he was: "For ye know the grace of our Lord Jesus Christ, how though he was rich, for your sake he became poor, that ye through his poverty might become rich." Yet he did not leave it to eloquence, even overmastering eloquence like this, to produce its effects unaided. He generated the motive power in superabundance, but then he did not neglect to provide the wheels, the bands, and all the mechanism necessary, to transmit that power to the point of fruitful application in actual work. It was Paul who, in just a pregnant line or two of one of his letters, struck out the plan for systematic giving, which is now almost universally acknowledged to be, for both

its immediately productive, and its permanently instructive, purpose, the most effective plan conceivable by the
wit of man (1 Cor. 16: 1-4) :

" Now concerning the collection for the saints, as I
gave order to the churches of Galatia, so also do ye.
Upon the first day of the week let each one of you lay
by him in store, as he may prosper, that no collections
be made when I come. And when I arrive, whomsoever
ye shall approve, them will I send with letters to carry
your bounty unto Jerusalem; and if it be meet for me
to go also, they shall go with me."

In quoting thus from his language a little more than
was absolutely necessary to set out Paul's plan for systematic giving, I have had a conscious object. I wished
to let my readers notice in what manner, with what
admirable business foresight, circumspection, and tact,
Paul arranges for the sending of the Corinthians' be-
nevolences to their proper destination in Jerusalem. The
Corinthian Church was to elect messengers, and Paul
would equip these messengers with letters of introduction
from his own hand. (The meaning may be that the
credential letters should issue from the church; but I
have preferred the marginal rendering, which, as I re-
consider this point, I find to be also the preference of
the American revisers.) And he would even go himself,
if it seemed desirable; but in no case alone, or as a sub-
stitute for the messengers elected by the Corinthian
Church; these men should by all means accompany him.

The reason for such precaution on Paul's part would
have been obvious enough; but we are not left to infer it.
In a subsequent letter to the same church, the Corinthian,
the apostle expressly states his reason (2 Cor. 8: 20) :
" Avoiding this," he says, " that any man should blame us
in the matter of this bounty which is ministered by us."
It should be left in no man's power to hint that perhaps
Paul converted the gifts meant for the distressed Christians in Jerusalem in some part to his own personal use

c

and advantage. Then follow these words, worthy to be written in letters of gold as a maxim of prudence for every trustee of charitable gifts: " For we take thought for things honorable, not only in the sight of the Lord, but also in the sight of men."   Paul might, of course, and no doubt he would, have had, silently within his own breast, the same delicate scruple of honor in the discharge of his fiduciary responsibility, without guarding himself, expressly and openly, as he did, for Christ's sake, against possible suspicion of malversation in office. For that intimate exercise of scruple he needed only to be absolutely incorruptible in heart; but to " take thought," as he did, and adopt the necessary outward precautions, he needed also to be, by instinct and by habit, a practical and practised business man. And such a man Paul was, to a degree not always recognized as it ought to be.

Measure now, if you can, the distance which separates such homely, painstaking, practical good sense as that just exemplified in Paul the business man, from the almost incoherent, almost rhapsodical, strain of the following language (2 Cor. 12: 2-4) :

" I know a man in Christ, fourteen years ago (whether in the body, I know not; or whether out of the body, I know not; God knoweth), such a one caught up even to the third heaven. And I know such a man (whether in the body, or apart from the body, I know not; God knoweth), how that he was caught up into paradise, and heard unspeakable words, which it is not lawful for a man to utter."

If ever there was mysticism, surely we find it here. In using this descriptive word, I do not mean to imply any doubt of the reality of that mysterious rapture, perhaps separating him from his body, of which Paul here speaks, and of which we are of course to understand that he himself was the subject. In the verses quoted, language breaks down under its vain effort to express what Paul indeed plainly declares to have been inexpressible. Was the man sane who could represent himself as having been the subject of such an experience? That transcendental language, observe, occurs in the selfsame letter which contains the wise fiduciary principle given here to illustrate the extraordinary sagacity in attention to details that was characteristic of Paul. The writer of those strange, those staggering, statements was perfectly conscious of their exceptional character. He almost immediately checked himself, and confessed that, for his own spiritual health and safety, he was afflicted as peculiarly as he was peculiarly honored. He then, with admirable sobriety, went on to say, " I have become foolish; ye compelled me." Yet it remains that there is no withdrawal, no abatement, there is increase rather, of his mystical claim. He avers that he might tell more of the same sort, and still be speaking only sober, absolute truth. Yes, the apostle Paul was a mystic, as truly as he was a master business man. His rich endowment of common sense he may be said to have needed, to act as a kind of ballast, keeping steady and safe the movement of a mind in him gifted with a quite extraordinary tendency to escape the limitations that bound it to the earthly sphere and to soar away into the realm of the supersensual.

14. PAUL AS A THEOLOGIAN

We have thus far, it will have been noted, throughout our whole discussion, dealt almost exclusively with the spirit and method of Paul as preacher, or with the traits in his genius and character that gave his preaching such power. It remains now to speak—very briefly it must be—of the *matter* of his preaching.

I have heretofore, as may be remembered, insisted very strongly that the idea of personal obedience to Christ was the animating and regulating principle of Paul's apostleship. That this idea did indeed occupy that place in his mind and heart, is evident from his own words, in what

may be called the inscription to his letter to the Romans:
" Jesus Christ our Lord through whom we received grace
and apostleship unto obedience of the faith among all
nations." But, notwithstanding the capital importance
thus attributed by me to the idea of obedience to Christ,
as controlling Paul's conception of his work and mission
in the world, it would be a mistake to imagine that I propose this idea as constituting the sum and substance, or
even the chief part of the sum and substance, of Paul's
preaching. Still, a part it was of his doctrine, a very
important part; this, besides being the informing spirit
and the guiding principle of his activity as preacher.

How important a part of Paul's doctrine the idea thus
recurred to necessarily was, will instantly be apparent
when once is fully comprehended what was the length
and the breadth and the depth and the height of that idea
as Paul held it. The inclusion of it and the application
of it were in his view absolutely universal. Richard
Hooker's famous apotheosis of Law was fully realized
in Paul's conception of the will of Christ as binding on
every soul of man. Hooker said: " All things in heaven
and earth do her homage, the very least as feeling her
care, and the greatest as not exempted from her power."
So, ideally, in Paul's view, the universe of beings, great
and small, owed fealty to Jesus. The following is his
mighty language; omnipotence seems to heave like a
ground-swell of the sea underneath it:

" Wherefore also God highly exalted him and gave him
the name which is above every name [that is, the name,
Lord], that in the name of Jesus every knee should bow,
of beings in heaven, and of beings on earth, and of beings
under the earth, and every tongue confess that Jesus
Christ is Lord to the glory of God the Father."

So much for the universal, all-embracing extension of
the sway of Jesus. The intension of it corresponds. For
the very thought of the mind is to be subject, as also
every impulse of the heart. Jesus, according to Paul,

is to be Lord of the belief of men. Whatever he says, is
to be believed, even as whatever he bids, is to be done.
There is no exemption, no exception, no escape.

As has previously been pointed out, Paul made the
most distinct and unmistakable claim to being trustee
of revelation, as to the gospel that he preached—revelation received without mediation of any sort, from the
risen and ascended Lord. This we know from his letter
to the Galatians. That revelation from Christ, Paul received in the spirit of absolute obedience on his own
part; and he everywhere proclaimed it with the demand
of absolute obedience on the part of those who heard
the proclamation. The obedience to Christ which he himself rendered, as well as the obedience to Christ which
he uncompromisingly challenged from others, covered
thus the whole range of doctrine inculcated by him.
Under the never-intermitting dominance of the idea of
subjection due to Christ as the revealing Lord, he
preached a vast system of doctrine—in fact, a whole
rational and practical theology.

There is one expression used by Paul that is sometimes
misunderstood to be a virtual disclaimer on his part
of any authority vested in him to govern the faith of
Christians. This solitary expression capable of such
misconstruction would, of course, be overwhelmingly
overborne by the quite unmistakable contrary tenor of
Paul's teaching in general; but it is perhaps worth while
to point out the true meaning of the apparently exceptional passage in question. In Second Corinthians, first
chapter, last verse, Paul says: " Not that we have lordship over your faith." " Have lordship " is a misleading
translation; the translation should be: " We are not lord-
ing it over your faith; . . for in faith ye stand fast."
Paul is not speaking at all here of the authority which
is his, least of all in order either to disclaim it or to
limit it; he is speaking of what he is at that moment
engaged in doing. He simply explains that he is not at

that moment exercising lordship over the Corinthians'
faith; on the contrary, he is merely helping their joy.
In point of faith they are not lacking; they already stand
fast in their faith.   Indeed, interpreted with wise consideration of the general tenor of Paul's Epistles, and
perhaps especially of his Epistles to the Corinthians, this
text yields an implication that Paul is conscious of having
the authority, which now, however, he is not exercising
—as there is no present need, the Corinthian Christians
being already fast in sound faith.

What were the chief points of that gospel which Paul
received by direct revelation from Christ?   As to two at
least of those points, happily the first extant letter to the
Corinthians removes all possible question or doubt.   He
says to the Corinthians: "I delivered to you first of all
what I also received, that Christ died for our sins according to the Scriptures."   He then proceeds to insist, with
much array of evidence, on the fact of Christ's resurrection.   This fact was a keystone fact in the Christian
faith, and as such Paul powerfully presents it.   But take
note of the first article of Paul's gospel; it is that "Christ
died for our sins."   This is simple language; it states a
fact and leaves the statement perfectly bare; that is to
say, it accompanies it with no comment, no theory.   The
fact, then, is here, of what has come to be called the
atonement; the fact, but not the doctrine—so far at least
as doctrine may be held to imply reason and philosophy.

But stay, perhaps we are hasty in excluding the element
of doctrine from this simple statement of fact concerning
Christ's death.   Let us see.   The immediate sequel makes
it plain that the subject which at the moment absorbed
the interest of the apostle, was the accomplished resurrection of Christ, and, with that, the future resurrection
of all the dead.   It is a thing therefore worthy of note
that, in hastening forward to contact and grapple with
this absorbing theme, he should, to the mere statement
that Christ died, have added the words, *"for our sins,*

according to the Scriptures." When he goes on to say that Christ " was buried," to *that* mere statement he adds nothing. There is doctrine, then, after all, found here— the doctrine that Christ's *death* was " for our sins."

That is an extremely simple phrase. What does it mean? Does it mean, can it mean, only that Christ died by reason of our sins; that, but for our sins, he would not have been crucified; that his crucifixion involved sin in those who were responsible for it? It is true enough that if those who put Christ to death had not sinned, they would not have put Christ to death. By reason of *their* sins, on account of *their* sins, Christ died. But Paul says, " for *our* sins "—evidently including with himself those to whom he was writing, namely, Corinthians who had nothing directly to do with the crucifixion of Jesus. The meaning, therefore, of the words " for our sins," in Paul's present use of them, must, interpreted by the general purport of his teaching on this subject, be that Christ died in expiation of our sins, that he died vicariously, that he died an atoning death. This is doctrine; and the fact that this doctrine is here introduced at all, is proof that it was a doctrine supremely important in Paul's view.

I am inclined indeed to believe that the doctrine of the atonement, interwoven as we find it in the whole warp and woof of Paul's epistolary writing, and therefore no doubt pervasive too in his preaching, was still a doctrine reserved by him for impartation and exposition to believers, and not a doctrine preached by him in the first instance to those who had not yet accepted Christ for Master. It is a doctrine which cannot, by any ingenuity, or any eloquence, of presentation, be commended to the natural reason of men. There must first be the obedient heart, before a mystery of grace like the atonement can be with hope proposed to human acceptance. The resurrection of Christ, on the contrary, was an historical fact capable of being adequately attested. Paul accordingly

at Athens preached Jesus *and the resurrection.* Such
preaching was exactly adapted to bring about acceptance
of Christ as Lord; and with Christ first accepted as
Lord, subsequent indoctrination in all the deep things
of the Christian faith was natural and easy. Those
mysteries, and mysteries they most of them are, were
accepted (when accepted) in acts of faith; that is, in
acts of obedience to Christ rendered by the loyal mind and
the loyal heart of him who had first accepted Christ for
Master. The faith exercised was itself obedience, obedience of the mind and of the heart. Paul so conceived it
and so represented it. Hence such expressions as these
from his pen: "obedience of the faith," "obeying the
gospel," "submitting to the righteousness of God,"
"obedient from the heart to that form of doctrine
whereunto ye were delivered."

The words just now italicized are significant. They
imply, as a necessary condition of discipleship, an attitude or a state of subjection to doctrine, on the part of
believers, entered upon in conversion; entered upon, that
is, in the very first act of obedience to Christ, namely,
the act of accepting him for Master. That accepting
Christ for Master was, in Paul's view, the simple, but
sufficient, test of the regenerate heart is shown in his
saying: "No man can say, Jesus is Lord, but in the
Holy Spirit."

Paul was a doctrinal preacher, he was eminently a doctrinal preacher, but his preaching of doctrine was always
in the spirit of challenge to obedience, obedience to be
accomplished by the mind and the heart. He seldom or
never argued for the distinctive Christian doctrines that
he preached, unless citation of Old Testament Scripture
be considered argument—but that, as I think, should
rather be considered pure appeal to authority. He announced his doctrines, he expounded them, he illustrated
them, but he did not try to establish them by reasoning
and by evidence. As to the facts that he preached, it

was otherwise. The fact of Christ's resurrection he argued for, he established it by testimony. That fact once proved, Christ's lordship was proved with it. Christ's lordship proved, the way was open to Paul for preaching the revelation of doctrine received by him from Christ, as matter of belief depending for certification on Christ's authority alone. It had by him been received, and it was by them to be received, by faith; by faith which, let me repeat it, was in fact obedience.

It is, of course, out of the question to offer here the briefest summary even of the doctrine that Paul preached; nor would it be to the purpose of the present discussion. Not a jot or tittle is to be abated from the inestimable value justly set upon Paul's writings as a source of Christian doctrine. Paul was the great theologian of the New Testament. But he *preached* his theology; and he preached it as theology ought to be preached—that is, with a view to its influence on behavior. He aimed to produce by it a full, intelligent obedience, outward and inward, to Christ. I attach as much importance as does anybody to orthodoxy. But there is something yet more important than orthodoxy, and that something is the spirit that produces orthodoxy, namely, the spirit of obedience to Christ. The tendency of these times in religion is to throw off the yoke of authority. What we need most of all is an era of obedience. That will bring about an era of orthodoxy. But the orthodoxy produced will still be an infinitely less good than the obedience that produced it. Not Paul as the theologian, but Paul as the bond-servant of Jesus, and the winner of men to bond-service in fellowship with himself—such is the Paul that by eminence the present age needs to recognize and to hail.

I regard it as an ominous symptom of revolt, on the part of current Christianity, against the mastership of Jesus—the disposition rife now to talk about return to Jesus from Paul. It is none the less revolt because it may

be unconscious revolt. With the most awe-inspiring attestation conceivable from heaven, Jesus accredited Paul
to be for all time his own chief prophet to the world.
How specious, how delusive, the dream of achieving a
superior fidelity to Jesus, by resorting to the words reported from his lips of flesh, through historians self-confessed, and by the Master declared, to be slow of heart
and dull of apprehension, and treating as of less import
the majestic revelation confided from heaven, by the risen
and ascended Lord, to the prepared and sympathetic
spirit of a man like Paul! What loyalty to Christ Jesus
is that?

Paul, like his Lord, was fond of paradoxes, and, like
his Lord, he presented in himself a miracle of paradoxes
reconciled. He was at once lowly and lordly. He rendered obedience, but he demanded obedience. The obedience he rendered was to Christ, and the very demand that
he sometimes made of obedience to himself from others
was made as part of his own obedience to Christ. Others'
obedience to Paul was thus in fact their obedience to
Christ.

That text which, at a point near the beginning of this
discussion of Paul as preacher, was said to be a text so full
and rich in revelation of the character of Paul's preaching, "We preach not ourselves but Christ Jesus as
Lord," is worthy of more study than we then gave it. It
has not only express meanings, but an implicit meaning.
Expressly, it disclaims and claims both at once. It disclaims for Paul the habit on his part of preaching himself as lord. It claims for Paul the habit of preaching
Christ as Lord. But the implicit meaning is important.
That meaning is, that Paul stood conspicuously before his
hearers in the attitude of one demanding obedience. The
charge against him of his antagonists evidently had been
that he was a domineering spirit. This charge would not
have been made unless he habitually demanded obedience.
Paul admits, nay, he insists, that in fact he did; but he

says it was not in effect obedience to himself that he demanded, but obedience to Christ. And it was to Christ, not simply as Christ is represented in the Gospels (the Gospels, indeed, as we have them, did not then exist), but to Christ as Christ revealed himself, apart from the Gospels, to Paul. Nobody can refuse to hear Paul without refusing to hear Christ; for Christ has chosen to speak through Paul.

15. PAUL AS A POET

It will be a surprise perhaps, but it will be no anti-climax, if I venture to follow the topic preceding with the topic, briefly touched, of Paul as a Poet. I inevitably think first of his exquisite canticle of love contained in the thirteenth chapter of First Corinthians. That chapter is doctrine to be sure, but it is doctrine conceived and conveyed in a form so instinct with imaginative literary charm that it rises buoyantly and, as it were, irrepressibly, into the upper air of poetry. I should be sorry, indeed, if treating it in this way shall seem to any to partake of dilettanteism on my part. The charm that I feel in this chapter, though truly a poetical charm, is subordinately poetical. For the finest charm of it is quite other than the charm of poetry, pure and high and noble as that charm to me is. Its finest charm is spiritual. That charm is transcendent, it is ethereal beyond the power of words to express. It soars into the empyrean of Christian thought and Christian emotion.

To appreciate it, one has to think how different it is from anything else contemporary with it or anterior to it, to be found anywhere, in human literature, or even in the Divine-human literature of the Bible. It is a strain of inculcation which to the thoughtfully discerning, is in itself sufficient to argue for it a Divine inspiration enabling the author. I can imagine that Paul himself, after producing that episode of his Epistle, regarded it with a kind of awe akin to worship, as if really it was the finger of God that wrote it. Let us conceive of Paul as on some suitable occasion relating to a friend his inward intimate experience in producing that passage. The passage itself, carefully studied, furnishes the means to trace the history of it as it entered and grew up in Paul's mind. " My soul," Paul may be thought of as saying:

> " My soul was worn and anxious with my pain
> At such distractions of the church of Christ;
> I found my peace at last in this thought, How
> Love would heal all, would gently join from schism,
> And in one bind the body of the Lord!
> A wish ineffable seized me to make
> Love lovely to those loveless ones. I had,
> With the wish born, and of the wish perhaps,
> A sudden vision that entranced me quite.
> I saw Love take a body beautiful
> And live and act in most angelic wise;
> It was as if a heavenly spectacle
> Let down before me with a heavenly hand—
> Not to be viewed with unanointed eyes;
> I touched my eyes with eye-salve and beheld.
> Then a Voice said, What thou beholdest, write.
> I took my pen and sought to catch the grace
> Of being and behavior shown to me,
> And fix it, as I could, in form and phrase,
> For those Corinthians and all men to see.
> A living picture, and a hymn, there grew.

> " Hymn I may call my eulogy of Love
> Then written, for indeed it seemed to sing
> Within me, as I mused it, and the tune
> Still to the hearing of my heart is sweet.
> I felt, and feel, a kind of awe of it,
> Myself that made it, for I did not make
> It wholly, I myself, I know quite well;
> A breath divine, breathed in me, purified
> My will to will it, and my soul to sing." [1]

Something such, self-evidently, must have been the way in which Paul's canticle of love was born. And does it not bespeak the poet as well as the saint? This one example may suffice to exhibit the soul of the poet in Paul;

[1] "The Epic of Paul," pp. 141, 142.

but his Epistles would supply many another example scarcely less striking.

I will not conceal my conviction that a crisis is to-day upon the church of Christ, as grave as any that ever has put her to test. It is not that there is so much disposition to depart from traditional orthodoxy. It is not that there is so much disposition to subject the Bible to criticism. These tendencies are not in themselves dangerous; they are even wholesome. Not in *themselves* dangerous; but, in so far as they are symptoms of revolt against Christ speaking through Paul, they are dangerous in the extreme. Paul, let it be well understood and remembered, is the chief voice of the glorified Christ, speaking to his church and to the world. When Christ met this man on the way to Damascus, in the glory and terror of that great light, it was as if a Voice uttered again from heaven the same words that once accredited the incarnate Son of God, and said also of Paul, " Hear ye *him.*"

Jesus is amply patronized now, admired, lauded—loved, I was about to add; but I remembered his own saying, " He that hath my commandments and keepeth them, he it is that loveth me," and then I wondered, Is he indeed loved? For with all the ascription to Jesus that is current and customary now in our speech and our writing about him, is he obeyed? Do we bow down to him as Master? Do we take upon us the yoke of his authority? As for the matter of attestation, what Jesus has given us, for obedience, through Paul, is not less, it is rather more, attested than what is reported as having been given us from his living human lips. For my own part, often, when I hear Jesus praised, as it is the fashion of our time to praise Jesus, I listen and seem to catch the tones of his voice saying over and over again those solemn words of rejection from his mouth, with their pendulum-like swing of rhythm: " Why call ye me Lord, Lord, and do not the things which I say?"

No persuasion enters more deeply into my mind, my conscience, and my heart, than the persuasion that I press the message chiefly needed by the church of to-day, when I present Paul as the highest human model for all preachers, and in especial when I most commandingly present him as, above all things else, the apostle of *obedience to Christ*.

CHAPTER II

PAUL'S CLAIM FOR HIMSELF

I

NEXT in degree to Jesus Christ, among all the personages of Holy Writ, Saul of Tarsus is at present engaging the thought and interest of men devoted to biblical study. It is really an impressive thing, to contemplate the array of books and monographs on the subject of Paul, many of them fresh from the press, that may be seen on the shelves of any well-appointed theological library. In all this great and growing literature, although much of it, especially of that part of it which is latest, has for one of its objects—in some cases for its chief object—to cast down the apostle from the throne of peculiar authority occupied by him so long as by eminence the doctor of the church and the source from Christ of its doctrine, there is scarcely anywhere the least disposition betrayed to disparage either the intellectual or the moral greatness of the man. And no wonder. For indeed it is quite impossible for any one to make Paul a subject of thoughtful and candid study without being thereby inspired with a deepening sense of the just title that is his to admiration and reverence.

It is equally impossible, however, to acquaint oneself with the latest literature on the subject, and not feel that the current tendency is strong, if not even prevailing, to reduce this great personality to the terms of quite ordinary human measurement, and to deny to him any title to be regarded as a peculiarly delegated and accredited *authority* in matters of religious faith. The cry "Back to Christ!" has often this meaning—a meaning which, if not consciously and purposely concealed by

47

those who utter the cry, is still not clearly apprehended always by those who hear it. It will be timely to challenge this popular religious rallying-cry and make it avow its true meaning. It will be timely yet further, to raise the question how far the true meaning of the cry is justified by the facts that exist in the case. I propose then to discuss briefly, first, Paul's claim—that is, the claim that Paul makes for himself, and, secondly, Paul's credentials—that is, the grounds of evidence on which Paul's claim is supported. This latter point, the question of Paul's credentials, will form the subject of a separate succeeding chapter.

II

I shall try to be candid and calm in discussing, but I shall not pretend not to be in feeling profoundly moved.

"Back to Christ!" I am ready to avow my conviction that that brief phrase, grown so common now, constitutes, in the mouths of some that use it, one of the most effective and most mischievous watchwords that ever allured and misled a credulous Christian public. It sounds so loyal, and it is sometimes so treacherous. It kisses the Master with homage, and in that kiss it betrays him. I charge nobody that cries "Back to Christ!" with conscious treason to Christ. But, conscious or not, the treason to Christ that I speak of exists; and, if not conscious, it is perhaps only the deeper and the more dangerous as being unconscious. It exists in effect, if it does not exist in purpose. It is with the effect, and not with the purpose, of treason that I deal.

As I have already intimated, some who cry "Back to Christ!" really mean, 'Away from the apostle Paul!' This meaning of the cry of course implies not only that between Christ and Paul there lies a difference, which undoubtedly is true, but also that the difference amounts to contradiction, or at least to irreconcilable mutual inconsistency, which I hold to be as undoubtedly false.

The watchword " Back to Christ!" presupposes of course that there is a way back to Christ discoverable. Say, then, we listen to the cry with all good sincerity. From our hearts we reply to it: ' Amen! Back to Christ be our aim. Show us the way and we will gladly walk in it. We eagerly desire the goal.' In perfect good faith, accordingly, I inquire, and I invite my reader with me to inquire, Where do we find Christ—the real, not the ideal, Christ? The answer is inevitable. Self-evidently, nowhere except in the New Testament. I mean not the subjective Christ, the essential Christ, the virtual Christ, of men's imaginations, but the objective Christ, verifiable from trustworthy documents. This Christ, I repeat, we can find nowhere if not in the New Testament. But where in the New Testament? Are we confined to the four Gospels for seeking him? So the cry " Back to Christ!" as often used, seems to imply. Let us not deceive ourselves. This implication is momentous. Its import is nothing short of appalling. *Is* there then no risen, no ascended, no glorified, Christ? For the four Gospels give us only the Christ that lived his human life on earth and died. True, they add that he rose from the dead, and even that he ascended into glory, but of the ascended and glorified life the four Gospels tell us nothing. Do we therefore know nothing of that transcendent life of Christ in glory with the Father? Are we left wholly to our imaginations to conceive of it, wholly to our unassisted faith even to believe in it? The cry, " Back to Christ!" meaning back to the Christ of the Gospels, would seem to imply this. But is such an implication true? Have we no documentary revelation of Christ, except that which subsists in the four-fold record of his thirty-three years of life on earth? Is there not some documentary revelation of the Christ that rose, that ascended, that forever sat down on the right hand of glory in the heavens? Evidently, if there is any such documentary revelation of the transcendent

D

Christ, we must look for it elsewhere than in the four Gospels. Where?—I repeat the question.

III

I reply, that in the New Testament Epistles, especially the Epistles of Paul the Apostle, we have what on the face of it purports to be such a documentary revelation of, and from, the risen, ascended, and glorified Christ. Is this ostensible revelation, purporting to be not only of, but from, Christ himself living and acting in the heavens —is it true? Can we trust it? They who cry, " Back to Christ! " meaning thereby, ' Back to the Christ of the Gospels alone,' would seem to answer: ' No, this ostensible revelation of, and from, the transcendent Christ is not true; it cannot be trusted.' Otherwise, why their summons to us to come back to the Gospels? If the revelation contained in the Epistles is a true revelation, why should we prefer the revelation contained in the Gospels? The revelation contained in the Gospels is of a Christ subject to limitations, a Christ humiliated. It is a revelation *of* such a Christ, not *from* him. It is a revelation given by men self-confessed to be comparatively incompetent even to understand their Master, much more, therefore, to report and represent him accurately and adequately. Besides being a revelation of Christ given by such men as I have now described, it is a revelation given by such men from memory, after the lapse of perhaps a score or more of years from the date of the events narrated and of the discourses ostensibly reproduced. I am now presenting the case on purely rational grounds, and I dispense for the moment with the idea of supernatural help afforded to the Gospel historians in the form of what we call " inspiration." If they indeed enjoyed such help—and I am far from denying that they did—they at least did not claim such help for themselves.

On the other hand, the apostle Paul explicitly,

emphatically, and most solemnly claims for himself that he received communications, not mediately, but directly, from Christ himself, the risen, the ascended, the glorified Christ. He claims also in express and unmistakable terms that he was *taught* by the Holy Spirit, was by the Holy Spirit given words wherein to impart what he received; that is, was "inspired," as we say. Further, Paul was a man of commanding natural gifts of mind, and his natural gifts of mind had been improved by long, sedulous culture. Morally too, and spiritually, he was by nature, perhaps beyond any other man that ever lived, qualified to know deeply and truly the mind of Christ. His loyalty, his devotion, to Christ was so intense that a loyalty, a devotion, more intense cannot even be conceived. Again, it is not necessary to suppose that any considerable interval of time elapsed between Paul's receiving of his communications from Christ, and his putting of them into written record. If now we add the important consideration that the communications concerning Christ which Paul received were communications not chiefly concerning the Christ subject to limitations, the humiliated Christ, but chiefly concerning the risen, the ascended, the glorified Christ, we surely shall feel the reason to be abundant why we should not disparage the revelation of Christ which Paul supplies, in comparison with the revelation of Christ supplied by the Evangelists.

Neither, indeed, of these two revelations of Christ ought to be disparaged in comparison with the other. They are both necessary, and they support and complement each other. We need that picture of Jesus, Son of man, moving here among men, which the Gospels afford us. Our Lord therein draws near to us and takes hold of our sympathies and our affections. But not less we need the majestic and awe-inspiring presentation of the exalted Christ, the Son of God, Assessor with the Father, which is given us especially in the Epistles of Paul. As I have said, the reason is abundant why we should not comparatively disparage this latter revelation of Christ.

That is to say, if this latter revelation, the revelation supplied by Paul, is a true revelation, then it is worthy of our trust. Is it such a revelation? But there is a question anterior even to that. Is it a fact that Paul *claims* for himself to have received communications, unmediated communications, directly from Christ himself, the risen, the ascended, the glorified Christ? Is it a further fact that he claims to have received such communications in a manner, in an amount, and in a kind, that quite distinguish him from the generality of Christians—quite distinguish him indeed from any one even of his fellow apostles? That these two claims are really advanced by Paul is, surprising to say, sometimes disputed by persons calling themselves evangelical Christians, and—what should be more startling still—occupying positions of responsibility and trust as teachers of ostensibly evangelical ministers and of supposably evangelical candidates for the ministry. A question then as to the very existence of such *claims* on Paul's part is raised; let us try to answer it out of Paul's own mouth.

IV

Paul wrote to the Galatian Christians these words— I ask that very particular attention be paid to them; they are very important words:

" For I make known to you, brethren, as touching the gospel which was preached by me, that it is not after man. For neither did I receive it from man, nor was I taught it, but it came to me through revelation of Jesus Christ."

In those words Paul states his fact in two ways: first, negatively, and second, positively. He did not " receive " his " gospel " " from man "; he was not " taught it." So much for the negative form of statement. The

positive form of statement is, that it came to him
"through revelation of Jesus Christ." Such language
from Paul himself would seem sufficient to establish it
beyond possible dispute that Paul claimed—whether in
accordance with truth or not, that at any rate he claimed
—to have received a personal communication directly
from Christ himself. Not "from man," but "through
revelation of Jesus Christ." What could be clearer, what
more decisive? But even language so clear, so decisive,
it is sometimes attempted to interpret in a manner to
avoid the natural and obvious conclusion which it seems
to contain. Those who say "Back to Christ," meaning
"Away from Paul," some of them, try to make out that
"revelation of Jesus Christ" does not mean "revelation
from Jesus Christ," that is, "revelation which Jesus
Christ made," but, on the contrary, "revelation which
was made of Jesus Christ." Paul's "gospel" would thus
become a doctrine which Paul arrived at by a process of
thought and experience going on in his own breast—a
process started and maintained in Paul's breast by the
exhibition made to him in the person and life of Jesus
of Nazareth. But would not a "gospel" so evolved be
emphatically what Paul expressly, and as if by special
prophetic foresight, declared that his "gospel" was *not*—
would it not be a gospel "after man"? Paul certainly
was a "man," and such a "gospel" as by the interpretation now in question is supposed, would be, even in an
eminent degree, a human product; something therefore
which Paul's phrase, "after man," would very exactly
describe. But Paul's "gospel," so Paul says, was *not*
"after man." Besides, the revelation or exhibition of
character in Jesus Christ, assumed by the interpretation now under consideration to have been the germ out
of which Paul, by brooding on it in thought, evolved his
"gospel," would—that special supernatural communication to him being supposed out of the question, which
indeed it is the very object of this interpretation to

dispense with—would, I say, necessarily be to Paul
"*through* man"; but, again, Paul distinctly affirms that
his "gospel" was *not* "through man."

Yet further: the whole tenor of the passage in which
occurs the language now under consideration forbids us
to suppose that Paul was thus earnestly insisting that he
—he by himself, independently of help or teacher—was
the originator of the "gospel" which he preached. That
he did *not* originate, that he did *not* evolve his gospel—
that, precisely *that,* is one thing that he was emphatically
asserting: he "received" it. The only question, as to his
coming into the possession of his gospel, that he dealt
with here at all, was the question whence and how he
received it. Was it *from* man? No. Was it *through*
man? No. Whence, then, and how? From Jesus
Christ, and by Christ's own revelation to him. This is
Paul's claim, whether the claim is in accordance or not
with truth. It is impossible to understand his language
otherwise. I may add that a commentator so well accomplished, so thorough, so sane, and at the same time so
free, as Meyer, unhesitatingly gives the interpretation
which I have ventured to declare the only interpretation
really possible.

Very solemn too, Paul's language becomes in putting
forward his claim. He says: "Now touching the things
which I write unto you, behold, before God, I lie not."
This solemn sacramental form of language Paul uses in
immediate connection with his putting forth of the particular claim now in question. His claim, then, is not
lightly made. Paul is serious in making it; he means
what he says; calls God to witness that he does not speak
falsely.

With Paul's language to the Galatian Christians agrees
his language to the Christians in Corinth. He says, concerning what he taught in Corinth as to the Lord's Sup-
per: "For I received of [from] the Lord that which also
I delivered unto you." This statement of Paul is still

more significant than to the reader of the English text it naturally appears. There is a peculiar emphasis on the pronoun " I." It is an individual, a personal communication to himself from Christ, of which Paul speaks. "*I* received of the Lord," he says. This statement, by the way, of Paul to the Corinthians throws a light of some importance on the meaning and inclusion of his word " gospel," used in the passage quoted from the Epistle to the Galatians. It seems to imply that the word " gospel," thus used by Paul, was used by him to cover the whole body of his apostolic teaching—as to substance, at least, if not also as to form. Loyal students of Paul—that is, students who trust him—will certainly, as to any given thing found in his teaching, feel safer in assuming that it is directly from the Lord than in assuming the contrary. The question, however, exactly what is the just inclusion implied in Paul's word " gospel," as thus used by him, is a separate and independent question which I do not now discuss, or even enter upon. It is enough for our present purpose that it includes something, and that whatever it does include, be it more or less, Paul claims to have " received " directly from the risen, ascended, and glorified Lord himself.

V

Although I thus waive discussion as to the exact limits of inclusion proper to be assigned to Paul's word " gospel," so used, it would be a serious omission not to point out that the claim which Paul makes to be recipient of direct revelation from Christ is at all events not a meager claim; but, on the contrary, a very large, an indefinitely large, an immense, claim. Hear what he tells the Corinthian Christians. He speaks of being " caught up into paradise," of there hearing " unspeakable words which it is not lawful for a man to utter." He says further that he was in danger of being " exalted overmuch " by this extraordinary experience of his, and that there was given him what he enigmatically calls "a thorn in the flesh" to guard him against such a spiritual danger. "The exceeding greatness of the revelations"—note the plural form of the word—is the strong expression that he uses.

It is impossible, therefore, either to deny or to ignore the claim which Paul makes to being, in a special, even a unique, sense, a chosen organ of communication from Christ, the risen, the ascended, the glorified Christ, to the church and the world. That claim, whether it is a true claim or not, stands out in bold, in commanding, relief, in two at least of the most important among Paul's Epistles, Paul's unquestioned Epistles, and it is water-lined inseparably into the texture of all his writings that survive.

Is this extraordinary claim a true claim? *Is* Paul the chosen organ of communication from the risen, the ascended, the glorified Christ that he claims to be? It is a question of the utmost moment to any one that believes there really lives a risen, an ascended, a glorified Christ to make communications to men, or that there did live such a Christ to make communications to men, at the time when Paul was engaged in doing his mighty work in the world—a work which somehow laid a more potent hand on nineteen centuries of subsequent human history than ever otherwise has been laid since Jesus Christ was crucified on Calvary.

We have thus raised the question, What are Paul's credentials? This question, as has already been intimated, it will require the room and scope of a separate chapter to answer. It is enough if in the present chapter it has been made clear and unmistakable that Paul at least put forth a stupendous claim for himself—a claim which it demands equally stupendous proofs to accredit and confirm.

CHAPTER III

PAUL'S CREDENTIALS

I

IN presenting, as in the preceding chapter I have done, the claim which Paul the Apostle prefers on his own behalf as selected and accredited organ and oracle of the exalted and glorified Christ, I make no attempt to conceal the fact that the claim thus preferred by Paul is one of a truly tremendous character and of truly tremendous proportions. If I may so far obtrude a matter purely personal to myself, I will confess that Paul's claim on his own behalf is even a thing staggering to my faith. I am constitutionally and habitually of a skeptical—that is, doubting and inquiring—turn of mind. In whatever sphere of things, I always believe with difficulty, and never fully believe except upon compelling evidence. It is therefore entirely in accordance with my natural bent for me to challenge Paul in his prodigious claim for himself, and to ask him to produce his credentials.

When, in confronting the problem involved, I am thus thrown back upon my instinctive skeptical attitude of mind, I feel it reassuring at the outset to note that Paul himself is perfectly conscious that his pretensions are something imposing, enormous. He does not, in the easy Oriental manner, claim for himself visions and revelations such as, though to Occidental minds portentous to the degree of incredibility, he nevertheless knew would, in the easy Oriental manner, be admitted by those to whom he wrote without question or difficulty—admitted, and at the same moment discounted as nothing really very exceptional in a human experience. In studying Paul's language, therefore, we have not to deal

with a case that constitutes simply one among many ex-
hibitions of an imaginative and exaggerating idiosyncrasy
pertaining to a particular race of mankind. Paul felt
the necessity of supplying objective evidence to sub-
stantiate his claim. Accordingly we observe that, when,
in writing to the church of Corinth, Paul put forward his
claim, he did not leave his claim unsupported. He appealed confidently to evidence that no one in that church
would dispute. Listen to his language: " In nothing was
I behind the very chiefest apostles, though I am nothing.
Truly the signs of an apostle were wrought among you
in all patience, by signs and wonders and mighty works."

" The *signs* of an apostle! " There were then recognized and unmistakable " signs " by which a true apostle
of Christ was accredited to men; and to such " signs "
of his own apostleship Paul could make his confident
appeal. But Paul in this text really understated his
case. He said he was " in nothing behind the very
chiefest apostles." The fact is that in one important
particular he was far before them all. One " sign " of
apostleship existed for him such as existed for none of
his fellow apostles. Paul was called to the apostolic
office not by Christ on earth, but by the Christ in the
heavens—not by the humiliated Christ, but by the Christ
risen, ascended, glorified. This was a distinction among
his brethren on which Paul himself never insisted—it
would not have comported with his exquisitely courteous
character to do so; but on the fact in his experience
which was the ground of the distinction he insisted again
and again.

The story of Paul's call to the apostleship is familiar—
there is hardly any story more familiar in the history of
the world—and I need not rehearse it. But this story—
that is, the story of Paul's " conversion," as it is more
commonly called—attentively considered, furnishes a key
to the solution of a highly interesting and most important
problem. The problem to which I refer is one which

few persons perhaps ever proposed to themselves. It is a twofold problem, but the solution is single. The problem is: To find the way in which Christ, supposed really risen and ascended to an invisible life of power and glory in the heavens, could best manifest himself as thus living and active, and could at the same time best accredit to men some new chosen representative and organ of his almighty mind and will. While Jesus was on earth in form as a man, he prepared the way for his church to expect—nay, even to demand—from her Lord some manifestation of himself to be made after he had withdrawn from ordinary human view, together with also some communication of vital truth additional to what he had taught up to the time of his death. Just before his death he said plainly to his disciples: " I have yet many things to say unto you, but ye cannot bear them now." He then added that the Spirit of truth should complete what he necessarily left thus incomplete, and lead his disciples into " *all* the truth." But in some transcendent way that Spirit was himself; for he said: " I will not leave you desolate; *I* will come unto you."

II

If, therefore, Christ on earth taught truly, it was to be expected as certain that he would somehow speak to men from heaven. In what manner could he do this, by means of what select signal example, so as best to assure his disciples then living, and at the same time his disciples to live in the future, that he was still alive, though invisible, and that indeed, as he had declared, all authority was given to him in heaven and in earth? If he should select from among his declared enemies the one man best known as such enemy; if he should choose the moment at which the persecuting zeal of that selected enemy was at its height, and, meeting him at midday under a blazing Syrian sun, should flash upon him from above a light that would make that meridian splendor seem like darkness; if he should at the same time speak to the prostrated man with an audible voice, and declare himself—the speaker—to be that very Jesus whom he was then persecuting; and if, as an attesting result of that Christophany, the persecutor should at once be transformed into the apostle—if, I say, such conditions as these were fulfilled, what way of exhibiting himself to mankind as really a risen, an ascended, a glorified Christ could human imagination conceive to itself more worthy of the Son of God, and better fitted to command the wondering and adoring belief and obedience of men?

I may venture to dwell a little upon the point that I am now making. What I submit to the leisurely consideration of candid and thoughtful men is this question: Let it be supposed for the moment that Jesus Christ did, as he foretold that he would, rise from the dead, and enter upon a new, a different, a transcendent, life of glory and of power in the heavens—how could he most fitly attest that fact to the world? Could it conceivably be done in a manner more fit than through the magnificent Christophany which, if the history of the Acts is to be trusted, occurred when the fanatic Pharisee Saul was arrested in his persecuting career on the way from Jerusalem to Damascus? I will defy the imagination of man to conceive a demonstration more majestically fit and convincing. Also I will defy the imagination of man to conceive of any evidence more commanding than in that same august Christophany was furnished, to accredit to the world an apostle called to his office—if indeed such an apostle were to be called to his office—by the Lord Jesus after his ascension to glory.

Of course I well know that a hypothetical fitness, such as I thus affirm to be found in the story of the conversion of Saul, does not prove that story to be true. I likewise well know that there is a disposition among critics of a certain order to bring the trustworthiness of the Acts into doubt. I do not wonder at this; for if

the Acts is a trustworthy book, then the argument is at
once overwhelmingly carried for a truly supernatural
Christianity. If, on the contrary, the Acts is not a
trustworthy book, or rather if the Christophany reported
in it as occurring to Saul on his way to Damascus did
not really occur, then there is an historical problem of
the very first magnitude left without probable, nay, in
my own opinion, without possible, solution. That problem is: How did Saul the persecutor become Paul the
Apostle? The problem is instantly and satisfactorily
solved by supposing true the story of the Acts. I repeat,
it is a problem without attainable solution on the hypothesis that the story of the Acts is false.

III

It is true—and it is worthy of note—that for the account which has been transmitted to us of the conversion of Paul we are indebted exclusively to the book of
the Acts. At first blush it might seem natural that Paul
should allude in his Epistles to the circumstances of his
conversion and of his call to the apostleship. This, indeed, he does; but it is mere allusion—he does not enter
into any such detail as to furnish confirmation of the
account which the author of the Acts not only himself
gives us in his own direct narrative, but also twice puts
into the Apostle's mouth as given by him in the course of
public addresses. The absence, however, of such confirmatory matter in the Pauline Epistles is no just occasion of surprise even, much less of incredulity. Nay,
rather, if such matter were found there, criticism (of
a certain sort) would say: ' It was interpolated to support the story in the Acts.' Or, if the references were
circumstantial and full, then the same criticism would
say: ' The story of the Acts was obviously constructed
out of the materials furnished by the Epistles.' There
is no possible silencing of criticism when the criticism is—
as biblical criticism is too likely to be—of a certain sort.

The sane and reasonable account of the matter is as follows: Paul's Epistles were addressed to believers, and in general to believers who admitted the apostolic office and authority of the writer of the Epistles. Paul therefore had in these no occasion to use the miracle of his own conversion as an argument. That use of the miracle had naturally already been made by the Apostle in person with those to whom the Epistles were addressed. If any doubt among them remained, appeal could effectively be made to " signs of an apostle " which they had witnessed with their own eyes. The two occasions on which Paul is represented as telling the story of what befell him on his way to Damascus were occasions on which he had to explain the course of his life to *unbelievers*.

But while thus, on the one hand, the Epistles of Paul do not furnish—as indeed they should not furnish—any direct and explicit confirmation of the wonderful and beautiful story told in the Acts of this great Pharisee's conversion, Paul's Epistles do, on the other hand, contain indirect and implicit confirmation of that story in the highest degree satisfactory to the wisely inquiring and wisely teachable mind. Observe that the whole character and the whole tenor of Paul's epistolary writing are precisely such as they would naturally be, and, so to speak, would inevitably be, if the story of the Acts is literally true. So much on the positive side. But, on the negative side, it is equally clear that the whole character and the whole tenor of Paul's epistolary writing are such as it would not be easy to account for on the supposition of any other experience of his in conversion than the one reported in the book of the Acts, or else of some experience substantially similar to that. For, throughout Paul's Epistles, the Christ whom he chiefly knows—almost the only Christ whom he knows—is the Christ entered forever on his invisible life of glory and of power in the heavens. To such a degree is this the distinction legible

on all the writings of Paul that it has supplied to some
modern critics of the Apostle a ground of objection against
him, or at least an occasion to disparage him as one less
worthy of trust, for the very reason that he did not, like
his brother apostles, deal with the historical Jesus of
Nazareth.

IV

I say "the historical Jesus of Nazareth," seeking thus
to distinguish between the earthly and the heavenly Christ.
But in truth the heavenly Christ is as "historical" as is
the earthly, if Paul is to be believed. The heavenly Christ
was in terms expressly identified with "Jesus of Nazareth." For did not the glorious and awful Being who
arrested Paul on his journey of persecution to Damascus
say, in so many words, to the prostrate Pharisee, "I am
Jesus of Nazareth"?

And, by the way, did not Paul ask the question, "Who
art thou, Lord?" in a way to seek and to obtain an
answer of needed *information?* And would he have
done this were the rationalizing explanation admissible
which undertakes to dissolve away the historical truth
of the narrative and interpret what occurred into a mere
subjective process that passed within the mind and imagination of an overwrought man? If, as the rationalizers
suppose, very improbably suppose, Paul, being at the
moment occupied with absorbing and discomposing re-
morseful thoughts of Jesus, and having, as the issue of
a silent and secret process now mature in his breast, become at length completely prepared suddenly to accept
for Messiah the very personage whose followers he was
then engaged in persecuting to the death—if, I say, under
such circumstances and conditions Paul was the subject
of an impression, very vivid, but purely imaginative, that
Jesus appeared to him and spoke to him, is it psychologically conceivable that he would have felt like asking
who he was? The very hypothesis that the apparition

was subjective, that it was self-engendered, excludes the possibility of such a question from Paul. It was the image of Jesus—Jesus himself—that, by the hypothesis, was conjured up before the imagination of the excited man—not some formless, mysterious fantasy whose *name* he must needs inquire. In short, the rationalizing explanation of the story of Paul's conversion is as arbitrary, as violent, and as destitute of external evidence in its favor as was ever any historical speculation conceived by the human mind. It could have been begotten only by a perfectly invincible *a priori* determination not to believe anything partaking of what the skeptic might choose to call " supernatural."

The alternative is rigorously unescapable: When Paul told the story which he told of his conversion, either he was a conscious impostor or else he was the weak-minded victim of pure hallucination—*unless* the story which he told of his conversion is a literally true story. That the sanest, most sober-minded, best-balanced, most steadily self-controlled, most practical, of all the great heroes of humanity was the weak-minded victim of a groundless hallucination which lasted him without intermission throughout a long career full of experiences well calculated to disabuse him of all such illusions—the idea needs but to be stated to be rejected as impossible. Equally impossible is the idea that Paul was a conscious impostor. There is nothing left possible for us but to admit that Paul's testimony *stands*—his testimony, I mean, concerning his own conversion and concerning his communications received immediately from the Lord Christ in the heavens.

v

But let us not be hasty. Let us fairly face the question in yet one other possible aspect of it before we insist on our conclusion as the only conclusion rationally admissible.

And is it not, let us ask ourselves, hasty on our part to conclude with such certainty that, because Paul was neither a deluded enthusiast nor a conscious impostor, therefore he was a witness to be trusted when he told a personal experience inherently so improbable as that of his miraculous conversion and subsequent supernatural receipt of special communication from heaven? Well, the attempt is indeed sometimes made to avoid the alternative which I have been declaring to be unavoidable. Matthew Arnold (in his " St. Paul and Protestantism ") has attempted this, with perhaps as much plausibility as the case admits. He says in effect: ' No, Paul was neither an impostor nor a weak-minded enthusiast—and yet the story which he told of his conversion is a story not to be taken as true. Paul believed it, Paul was a thoroughly sound-minded man, and—Paul was profoundly mistaken in a capital matter of his own intimate personal experience.'

And Matthew Arnold, having found this out, explained it all—quite to his own satisfaction, if not to ours! This was the way of it—according to Arnold: Paul lived in an age and a country in which supposed miracles were common occurrences. It never entered Paul's mind to doubt the reality of such occurrences. It was perfectly natural, therefore, that Paul should attribute his own conversion to a miracle. Such, in short, is Arnold's disposition of the matter.

To a logical mind, the conclusion drawn by Arnold does not quite necessarily follow from his premises, even let his premises be supposed true. But are his premises true? Is it a fact that in Paul's time and in Paul's local environment miraculous occurrences were the every-day sort of thing that Arnold lightly represents them to have been? The answer to this question must be a decisive, No. One unquestionable historic instance will suffice to establish the negative. John the Baptist was a contemporary of Jesus and of Paul. He was a very conspicuous figure

E

in the Jewish life of his day—more conspicuous figure there was none, except Jesus himself. John the Baptist was a great religious teacher; he had a universal and splendid popular fame as a prophet—that is, as an accredited voice from God. This was John the Baptist's recognized character, and *yet no miracle is attributed to him*. If the country and the age were such as Matthew Arnold so confidently assumes that they were, it is impossible to account for the fact that not a single story of miracle wrought by him has attached itself to the name and memory of John the Baptist.

Incidentally, and therefore more strikingly, confirmatory of the argument supplied in the instance of John the Baptist against the notion that miracles were accepted as every-day occurrences in that age and in that country, is the account in the Gospels of what took place when John's messengers came asking Jesus on behalf of their master whether or not he, Jesus, was the expected one, the Messiah. " In that hour "—note the strikingly exact designation of time—" in that hour he [Jesus] cured many of diseases and plagues and evil spirits; and on many that were blind he bestowed sight." Such miracles, then and there notably multiplied, Jesus treated as a sufficient sign to John of his own unique office of Messiahship. This of course he could not have done either if John himself also had been believed to work miracles, or if miracles were freely imagined by the people of that time and place to be of frequent occurrence.

The total absence of miracle-working tradition in John the Baptist's case is of the highest historic and argumentative significance. It is alone sufficient to show that Arnold's assumption about Paul is an unwarranted òne. But this is not all. Arnold occupies much space in reciting a case of alleged witchcraft in which Sir Matthew Hale was involved as judge. That enlightened jurist, that excellent man, avowed his full belief in the reality of witchcraft—he even sentenced to death certain women accused of being witches. The explanation offered is that Matthew Hale was not superior to the prevalent superstition of his age. The same, it is then inferred, was true of the apostle Paul. Such is the reasoning of Arnold, and such the way in which he attempts to save the sound-mindedness of the Apostle and his moral integrity, at the same time that he discredits that apostle's testimony concerning a certain personal experience of his own. Paul believed in the miraculous, and *therefore* he mistakenly believed in the reality of something extraordinary that suddenly and unexpectedly happened to him—or rather that suddenly and unexpectedly *seemed* to happen to him—one day at midnoon as he journeyed to Damascus. Nothing at all really happened to him—*to* him, nothing; something probably happened *in* him, yes; but because he believed that miracles might sometimes occur, therefore he believed that on a certain occasion a certain miracle did occur in his own experience! That, in a nutshell, is Arnold's argument; and that, in a nutshell, is necessarily the argument of any one who undertakes to save Paul's character as a sane man and an honest, while he rejects Paul's testimony concerning the circumstances of his own conversion.

Arnold's labored parallel between the apostle Paul and Sir Matthew Hale is a fallacy in reasoning. The parallel assumed does not exist. The difference between the two cases is a vital difference. Sir Matthew Hale, in the case involving him, was not a witness, but a judge. He did not give testimony—he judged testimony. Sir Matthew Hale did not pretend to have had experience of his own in the matter of witchcraft. If he had affirmed that he himself was a wizard, and that he could, by collusion of the Evil One, exert a supernatural power of harm—or rather that in a particular case he *had* done so—then his case would be approximately parallel to that of the apostle Paul; for both men would then be witnesses, ostensibly testifying of personal experiences of their own. But had Sir Matthew Hale so testified, I venture to say that Arnold would not, toward the close of the nineteenth century, have been found standing up for the balance and sound-mindedness of such a man; I venture to say, further, that such a man would not enjoy the reputation that, despite his error concerning witchcraft, Sir Matthew Hale does enjoy for sane judicial qualities. No, the alternative is absolutely rigorous and unescapable: If Paul did not tell the literal truth about his experience on the way to Damascus, he was either an impostor or a weak-minded victim of delusion. That it is impossible to regard him as either of these Arnold expressly confesses; and he emphasizes his confession by the desperate attempt that he makes to save the Apostle's sound-mindedness while rejecting his testimony concerning a certain personal experience of his. There is nothing—nothing whatsoever, it may with all confidence be asserted—nothing dependent on human testimony better ascertained, more certainly true, than the story told in the Acts of the Pharisee Saul's conversion to Christianity and his call to the apostleship.

VI

While some misjudging Christian thinkers are, as the watchword " Back to Christ! " means in their use of it, seeking to rid themselves of the authority of Paul (in order to escape the idea of a vicarious atonement and a suffering Saviour, falsely supposed to be Paul's idea instead of Christ's), a different class of Christian thinkers unfriendly to Paul are seriously pointing out that it was Paul, not Jesus, who initiated the notion of giving the gospel to the Gentiles at once, and of dispensing the Gentiles from the necessity of becoming Jews. What if the watchword " Back to Christ! " in the sense of ' Away from Paul! ' should be insensibly leading the Christian world out from the liberty which, thanks to Paul, it has so long enjoyed, toward the old bondage of Judaism again? But, you will at once exclaim, there are Christ's own words, "Preach the gospel to every creature!" Yes; but what if those words were never uttered by Christ? What if they were indeed, as a critic of the class last alluded to suggests, simply "a magnificent afterthought" attributed to Jesus as expressed by him on a certain "alleged occasion"? If criticism wants to make out a case, it is a pity that any text should inconveniently stand in the way. Perish the text—long live the case!

Meantime the obvious solution of all difficulties is to admit that the testimony of Paul stands. It ought to stand; it is buttressed by nineteen finished centuries of Christian history. For all this history is in a manner an attestation of the truth of the testimony of Paul. That testimony, admitted true, explains the miracle of the history—a miracle unexplained, nay, a miracle impossible, on the supposition that the testimony was false. Such a history could not have started—such a history, once started, could not have continued and have accomplished itself—on the basis of a lie so audacious as would be the story of that Christophany to Paul on his way to Damascus, if the Christophany alleged did not occur. There are such things as historic impossibilities, and the career of Paul, together with the long sequel to that career brought forward to this living moment of time, is an historic impossibility if it be not true that Paul miraculously saw Jesus and heard his voice after Jesus had ascended to glory and power in the heavens.

And if Jesus did indeed ascend to glory and power in the heavens, and if he wished to signify that fact to men beyond the possibility of reasonable doubt, what is there incredible, what is there that we might not naturally expect, in a manifestation of himself such as that made to Paul? We must beware of the subtle and secret infidelity toward Christ that tempts us to doubt Paul's apostleship and authority. In such doubt we are doubting

not so much Paul as Christ himself. It is the leaven
of unbelief. It is the disposition to deny the supernatural. Under the guise of paying homage to the earthly
Christ we are in danger of doing a deadly dishonor to the
Lord Christ in heaven.

What I affirm is that as between the two—namely,
Christ through the Gospels and Christ through Paul's
Epistles—Christ through Paul's Epistles is the *better*-
attested Christ. If we have reason for rejecting the
Christ of Paul's Epistles, we have more reason, rather
than less, for rejecting the Christ of the Gospels. And,
further, I deliberately avow my belief that if so-styled
and self-styled " scientific " study of the New Testament
succeeds in setting aside Paul's representations of Christ
and of Christ's teaching, as simply one great man's individual and subjective way of conceiving things, and as
therefore of no peculiar and binding authority—then the
time is not far off when the Christ of the Gospels will,
by the same rationalistic and naturalistic methods mask-
ing under the name and pretense of " scientific," be reduced to the quality and dimensions of a *man* not so very
different from other men. That is the natural, the logical,
the inevitable, issue to which tends the spirit that will
not loyally receive the apostle Paul as the Lord Christ's
attested and authoritative voice speaking from heaven.
Already the miraculous birth of Jesus is brought into
doubt by the effect of the teaching given to some of the
candidates under instruction to prepare them for the
pastorship of evangelical churches. The keystone fact of
the resurrection of Christ will, in natural sequence, be
volatilized away by " scientific " explanations; and, in
short, we shall in due time have nothing left to us to
take the place of a Divine Saviour lost, but the beautiful
and pathetic legend of a life once fondly idealized as
perfect, but found out at last to be flawed with many
shortcomings—ignorances, petulances, errors of judgment, overweening assumptions, and self-assertions—

sadly offsetting its laborious beneficence, its intuitions of wisdom, its willingness to suffer for the truth.

VII

It is idle—it is worse than idle—to ignore fact; and the fact is that we are involved in an era of rationalism threatening to be as fatal to evangelical Christianity in America as was the rationalism that in the first half of the nineteenth century swept like a wave of desolation over the Protestant churches of Germany. It is no less rationalism because it calls itself by another name. " Scientific " Bible-teaching is often rationalistic Bible-teaching pure and simple. When and where it is such, then and there let it confess itself such; at least let it be exposed and recognized as such. " Back to Christ! " is one of its favorite cries. That cry, fair-sounding as it is, is not seldom a suspicious cry. It sometimes means: " Give up the Christ that Paul reveals, and confine yourself to the Christ revealed in the Gospels." In other words: " Give up the Christ that now reigns, and keep only the Christ that once served; give up the Christ declared to be the Son of God with power by the resurrection from the dead, and keep only the Christ that was humbled and that suffered as a man; give up the Christ that is eternally set down in glory at the right hand of the Father, and keep only the Christ that hung in shame between two robbers on the cross; give up the Saviour and the Lord, and keep only the teacher and the example." That is what " Back to Christ! " may mean. We must beware lest it mislead us. Our option is not, Christ or Paul; " God forbid! "—so I seem to hear Paul himself, after his manner, fervently saying. Our option is not, The Christ of the Gospels or the Christ of Paul's Epistles. Our true option is, ' The Christ partially revealed in the Gospels, or the Christ far more fully revealed *both* in the Gospels and in the Epistles.'

The watchword, then, ' Back to Christ *from* Paul,'

I would replace with the watchword, 'Back to Christ *through* Paul.' One word, however, of explanation is necessary: It is not the Paul of the theologies and the creeds, it is the Paul of the Epistles, that I mean.

Paul's claim for himself, I admit, is stupendous; but his credentials, I insist, quite fully correspond.

CHAPTER IV

PAUL AND THE HEAVENLY CHRIST

I FEAR it is not adequately considered, among even the more thoughtful Christians of our day, how much we still need the contribution made by the apostle Paul to the most vital parts of the religious creed by which the church of Christ, without distinction of sects, professes to live, and but for which indeed it could not continue to live. As I have already tried to render clear, the cry, so rife everywhere about us, " Back to Christ! " really means, from the lips of many who utter it, ' Away from Paul! '—nay, even almost, ' Away with Paul! ' With many zealously active and widely influential Christian teachers and writers the feeling has been growing stronger every day, for now a decade of years or more, that the apostle Paul has too long been suffered to dominate, too exclusively, our conceptions of Christianity. The view has been propagating itself by boldly declaring itself, the view, I mean, that the proper way to regard Paul's writings is to regard them as setting forth not authoritatively the true doctrines of Christ, but only as setting forth one great mind's own individual way of conceiving those doctrines. The doctrines themselves, it is urged, in their unadulterate purity, are to be sought in the words of the living Jesus, as those words are reported by the four Evangelists, but especially by the three synoptic Evangelists so called, Matthew, Mark, and Luke. The records of these historians, we are told, are to be sifted carefully; for the truth which they give is mingled with error—the error of imperfect report and imperfect transmission. Besides this, so we are further given to understand, there is the error, an uncertain amount, to which

73

Jesus himself, as proved by his own admissions of igno-
rance on some points, was liable.

To this pitiable state of hopeless incertitude as to what
we may hold for true in religion, we are reduced by the
methods of biblical criticism at present so widely in
practice.

In such a condition of things, our need of Paul is a
crying need. Without him, the Lord himself, whom, as
risen from the dead and glorified in power on high, Paul
thought he was serving throughout that flaming missionary career of his, is on the very imminent breaking verge
of being quite lost to the church, degraded from the
rank of a Being who had existed before the world was,
through whom indeed the world was made, and who now
lives and reigns in the heavens, to the rank of a man who
was singularly good, who was gifted with singularly fine
and clear religious intuitions, but who was simply a
better specimen of humanity than any that had before
appeared, or any that has appeared since. We are this
moment unconsciously on the steep decline of the way
toward reproducing in ourselves that experience of Mary
bewildered at the tomb of Jesus: "They have taken away
the Lord and I do not know where they have laid him!"

A signal, a capital, fact it is in the life of the Christian
church, at this very moment, as it always has been, that
for a Saviour and a Lord who now is, and who is active
still with all power in our behalf, a living, an ascended,
a glorified Christ, who can forgive sin, can raise the dead,
can take us to himself where he is in the heaven of
heavens with God—for this Christ Jesus, the Christ
Jesus in whom we have trusted as an almighty redeemer,
to whom we sing our songs and pray our prayers—it is,
I say, a fact not to be lost sight of that for this Christ
Jesus, clearly defined in conception, vividly figured in
imagination, firmly adhered to in faith—we are chiefly
indebted to the Apostle Paul. It was to render this
immortal service to his church that Jesus Christ fitly, in

the case of one of his apostles, and that one the greatest,
waited till after his own resurrection and after his own
ascension to glory before calling him to that task of apostleship for his Lord which, to the everlasting profit of
mankind, he fulfilled so faithfully and so well.   It well
behooved that the great apostolic witness to the transcendent, supramundane person and activity of Christ
should be summoned to his mission by a Christ that had
already reentered his eternal, transcendent, supramundane sphere of power and glory, and that visibly and
audibly he should be summoned *thence,* as, in fact, Paul
was.

It is true, of course, that the preexistence of Christ
and his exaltation to eternal glory following his death,
are both of them facts plainly enough announced in
words of his own, spoken during his earthly life and reported by the Gospel historians.   But it is Paul, and
Paul alone, of the New Testament writers, who gives
these two facts that comparative prominence which, it
must be conceded, properly belongs to them, if they are
indeed facts, facts of history, and not fictions of the
imagination.   Paul makes almost nothing of the earthly
life of his Lord—so completely do the heavenly life that
his Lord lived before the world was, and the heavenly
life that his Lord resumed after he was crucified, usurp
the rapt faith, the kindled imagination, the adoring affection, of the great apostle to the Gentiles.   So strikingly
is this the case, that this conspicuous characteristic feature in Paul's Epistles is even sometimes made a point
against him, as if the things, some of them at least, that
he relates soberly about himself in his relation to Christ,
were too much in the air to merit serious heed.   But
this objection is the objection of very wrong-headed
criticism.   Nothing about Paul is more solidly real, more
inexpugnable, than his common sense, his perfect sanity.
He is to be believed altogether in what he testifies or not
believed at all.

That Paul occupies himself to such an extent with Christ's person and Christ's activity in the supernatural sphere, is quite as it should be; for if, previously to that ever-memorable noonday which found Paul a persecutor on his way to Damascus, he had known Christ " after the flesh," subsequently to that experience of his he knew him so no more.   Paul's glances at Christ's earthly life are invariably glances merely.   What he dwells on is his Lord's power and glory before and after the period of his humiliation in the flesh.   It was needful for the Christian church that there should be one potent spirit among the apostles, prepared by such an experience as Paul's experience was in being called to his apostleship by a supernatural voice from heaven—by a voice self-certified as the voice of Jesus of Nazareth, risen from the dead, ascended, and glorified—that there should, I say, be one spirit among the apostles, so endowed by nature and so qualified by unique experience as was Paul, to lay a commanding and an enduring emphasis on the vital fact that it was not Jesus as a man among men, but Jesus as supreme Divine Lord over men, that was Saviour of the world, if the world had a Saviour.   The Christian church cannot afford to obey the call " Back to Christ! " if that call be understood to mean back to the earthly Christ of the Gospel histories away from the heavenly Christ of the Epistles of Paul.

The tendency, now so strong and prevalent so widely, to deal with Jesus on severely "scientific" principles of historical criticism, simply as a man who lived once in Palestine, and whose words and deeds were very imperfectly reported by very ill-qualified biographers, biographers that must be halted with challenge at every point and not confidently relied upon, unless they *all three* happen to relate the same thing in the same way—I say all "three," not all *four,* because John is to a great extent discredited and counted out (sometimes) as not John, but, according to one hypothesis, another man by the name of John!—this tendency, however it may suppose itself to be peculiarly loyal to Jesus is, in deepest truth, the most specious and the most dangerous disloyalty to him that he has ever encountered in all the centuries since he finished the work on earth that was given him to do.

Let it be duly considered, if Christ comes at length to be measured by this rule, the time will then not be distant when he will be still further reduced; and from being the preeminent, the ideal, the flawless man, will be found out to be at best a man not well enough known to deserve such distinction, and, at worst, a man shown to have had his limitations, his weaknesses, his infatuations, even his faults of temper in speech and in behavior, such as bring him down after all quite comfortably near the level of the better sort of average human nature. This is the inevitable logical end, in effect upon our conception and estimate of Jesus, to which the current disparagement of Paul as accredited authority in Christian doctrine—a disparagement carried forward in the interest of ostensible superior fidelity to Jesus—is swiftly though unconsciously tending.

Already, for an ever-increasing number of " scientific " biblical students and teachers, the aureole of exquisite miraculous story that surrounds and beautifies the birth of Jesus, is dissipated under the solvent searchlight of historical criticism, and he becomes merely the natural— " natural," also, in the ambiguous sense of the term! —son of Joseph. His resurrection from the dead is similarly volatilized away into a posthumous revival of beneficent influence. The quasi-historical documents that seem to teach something more real, more substantial, than this are admitted to be interesting *memorabilia* of a notable personality that appeared once in Palestine, but they are held to be destitute of such credentials for accuracy as could commend them to the confidence of the trained historical scholar and critic.

In such a state of the case, our present need of Paul is incalculably great. Let the Gospel accounts of the resurrection of Jesus be given up as non-historical, there still remains the unquestionably historical and authentic testimony of Paul. This testimony is such that no fiercest crucible fires of historical criticism can possibly in the least affect it. Nothing even conceivable, except the actual literal resurrection of Jesus Christ from the dead, can account for the undoubtedly historic phenomenon of the apostle Paul, his career and his written words.

Our need of Paul is great, but God has graciously made Paul equal to our need.

CHAPTER V

JESUS CHRIST VERSUS HIS APOSTLES

IS the title of this chapter startling? It is not more so than, to loyal Christians, ought to be that tendency in current religious thought which has suggested my use of it. For there is indeed now in course of litigation before the bar of public opinion a case that may fitly be entitled, after the manner of lawyers, "Jesus Christ *vs.* his Apostles." It is, to be sure, not a real case, but one purely imaginary; still, purely imaginary as it is, it is a case of vital importance, and it is at this moment litigated actively.

Strange to say, the case at its present stage seems to be going against Jesus Christ—really against him, though ostensibly in his favor. To heighten the paradox that exists, while the case is thus, as I have said, just now going against Jesus Christ, it is going also against his apostles. Plaintiff and defendants will suffer together, if the decision which at the actual moment seems imminent is finally reached.

I shall make the impression of speaking in parable; and I hasten to explain myself. There is a quite illegitimate issue being forced into controversy, as between Jesus Christ and his apostles (as between Jesus Christ and by eminence his apostle Paul), which may be stated thus: "Is the authority of Christ's apostles, notably of Christ's Apostle Paul, equal to the authority of Christ?" If there were any legitimate issue of this sort possible to be joined in the premises, of course the answer would have to be a negative one, namely: "No, certainly the authority of the disciple cannot be equal to the authority of the Master." And such is, in fact, the decision being now inconsiderately rendered, and to a wide extent

79

inconsiderately accepted as sound. The cry "Back to Christ!" is the plausible popular form which this decision, rapidly crystallizing itself, most frequently takes. The expression sounds as if it did honor to Christ; but, when uttered in the sense just indicated, it in reality does him the deepest, the most deadly, dishonor.

Do we Christians believe that Christ now lives? That he reigns? If we do not, then we discredit not only the apostle Paul, but Christ himself; for the historical Christ, Jesus of Nazareth, declared this, and in effect declared it repeatedly, as once at least, with emphasis the most sublimely awful, he expressly declared the fact before the council of the Jews in these words: "Henceforth ye shall see the Son of man sitting at the right hand of power, and coming on the clouds of heaven"—august averment, which must be understood as having meant, when made, that the maker of it would live a life thereafter (observe the adverb, "henceforth," "from that time forward")— would live a future life indefinitely prolonged in possession and exercise of sovereign authority and power to rule. We must not limit the interpretation by carelessly taking the reference to be simply to a single event, even so solemn an event as the second coming of the Lord. (Of course I do not forget that this is "apocalyptic," and that, in the view of rationalistic criticism, "apocalypticism" has had its day and "passed.")

If we believe the historical Jesus making such a declaration as this, then it becomes to us not only probable, but morally certain, that this now living and reigning Christ will make some unmistakable manifestation of himself as thus living and reigning. With this idea, antecedently probable, accords what he said to his disciples in his very last discourse to them: "I have yet many things to say unto you, but ye cannot bear them now." Christ would then in due time resume his communications to his apostles, and this would necessarily be after his crucifixion, his burial, his resurrection.

But after his ascension?

Well, almost certainly Christ would after his ascension manifest himself in some absolutely convincing manner to those who believed in him or to those who would believe in him because of such manifestation. There was overwhelming antecedent probability that Christ, if indeed living and reigning still, would show himself as thus living and reigning by some such demonstration as that which actually occurred in the conversion and calling to apostleship of Paul.

And it would be astonishing if, in addition to the college of apostles appointed during Christ's earthly life, there should not be chosen at least one apostle, otherwise endowed and otherwise disciplined than were any of these, to receive from Christ such additional communications of his mind as were at the same time peculiarly fit to his state of exaltation and, for that very reason, more difficult for those fishermen of Galilee satisfactorily to grasp and effectively to impart to mankind. Exactly such a choice of apostle—which, since it has been made, we are thus able to see was, as it were, indispensably necessary—gave Saul of Tarsus to the Christian church. Safely reasoning backward, we are able also to see that the choice made should have been made in some such extraordinary manner as that in which it was made in the case of Paul. In no other way could the continuing life in glory and in power of the risen and ascended Christ be so well evidenced to men.

And now, in this new apostle, called and accredited by the exalted and glorified Christ, there was raised up that adequate personal medium through whom the reserved communications, foreshadowed by Jesus when about to suffer, could be made successfully to his church. These reserved communications are, in fact, stored up for us most largely in the Epistles of Paul. To "hark back" from Paul's Epistles to the Gospels is only to "hark back" from Christ speaking in his exaltation to Christ

F

speaking in his humiliation. We cannot too heedfully and too obediently hear what is said to us by the humiliated Christ; but surely we should not disparage in comparison what is said to us by Christ in his exaltation. I prize the four Gospels as of inestimable worth, but I do not hestitate to say that in my own opinion Christ Jesus is more fully, more effectively, set forth, not of course in the facts of his earthly biography, but in his spirit, his person, and his character, by the apostle Paul than by any one of the Evangelists—nay, than by all the Evangelists taken together. We cannot afford to forsake Paul.

Perhaps the personal allusion will be pardoned if I say that it is a letter lately received by me from a correspondent, of whom I know nothing except what his letter reveals, that has set me upon the present tenor of thought. This correspondent had read the preceding chapter as published in a monthly magazine. Quite illegitimately, but perhaps, in view of current theologic thought, not unnaturally, my correspondent felt in my argument for Paul some implied derogation from Christ. The precise reverse of this was in truth the intention, as it was also, I think, the proper tendency, of my argument. To make Christ more, not to make Christ less, was what I aimed at; not to set forth Paul as a rival of Christ, but to set forth Paul as the chosen best human representative of Christ.

A few years ago, I remember, a religious body of some importance discussed publicly for one of its subjects the question, " Is the authority of the apostles equal to the authority of Christ?" I quote from memory, but such, I am sure, is the substance, if not the exact form, of the question thus discussed. The question so stated was a misleading question. There really is, there really can be, no question as to the equality or the inequality of the apostles' authority with the authority of Christ. The apostles never either exercised or claimed *for themselves* any authority whatever, whether equal or not equal with Christ's authority. They simply represented Christ, and if they seemed to exercise or to claim authority, it was always Christ's authority, not their own, that they exercised or claimed. There are therefore no two authorities in the case that admit of being compared and measured one against the other. The question should have been stated in some such way as this: Is the authority of that Christ who is represented by the apostles in their letters or in their extant reported discourses equal to the authority of that Christ who is represented by the Evangelists in the Gospels?

The true answer to the question thus properly stated is sufficiently indicated in a remark let fall by that prince of exegetes and that prince of homilists, both in one, Dr. Alexander McLaren, on the signal occasion when his fellow ministers in Great Britain did themselves honor by honoring him in a great ovation on his completing the fiftieth year of his fruitful and illustrious ministry. " I have preached Christ," he said (again I quote from memory, but with absolute confidence) ; " not the Christ of the Gospels alone, and not the Christ of the Epistles alone; but both the Christ of the Gospels and the Christ of the Epistles, and I have found them not two different Christs, but one and the same Christ, both of them." That, I repeat, is the true solution of the question of the relation between Christ as reported in the Gospels and Christ as reported in the Epistles.

I used the plural number in writing the title of the case, " Jesus Christ vs. his Apostles." But the apostle Paul so much overshadows his fellow apostles that these, I thought, might well enough be left out of present account, while the case was discussed as if it were entitled, " Jesus Christ vs. the apostle Paul." It is of course true enough, as in my own view it is quite the reverse of regrettable, that Paul has to an extraordinary extent dominated the religious thought of nineteen Christian

centuries. But if he has done so in a way to relegate
Jesus to comparative obscurity, that result certainly is
one for which Paul cannot be held to blame, as it is one
which Paul himself, far more than any other, would
deplore. For the exaltation of Jesus is the master-key
to the life and the writings of this great man. For example, the first ten consecutive verses of Paul's first
Epistle to the Corinthians contain the name of Christ,
always in a way to glorify him and make him all, *ten* times.
No parallel exists in history to the subordination, the
effacement, of self in deference to another, that is exhibited in the attitude assumed by Saul of Tarsus toward
Jesus of Nazareth. There have been instances of men
of a certain secondary or dependent type of character
completely taken possession of by master spirits met
among their fellows living or dead. But where is the
second instance of a man, himself so unquestionably born
to be monarch of his fellow men as Saul of Tarsus
demonstrably was, falling so absolutely under the sway
of another as Saul of Tarsus fell under the sway of
Jesus of Nazareth? Paul's prostration before Jesus was
such that it might almost be called abject, if the idea of
abjectness admitted of being associated for one moment
with a personality like Paul's.

The notion, therefore, of any pitting of Paul against
Christ in the way of estimating their comparative authority is a notion peculiarly abhorrent from the whole
tenor and spirit of Paul's writings. Those writings are
one continuous tissue of adoring glorification, on the
writer's part, of Jesus Christ. "For me to live is
Christ" is the key which Paul himself supplies to the
whole problem of his life. In Paul's view, Paul was nothing and Christ was all. The true aim in critical ("scientific") study of Paul the man and Paul the writer could
in no other way conceivable be missed more widely than
by raising an issue between him and Jesus, and asking,
Is Paul of equal authority with Christ?

The entire discussion, to the logical mind, narrows itself down to this: Is Paul a man to be believed in what he
solemnly asserts? Was he sane and was he truthful? If
he was both truthful and sane, then he had immediate
personal communications from Jesus, risen, ascended, and
glorified in the heavens. These communications made
Paul an apostle of Christ and furnished him with the
gospel that he preached. If Paul is to be believed in what
he solemnly asserts, he became, miraculously became, the
recipient and the communicator of doctrine proceeding,
without intermediary, from Jesus Christ seated on high
in glory and in power. In short, Paul became an organ
through whom Jesus Christ, now ascended, would in part
exercise that authority which, about to ascend, he, according to Matthew's Gospel, declared was in absolutely un-
restricted plenitude given to him in heaven and in earth.
If Paul was a man of sound mind and a man of veracity,
instead of its being his own authority that he exercised as
apostle, it was simply Christ's authority delegated to him
that he exercised; and he was under compulsion to exercise it; he would have failed to exercise it at his peril.

Fortunately for us of this day, Paul's right to exercise
Christ's authority was sharply challenged by his contemporaries, sharply and frequently. I say " fortunately
for us," because in that way Paul's right to exercise
Christ's authority was *proved* as it never otherwise would
have been proved. Paul's expressions as to this point
are of a nature to leave no doubt whatever in any mind
at once intelligent and candid, that he could appeal to
evidences of his apostleship—in other words, of his right
to exercise Christ's authority—evidences perfectly well-
known to those to whom he was writing, and evidences
that they, however much tempted to resist him, could not,
and therefore would not, dispute. When, for example,
we read Paul writing to the church in Corinth (which
contained members that were anxious to disparage him),
" In nothing was I behind the very chiefest apostles,

though I am nothing. *Truly the signs of an apostle were wrought among you in all patience, by signs and wonders, and mighty works"*—when, I say, we read such expressions from Paul, several things become plain to us:

One thing is, that that age was not so weak-mindedly superstitious and credulous as not to need " signs," or proofs, of an astounding claim like Paul's—a claim, namely, to nothing less than delegated authority from an invisible Being in the heavens who identified himself as one and the same with the once crucified Jesus of Nazareth. A second thing is, that in Paul's case those needed signs were actually supplied, and supplied in abundance and in power. It was not merely before persons eager to welcome and accept them that they were supplied; they were supplied before persons some at least of whom were bent on ignoring and denying them if they could. Read again the foregoing citation of Paul's words, and observe the perfectly confident tone in which he expresses himself. It is inconceivable that a man like Paul should stultify and shame himself by appealing to ostensibly notorious supernatural credentials for his apostleship, if it was open to his adversaries to reply: 'Nay, but we are by no means aware of any such attestations of his presumptuous claim as would be those things of which he thus speaks.' I repeat, it is inconceivable that a level-headed man like Paul should lay himself liable to be discredited through a *false* appeal of his own to testimonies on his behalf which were capable of being met with a simple denial of their reality. No, the risen, ascended, and glorified Lord Jesus supported this chosen apostle of his with those special signs in his favor required by the fact that he was called in the exceptional manner which in this respect differenced Paul from all his fellow apostles. Paul's credentials as apostle, that is, as wielding the authority of Christ, are commanding and they are complete. It should be well understood that REVOLT AGAINST PAUL IS REVOLT AGAINST CHRIST.

CHAPTER VI

TWO COMMON-SENSE VIEWS THAT MAY BE TAKEN OF THE HISTORICAL PHENOMENON OF PAUL

FIRST VIEW

TWO " common-sense views," my chapter title says— two soundly scientific views it might as well have said, for soundly scientific I hold indeed to be the two views I am now about to set forth.

Certainly, the apostle Paul presents a problem in history remarkable enough to be well worth attentive study. Let us linger to study it attentively in the light of simple common sense.

I

In the first place, then, Paul is an undoubted fact. I know of no one skeptical enough to call the fact of Paul in question. The fact of Jesus some affect to doubt. I never heard of any one's doubting the fact of Paul. [I should have written, I do not *remember* having heard of any one's doubting the fact of Paul. Everything is possible in the realm of skepticism, especially skepticism dealing with Scripture, and I might well have presumed that some one somewhere had raised a question as to the reality of Paul. A vigilant reader of the present chapter has kindly advised me that " Van Namen in Encyc. Bibl., III, col. 3632, mentions a certain E. Johnson who did so doubt." Thus reminded, I now seem vaguely to recall having met with this " certain E. Johnson " before.]

But Paul, the admitted fact, is more of a problem in history than many people ever have bethought themselves to consider.

87

Besides the fact *of* Paul, what are the facts *about* Paul?

The answer to that question will make plainly appear what an extraordinary historic phenomenon Paul is.

For the purpose of learning what the facts are about Paul we have but the one source of information to which to go; we must take recourse to the New Testament. But we need not go to the New Testament in any blind spirit of childish belief. We may ignore entirely all questions relating to the " inspiration " of Scripture, Old Testament or New, all questions relating to the " inerrancy " of the history contained in those great literary monuments; and may use the ostensible record of special divine revelation which they present simply as so much " source " of material for our investigation and study, appraising it freely for its trustworthiness precisely as we should appraise any other document whatsoever submitted to our hand. Of course we cannot abruptly dispense altogether with the New Testament, for in that famous body of literary and historical documents we have what is absolutely our only source of original, direct information, or of even ostensibly original, direct information, concerning Paul's character and career. But when I say this of Paul's " career," I need to qualify my statement by saying " concerning Paul's career *run while he lived.*" Of Paul's career run since his death, all subsequent history is an abounding, an inexhaustible, source of information. No other human being, in all the tide of time, has ever lived, and certainly no other human being does now live, such an inextinguishable, such a penetratively, pervasively, influential posthumous life as undeniably has been, and still is, the posthumous life of Paul. I have thus already, as it were incidentally and unexpectedly, struck one point at which we may, by exception, dispense with the New Testament altogether. For, inquiring, What do we know of Paul? we may for the moment look quite

away from the New Testament for our answer and find
Paul a living force everywhere present in the thought,
the literature, the life, of to-day. Everywhere present;
that is to say, among all the races of mankind that make
history and that write history. This is a fact which
is its own evidence. We have, therefore, in this fact
a starting-point for our discussion which is beyond all
possible dispute. The fact is certain with a certainty
which, though not mathematical, is, were that possible,
even more certain than mathematical; for it dispenses
with demonstration, or rather transcends it.

How did this extraordinary fact come to be? What
constituted, what constitutes, Paul the historical phenomenon that he has been and is? That question is
our problem.

In the attempt to solve the problem we most naturally take our course by regress to the past. How long
has Paul been the potency that he now is? At what
point of time and of history did he begin to be such?
This question takes us back to the New Testament,
our only record, our only even ostensible record, of
the beginning of Paul's continuous and unending career.
Through what to some minds might seem an unmistakable ordering of divine Providence, but what we
here, trying to be as scientific (even in the strained
" modern " sense of that word) as possible, may call
simply a fortunate circumstance, a very great part of
the available record, indeed nearly all the part that we
need to use, subsists in the form of a literature written
by Paul himself, and, as to the point of authorship,
authenticated to us for Paul's as satisfactorily, I suppose, as any other literature in the world, ancient or
modern, is accredited to its author. At any rate, the
really material things for our present use are contained
in writings, ostensibly Paul's, which are universally conceded to be genuine. (We need not consider one or
two freaks among critics, who, as the last chance left

them to be original and startling in destructive criticism, have called in question everything extant purporting to be from Paul's brain.)

From this record of the beginning of things with Paul, we know that he was a Jew; that he was a Jewish Pharisee; that he was a zealot, not to say a bigot, Jewish Pharisee; that he was intensely a Jewish patriot, intensely a devotee of the Jewish religion as that religion was understood by the most fanatically strict legalists of his time; that, as an inevitable consequence of being such, he hated, or would have hated had he not despised, Jesus Christ, hated Christ's disciples, hated them violently, cruelly, to imprisonment, to scourging, and to death; that not content with thus persecuting them at home, he hunted them to persecute them abroad; that then, suddenly, with no forewarning, no preparation, that appears anywhere hinted in the record, he was arrested, while in the very act and article of one of his mad, murderous, persecuting foreign raids—suddenly arrested, how, shall we say?—for we wish to remain, up to the last point possible, strictly scientific and indisputable.

Let us say, then, that Paul was arrested on his way to Damascus by an extraordinary, a compelling, *experience* of his—an experience which not only arrested him, but turned him short around in his course, entered into his being, his innermost being, took him helplessly captive; nay, such is the paradox existing in the case, took him joyfully captive, subjugated him utterly, transformed him, made him an inconceivably different man—inconceivably different, yet remaining inconceivably the same—and set him forward irresistibly, conquering and to conquer, on the endless beneficent career that for nineteen centuries since he has run.

The facts concerning Paul, the unquestionable, the scientifically ascertained and authenticated facts, are such as they have now been stated to be. The marvel, the miracle, of them, so stated, is immense, but, so stated, they have been understated immensely. The all-transcending wonder is that Paul, the proud, the lordly, the imperious, imperial Paul, from ineffably despising Jesus of Nazareth, became, in a moment, in the twinkling of an eye, not merely an obedient bond-servant, but a boundlessly adoring, an ineffably passionate, devotee and worshiper of him. That also is a fact which indisputably stares in the face of every one that reads the New Testament Epistles of Paul.

Candor, with vigilant care to be accurate, compels us to remind ourselves that we go outside of Paul's own writings to learn the fact that the transforming experience referred to of Paul occurred suddenly when he was on his way to Damascus for the purpose of persecuting Christians. This particular fact regarding Paul is known to us, not from Paul's writings (although a tolerably distinct implication of the fact is indeed contained in the first chapter of Galatians), but from the report of it contained in the New Testament book entitled "The Acts." So few doubt the truth of this narrative that it may be regarded as a part of scientifically accredited history. Though Paul does not appear as himself writing the narrative, he does appear as himself giving it form in a credibly reported address or discourse of his—an address which it is not unlikely he repeated with his own voice to the historian who reported it in writing—singularly enough, for all future generations of mankind to see.

II

It is not careless exaggeration when I attribute to Paul so much influence, extensive and intensive, in the world. The simple fact is that Paul's influence is felt wherever the influence of Christianity is felt. So much is this the case that some thinkers, not altogether without specious grounds for their contention, have undertaken to maintain that Paul, and not Christ, is the true founder of Christianity. That watchword so often heard, " Back

to Christ! " is really a futile, a fatuous, summons bidding
us away from Paul, from Paul mistakenly conceived to
be having too much influence with men, mistakenly conceived to be, indeed, almost superseding Jesus Christ.
This is an unconscious, an unintended, but a quite unmistakable, tribute to the prodigious power exerted by this
extraordinary man—extraordinary historical phenomenon,
I should say rather, for it is less as an extraordinary
man than as an extraordinary historical phenomenon that
he is constantly regarded here. Paul's attitude toward
Christ, his absolute, self-effacing, subjection to him, his
eager subservience, even over-insistent, over-demonstra-
tive, were that possible, his adoration, his worship, of
Christ, makes it of course absurdly impossible to fix such
a crown of dishonor, pretending to be honor, on Paul's
head.

What, however, must be admitted to be true, is that,
from the point of view of mere scientific history, Paul
was from the first, and he has been ever since, the chief
human agency in achieving for Christianity its age-
long, world-wide, as yet very imperfect, conquest of mankind. That narrow-minded, blindfold, Jewish Pharisee,
intent on nothing but sentencing himself to ridiculous
defeat and everlasting oblivion, as adherent and advocate
of a hopelessly obsolescent religious cult, became somehow the most broad-minded, the farthest-seeing, man of
his time or of any time—achieving therewith for himself, what he never dreamed of achieving, what he never
desired to achieve, a personal fame constantly coex-
tensive with the constantly extending uttermost bounds
of the civilized world, and a fame not less, nay, more
rather, enduring and deathless than the earthly future
of the human race itself. (If this last suggestion cannot
claim to be exactly scientific, let it be indulged nevertheless, as merely a passing individual prognostic in a very
high degree probable.) The result is that what, from a
purely scientific point of view, appeared to be a delusion

(easily referred to a recognized class of such by latter-day psychologists!) misleading a few commonplace, ignorant enthusiasts, became the sober devout belief of the most enlightened intellects in every succeeding age, and what (still from the purely scientific point of view) looked like an insignificant ephemeral Jewish sect was widened into a world-embracing, seemingly indestructible, religious community of human souls. All this stupendous result because of Paul, and all because of Paul's having that "experience" of his on the way to Damascus. I make this affirmation, be it remembered, as an affirmation absolutely incontrovertible from the scientific point of view.

III

It will be noted that I have avoided saying "occurrence," or using any word of similar import, to designate the cause of Paul's remarkable transformation, and of the prodigious consequences that followed from that. I choose to abide within the bounds of the rigorously scientific. It is, I take it, scientifically certain that Paul had the *experience* in question. As to what objectively and observedly *occurred,* there of course could be, and so there of course have been, doubts raised, doubts imagining themselves to be by eminence scientific. Let us confine ourselves to what cannot scientifically be brought into question, namely, to that *experience* of Paul's.

What was that experience? We have now asked a question which admits of being answered scientifically. Paul thought that suddenly, at high noon, he saw a great light which blinded him. He thought he heard a voice from above, calling him by name and asking him a question to which he replied, or shall we say thought he replied, by asking back a question in return. Paul asked, or at least thought he asked, who it was that thus challenged him, and he thought he got the reply that it was the very Jesus of Nazareth, whom he was that moment engaged in persecuting. Paul hereupon was overwhelmed, or thought he was overwhelmed, into asking, or into thinking that he asked, what the person speaking to him, or imagined to be speaking to him, would have him do. This implied that he was instantly ready to obey the person, real or imaginary, who he thought was addressing him. He got his orders, or thought he got them, and proceeded to fulfil them. This very last clause we need not affect with the alternative, " or thought he proceeded to fulfil them." It is objectively, scientifically, certain that he did proceed to fulfil those orders, whether they were real or imaginary.

Now what did Paul do in fulfilling those real, or imaginary, orders? Well, remaining carefully scientific we are obliged to say that he simply went about preaching Jesus as Lord (for this, as the character of his preaching, we have Paul's own testimony) and wrote letters, of which a few survive, to the scattered communities of persons whom he succeeded in convincing of the truth of his message. And is this all that Paul did? Yes, or No? We hesitate in replying, for, in what purports to be a conscientious, intelligent account of his activity, it is stated that certain supernatural results attended his course. Indeed, Paul himself says this, but we are undertaking to treat our subject scientifically, and we put such supernatural incidents out of account. Preaching, then, mostly itinerant preaching, and occasional letter-writing to obscure little communities, composed almost exclusively of very obscure people, many of them slaves—such preaching and such letter-writing was all Paul did? All, absolutely all, in the view of pure science, that is, pure historical science, as such science is generally now conceived when applied to Scripture history. And the prodigious, the incalculable, result was in this manner brought about? It is staggering, but we are " scientifically " (I now affect the word with quotation-marks), we are " scientifically " bound to answer, Yes.

IV

Such, as I have thus very inadequately indicated, is the historic phenomenon, Paul. The problem of the phenomenon is, How account for it? The solution of the problem is either simple and easy, or exceedingly complex and difficult—according to the method we adopt in attempting to solve it. There are two methods possible, only two; the alternative is rigorous, it is necessarily either the one or the other. Of these two methods the one is scientific, and now I mean truly scientific. The other, while it lays claim to being scientific, peculiar claim, is in fact, so I hold, as unscientific, as anti-scientific, as possible. Nevertheless, since its scientific pretensions are great, let us recognize them by giving it an adjective in accordance at once with its claim and with its character, and call it briefly pseudo-scientific. (The adjective is objectionable as hybrid, but it is good enough for the thing it describes.)

That method which I pronounce truly scientific consists in accepting New Testament history as substantially true history, and therefore in assuming that what Paul thought happened to him, that memorable day, did really happen to him; namely, that he did objectively see that great light; did objectively hear that great voice, and did not merely imagine them. He assuredly, unless the narrative falsifies, did objectively fall to the ground, objectively become suddenly blind, objectively have scales of searing form on his eyeballs, scales, or seeming scales, which, at any rate, were objective enough subsequently to fall off—objectively fall off! These points in the circumstances, these, at least, were real and objective. What was it made them real? Was it Paul's sudden new state of mind? What created that sudden new state of mind in Paul? But we must for the moment repress these questions which spontaneously start. In brief, the method that I have been pointing out approvingly, for the solution of the problem presented in the historic phenomenon of Paul, is scientific. Why? Because it proceeds according to the evidence in the case. The hypothesis that that evidence is sound and true, satisfies completely every condition of the problem. It removes every difficulty, it leaves nothing unexplained. This, I submit, no other conceivable hypothesis will do. That hypothesis, therefore, is scientifically—not mathematically, but scientifically—established.

V

What about the pseudo-scientific method, the method which assumes that, contrary to the evidence, nothing happened to Paul that day—nothing, that is to say, peculiar? What solution of the problem of Paul does that hypothesis offer? Let us see.

We have, to be sure, prejudged the case we are about to try, by applying the word "pseudo-scientific," but let us nevertheless do our very best to make our pseudo-scientific hypothesis work. It is understood that there is no question now anywhere as to the substantial trustworthiness of the narrative of Paul's conversion. The pseudo-scientific hypothesis admits that, and seeks its solution of the problem presented in Paul, by putting a peculiar *interpretation* upon the narrative. The narrative is true, but it must be interpreted. The correct interpretation, so the pseudo-scientific hypothesis maintains, is that Paul was excited, and that he *imagined* the outward incidents related; that is, the great light and the great voice, with the colloquy that ensued. Did he *imagine* that he fell to the ground? I have never seen any exhaustive attempt to construe according to the pseudo-scientific hypothesis all the details of this simple, yet confessedly remarkable, narrative. I do not pretend therefore to know the best that the pseudo-scientific hypothesis does with the alleged falling of Paul to the ground. The grotesque suggestion of a sunstroke has been made. Well, a powerful sunstroke might doubtless lay a man suddenly prostrate. But it would be a sunstroke extraordinary to the degree of bordering on the supernatural (which is to be shunned), that should set the prostrate victim to imagining not only a great light, but a great voice, and therewith words back and forth forming a colloquy. And then the *blindness* continuing for days thereafter, while the subject was able to walk and to talk, with at length the seeming scales shed from the eyeballs. The sunstroke fails to account for these things. Besides, how should a sunstroke produce the alleged *kind* of colloquy, and, more unaccountable than all, the lifelong subsequent result of persecution changed into apostleship? A sunstroke converting Saul into Paul!

But there is the alternative conjecture of epilepsy. Pure conjecture, there being no least hint of epileptic condition in Paul. Epilepsy would indeed account for the falling of Paul to the ground, but epilepsy would be as ridiculous as sunstroke, to account for the alleged incidents, and the undoubted consequents, of the fall. In short, the pseudo-scientific hypothesis breaks down at once as soon as you begin seriously to apply it.

We have left, however, as a possible producing cause, or at least condition, of Paul's experience, an excited state of mind on his part. We need not doubt that this condition really existed in the case. The history informs us that Paul, bound for Damascus, went breathing out threatening and slaughter against the disciples of Jesus. That, of course, implies an excited state of mind in him. But it also unmistakably implies mental excitement *of a certain sort*. Now mental excitement is undoubtedly a powerful producing cause. But producing cause of what? Why, naturally, of effects having some relation to the nature of the excitement. And we are asked by the pseudo-scientific hypothesis to suppose that excitement due to ravening, bloodthirsty motive and purpose directed against a particular name, name hated and despised, would

G

stimulate the man actuated by that motive and engaged in executing that purpose to fall prostrate in act of sudden abject devotion to the late execrated name, and keep him ever after, in the face of every danger, every shame, every suffering, a passionately loyal champion of the cause which, up to that moment, he had exerted every energy, and practised every severity of punishment, to overthrow! Yes, even that is what the pseudo-scientific hypothesis requires us to suppose.

VI

Unless, indeed, recourse be taken to conjecture of a different kind of excitement for Paul, and it be now no longer the excitement of vengeance to be wreaked upon an accursed crew of wretches everywhere spoken against, and have become instead an excitement of recoil from what he was doing, and of remorse for what he had done. Not the shadow of hint in the record going to show the probability of this—pure groundless guess, all in the air. But let the improbable conjecture be for a moment entertained. What explanation does it afford for the things that happened? Sudden access of remorse hurling its subject to the ground, causing him to imagine a great light, a great voice, creating in him the hallucination of a colloquy between himself and an imaginary being of awful power and awful glory, who identifies himself with that despised Nazarene lately crucified as a malefactor! And then—for a climax of grotesque absurdity—remorse driving its subject blind, and sealing his eyes with material scales that soon after visibly cleave off! Is not such "scientific" explanation worthy of being called "pseudo-scientific"?

But the pseudo-scientific method of dealing with Scripture is resourceful, and at the end of all other expedients it holds one master expedient always in reserve. It can criticize its "sources," and find unhistorical any element of a narrative which proves to be otherwise unmanageable in its hands. Here, having easily disposed of the great light and the great voice, as products of an excited sensibility playing upon an overwrought imagination, it can proceed to say: ' The historian, and perhaps the apostle himself, exercised a characteristic Oriental freedom in dramatizing, in appropriate outward circumstance, what in fact was simply a vivid inward experience of Paul's. Understood with Western literalism, the narrative is unhistorical; but understand it scientifically, in the manner just suggested, and it becomes trustworthy enough to be fairly adjudged historical; such enlightened treatment of the text is not destructive criticism; it is, on the contrary, constructive, and in the best sense conservative, criticism; it saves the narrative to even the most advanced modern scientific mind.'

But, alas, what, even so, has this shallow, self-complacent pseudo-scientific process really accomplished toward solving the problem presented in the historic phenomenon of Paul? Nothing, absolutely nothing, nay, even less than nothing; for it has merely volatilized utterly away the only explanation ever offered of that "vivid inward experience" which confessedly turned Saul into Paul. The kernel of the problem, namely, the question, What *caused* that vivid inward experience of Paul's? remains absolutely untouched, as whole and as obstinate as ever, no solvent force has even reached it, much less subdued it into happy scientific solution. Besides, nothing could be more opposed to a true scientific treatment of history, than arbitrarily to inject into a sober, commonplace narrative like Luke's, an episode, such as that supposed would be, of imaginative extravagance by way of lively dramatic representation.

I have not been able completely to repress my sense of the preposterous, felt by me to inhere inextricably in the pseudo-scientific treatment of this subject; but I have honestly sought, nevertheless, to give it fairly every advantage that it deserves in the forum of reason and

common sense. I conclude that the historic phenomenon
of Paul admits no possible adequate explanation that
does not involve the acceptance of the New Testament
narrative of his conversion as true. But if that narrative is true, then the four Gospels might be relegated
to the limbo of things utterly negligible, and Paul alone,
regarded simply as an historic phenomenon, constitutes
evidence amounting to demonstration—scientific, not
mathematical, demonstration—for the uniqueness of the
personality of Jesus, and for his exaltation after death
to a degree of power and of glory not to be distinguished
from authentically Divine. It proves him worthy to be,
and it proves him to be, the rightful supreme Lord
of all human souls, and a Saviour able to save unto the
uttermost all that accept him as such.

SECOND VIEW

I

The subject with which we are here dealing is one
that, on intent consideration, proves many-sided; it teems
with almost endlessly various and often truly surprising
suggestion. I am impelled to introduce abruptly at this
point, postponing for the purpose return to the main
double argument of the present chapter, a suggestion
which forces itself upon my mind, and which seems to me
to possess a very considerable apologetic potency and
value. Although the suggestion is in the nature of a
note, I do not print it in a different type at the foot of
the page, but place it rather within brackets in the body
of the text, undistinguished from that in typography. I
thus seek to give it the emphasis which I think it deserves.

[The suggestion is this: How are we to explain the fact
—a fact which nobody can possibly dispute—that Paul
came somehow, and came very suddenly, to conceive his
peculiar passionate personal *love* for Jesus Christ? Consider, he probably had never seen Jesus, even casually, in

the flesh, at any rate, had never become attached to him in affection, nay, but the violent reverse of this had obtained; Jesus had never wrought him, and had never engaged to work him, anything but injury of the most serious possible kind and degree, so far as the external, material good of life was concerned—now the problem, the psychologic problem is, How, and why, did Paul, from a certain definite point in his experience, come to *love* Jesus so? Evidently, Paul's was not the love of a pupil to a teacher—a teacher unseen, a teacher never seen by his pupil, a teacher now not living to inspire or to receive such tribute of devotion. Evidently again, Paul's love for Jesus was not the love of a servant for his master; Paul's love for Jesus was a passion that infinitely transcended all bounds, the widest conceivable, of such sentiment as either of these or as both of them, coexisting and reenforcing each other, and thus blended together into one, could be imagined to inspire. The transcendence was not simply a transcendence of degree; it was still more remarkably a transcendence of kind. It could indeed be conceived that Paul might in some way be convinced, as Tolstoy, for example, was convinced, that Jesus was supreme in religious, in ethical, in social, wisdom and doctrine, and that therefore he was worthy to be revered, worthy to be followed and obeyed as Teacher and as Master; but this supposition leaves utterly unaccounted for the intense, the all-absorbing, the indescribably passionate, *peculiar* personal love of Paul for Jesus. The psychologic problem of that love remains unsolved.

Will it be said to me, Really, you find a mystery where there was no mystery to be found? The ardor of Paul's devotion to Jesus was much a matter of personal temperament with him. Your own words may be quoted against you. You said, very justly: " Whatever Paul thought he thought passionately, whatever he believed he believed passionately; in short, he was passionate in whatever he did."

Yes, I reply, and that accounts for the *intensity* of Paul's love for Jesus. But it is not the intensity of it that constitutes the problem; it is the kind, the quality, of it. Every thoughtful, discerning reader of Paul's Epistles must feel the difference in *kind* between the emotion with which he loved Jesus and the emotion with which he loved any one else in the world. Raise the power of his love for any fellow man to whatever degree you will, and you do not get the *kind* of love that Paul lavished on Jesus. What is the secret of it, what the solution of the problem? There is only one solution of it philosophically, scientifically, possible. The love of Paul for Jesus was a supernatural love; that is, it was a love supernaturally begotten, supernaturally nourished and sustained. It was love not simply for a Teacher, a Master, but love for a *Saviour,* a suffering Saviour, a Saviour who died to save, a *Divine* Saviour being a Saviour who *could* save, nay, who *had* saved *him,* Paul, chief of sinners. Here, to whoso deeply considers, is argument sufficient to prove the saviourship of Jesus, his saviourship by suffering and by death, his Divine saviourship.]

Hitherto we have been contemplating Paul from one particular angle of vision. But this extraordinary man, in yet another view of him, independent of that which, under the title, " First View," was presented, is in himself alone, unsupported by other evidence, a voucher, to the candid scientific mind, entirely adequate, for the truth of Christianity.

For this second view, we set quite aside that narrative in the book of the Acts which purports to give the circumstances and incidents of the conversion of Paul. We say, Of the manner in which this man was converted we know nothing. We know only that he was converted. That certainly is a fact needing no evidence. But it is a very remarkable fact, well worthy of being deeply studied for the momentous implications that it contains.

Paul somehow, no matter how let us for the moment say, became convinced that Jesus of Nazareth was *his* rightful Lord. We need not for the moment insist that Paul became convinced of the bodily resurrection of Jesus Christ from the dead. His language indeed, in his Epistles, fairly interpreted, signifies that beyond question. But since, in some quarters, the effort is now influentially made, to put a different interpretation—an extremely forced, artificial, arbitrary interpretation it seems to me to be, on Paul's language bearing upon the point, let us waive this conclusion, and say simply, At all events, Paul came to believe that Jesus Christ was living after his crucifixion, that he was exalted to a degree of power and of glory beyond the imagination of man to conceive, and that he was actively exercising a sovereign dominion in all created worlds.

That Paul should, *in any manner,* have come to entertain this belief is, antecedently considered, as incredible a thing as it is possible to conceive, regarded simply in the light of a phenomenon occurring in the realm of human psychology. Take account of the elements of improbability subsisting in the case: Jesus Christ was a man of whom, so far as appears from any extant record, Paul knew nothing save by common report, report obviously had by him from sources bitterly hostile to his name. He thus knew that Jesus Christ was hated, or was despised, by the class of Jews to which he himself belonged, the ruling class, the aristocracy of the nation, that by these he was regarded as a base-born, mischievous pretender and impostor, that as such he was hooted to the cross by a mob that the rulers, Paul himself, for aught we know, among them, set on to cry, Crucify him! Crucify him! So possessed was Paul by this sentiment as to Jesus that he made it the chief business of the strenuous life, which it was deep in the nature of the man always to live, to trample that name under foot, stamp it into the dust, efface it from human memory. His conscience was enlisted in this cause. He verily thought—this we know from his own declaration —that he ought to do what with his whole soul he did. Moreover, his personal hopes and ambitions were engaged on the same side with his conscience. His prospects of success in life, of making a name for himself, of conquering for himself a commanding position in that Jewish polity which was all the world to Saul—these committed him, as strongly as ever man was committed to any course of conduct, to a course of implacable antagonism to Jesus Christ. And he had already now won an illustrious reputation among his countrymen as champion of the ancestral Jewish faith against the monstrous upstart creed, the abominable heresy, of a crucified Nazarene accepted, forsooth, for the nation's Messiah!

Such, on the one side, was the conspiracy of conditions rendering it incredible that ever Paul should be converted into a Christian—that haughty spirit humbled into a disciple, an adorer, of the crucified Nazarene! In other words—to repress the exclamatory words of wonder that will irrepressibly start, and put the matter into a form of simple, sober expression—it surely required some extraordinary compulsion of evidence to overcome, amid adverse conditions so powerful, such obstinacy, such fanatical fury, of unbelief (to use no stronger term) as originally was Paul's.

But we have considered thus far only one side of Paul's case; namely, what he would have to give up, the sacrifice he would be obliged to make, before allowing himself to be convinced that Jesus was Christ. Now look at the other side, and measure, if you can, the magnitude of the positive hardships and sufferings that would be involved for him in his becoming a convert to Jesus. He has himself given an eloquent account of these. That account, simple enumeration as it is, has a quality in it, a quality of self-evidencing truth and genuineness touched with generous passion, which places it among the most living classic passages of literature. Contrasting himself with certain false teachers not named, and interposing by the way an expression of the almost disdainful recoil that he feels from such necessary self-vindication as he is about to indulge, he says:

"I am more; in labors more abundantly, in stripes above measure, in prisons more abundantly, in deaths often; of the Jews five times I received forty stripes save one; thrice I was beaten with rods; once I was stoned; thrice I suffered shipwreck; a night and a day I have spent in the deep; by journeyings often, by perils of rivers, by perils of robbers, by perils from my countrymen, by perils from the heathen, by perils in the city, by perils in the wilderness, by perils in the sea, by perils among false brethren; by weariness and painfulness, in watchings often, in hunger and thirst, in fastings often, in cold and nakedness."

The persecutions that he had inflicted, and more and worse, would be retorted upon him. Those whose esteem he had previously courted would now account him an apostate and a renegade, they would cover him with obloquy and scorn, he would be an outlaw in their sight, they would thirst for his blood. "We have become the filth of the world, the offscouring of all things," is Paul's own language, which not only describes vividly the fact, but betrays the exquisite sense of the fact that ate into Paul's heart.

If it be objected that all this consequence of his conversion Paul could not have foreseen, and it could not, therefore, have entered into the conditions of the case to increase his unwillingness to be convinced and to create a corresponding necessity for overpowering evidence to convince him, it may be replied, Perhaps; but when the trials came, then at least he knew them, and then he needed the support to his faith of evidence the most reassuring conceivable. Let it be borne in mind that it is by no means simply the solitary first act of Paul's being converted that constitutes him such a witness as he is for the truth of Christianity; it is also, and hardly, if at all, less, the fact of his continuing, through all those troublous years of his apostleship, the absolutely unshaken pillar of testimony for Christ that he was, down to the day when he was offered up on that altar of sacrifice.

II

I have experienced a certain difficulty of which I must now speak in treating this part of my subject. Our present concern, be it noted, is with Paul regarded as a witness, a bearer of testimony. But of what was he a witness? What testimony did he bear? If the record in the book of the Acts may be trusted, he testified as witness that Jesus Christ, after his crucifixion, appeared to him in a light of insufferable glory, and spoke to him with such a voice as commanded instant belief and instant implicit obedience. In his own acknowledged writings, he testified further that Jesus Christ subsequently made frequent immediate communications to him, revealing to him in fact the gospel that he should preach. But this testimony, of supreme importance, if true, partakes of the character of that " supernatural " which we agree for the time to exclude. Still, there is no other testimony extant, in the ordinary sense of the word " testimony," proceeding from Paul. He appears even singularly devoid of personal knowledge that would enable him to testify respecting Jesus as a man among men. One wonders how Paul could have escaped knowing, as apparently he did escape knowing, at first hand, much of the great words and the great works of that illustrious life which, through three years, the most momentous of human history, had so illuminated the land. The fact has to be recognized that, unlike his brother apostles, Paul had no testimony to bear concerning the Jesus who lived and died, but only testimony concerning the Jesus who rose from the dead and ascended to glory, which testimony, transcendently important as it is, we must now, with effort, keep out of our view.

Do we, therefore, have to abandon our argument from Paul regarded as a bearer of testimony? As strictly a *bearer* of testimony, Yes; but as something much more than that, as *being* testimony, No. We are completely free from the necessity in his case of appraising the trustworthiness and value of what he may be found to testify. Paul as a convert, however he became a convert, is in himself his testimony, and he, personally considered, cannot be gainsaid. It is as if a colloquy like this should take place, Paul being in the witness-box and Christianity on trial :

What testimony have you to offer on behalf of Christianity?

Myself.

But who and what are you?

I am Paul, a bond-slave of Jesus Christ.

How came you to be a bond-slave of Jesus Christ?

You would not believe me if I should tell you.

What convinced you that Jesus Christ was worthy to be your Master and was in fact your Master?

As I said, you would not believe me, if I should tell you.

What, then, can you offer in the way of testimony on his behalf?

I can offer myself—myself in the character of his bond-slave.

But how did you become his bond-slave?

I do not wonder that you wish to know, but I tell you plainly, you *cannot* know, for, despite your wishing it, you *will* not know, you refuse to know. It is testimony enough that I, Paul, *am* Christ's bond-slave. How I became such, does not matter as affecting the truth of my testimony.

But it would be a satisfaction to know through what process it was that you came into such a remarkable relation to Jesus of Nazareth. There must have been some evidence brought to bear upon your mind which convinced you that this Galilean rustic was a being to be worshiped by you instead of a being to be despised. That was a tremendous revolution to take place in your mind, and it must have had a tremendous producing cause. Now please tell us plainly what was that producing cause. It was, of course, evidence of some sort. What was the evidence? It cannot have been the evidence supplied in the alleged miracles wrought by Jesus. For in the teeth of that evidence you stoutly disbelieved. It cannot have been the evidence consisting in the reports popularly current that Jesus rose from the dead, for these reports you discredited. Now what would be desirable is some rational, credible account of the way in which you did finally make the great transition from being a violent disbeliever to being the ardent believer that you became.

In the extant records of your life, and in the extant letters that you wrote, there does not appear any least hint of *progress* on your part from a state of opposition to Jesus Christ toward a state of absolute submission to him. It is contrary to the very first principles of scientific human psychology that you should have made that stupendous transition without some traceable steps of approach to the crisis of the change. But we are absolutely in the dark concerning such steps. All seems as sudden, as abrupt, as a stroke of lightning. It bewilders one who would like to have reasonable explanations of things. If one could suppose an access of secret remorse on your part in view of the miseries and the murders you had caused. But your self-accusations are all in view, not of your wrongs against fellow creatures, but of your sin against Jesus Christ. Now, of course, you could not have had a sense of sin as against Jesus, *while* you verily thought you ought to do what you did against him. That remorse could not have visited you until *after* you had changed your opinion of his character. That remorse, therefore, could have had no part in making you change your opinion of his character. We are still at a loss to account for your change of opinion in this regard. You do not furnish us even a *clue* to guide us. We seem to be in the presence of a momentous effect produced without a cause. It is extremely perplexing to the scientific mind. To be sure, there is that *experience* of yours on the way to Damascus. But what produced that experience? Here *you* are, we are compelled to admit it, an embodied testimony, incapable of being gainsaid, in the mere fact that somehow you became a Christian. It is impossible to account for you *as a Christian* on scientific principles.

III

The colloquy we have been supposing obviously lacks verisimilitude, and we may freely make that lack still broader and franker by a bold anachronism. Let Paul become sufficiently a " modern " man to make in his turn certain inquiries.

He asks, What scientific principles forbid your taking my testimony for true that Jesus appeared to me that day, in power and in glory capable of suddenly convincing me that he was Lord of all?

That, Paul, would be supernatural, and science will not permit us to believe anything supernatural.

But, pray, why not?

Why, for the very good reason that, in the view of science, everything in the universe is subject to law, nothing can be supposed to break the uniformity of nature.

What, then, is this law, this uniformity? Can it be stated in plain terms?

Yes: Like causes under like conditions always produce

like effects. The operation of that law produces the uniformity observable universally in nature. Given a certain effect, there must be assumed a cause equal to producing it. Now, what we seek, and seek in vain, is the producing cause of your change of opinion as to Jesus.

Well, is not the cause I assign fully equal to producing the effect you see in me? Wherein is involved the violation of scientific principles?

You see, Paul, your case has no parallel, it is unique.

Is it, then, a scientific principle that a thing can not be admitted to have happened at all if it has happened only once? But how can it be scientifically made certain, as to any given incident or event, that it is without precedent, without parallel; that, in fact, it, or the like of it, has never occurred before, may never subsequently occur again? That which is supernatural, you say, does not occur, never has occurred, never will occur. How is it possible to prove this?

There is no need, now we can answer confidently, to prove it. It is a first principle, a necessary postulate, of science, the very foundation on which the whole structure of science is built.

Science, then, is built on the assumption, without proof, that the supernatural is a figment of the human imagination; that the supernatural, in fact, does not exist. May I ask, what do you mean by the word "supernatural"?

We mean something out of the natural order of things, something that does not conform to law, something that is not subject to the omnipresent principle of cause and effect.

Now, may I ask further, What is there in the case under present consideration that answers to this description?

Why, all the alleged circumstances of your conversion. These are extraordinary, too extraordinary for the scientific mind to give credence to—unless, indeed, they can somehow be so understood and interpreted that they will fit into the universal uniformity of nature.

Yes; I understand, then, that what you mean by supernatural, as applied in description of the circumstances of my conversion, is really nothing more nor less than that those circumstances were very unusual—which, of course, is quite true. That they were supernatural in the sense of not fitting into the order of the universe, of not falling under the dominion of law, is far from being apparent.

But, Paul, the improbability, the staggering improbability, of them!

Yes; I felt that strongly myself—at one point. It was difficult beyond measure for me to believe that Jesus of Nazareth, the crucified, was a being able to speak to me in such a voice out of such a light. That is, it would have been immeasurably difficult for me to believe this, had not the difficulty, the seeming impossibility, been instantly, overwhelmingly, overcome, overcome in the very act and article of the announcement so made that it was he. It cannot surprise you, it cannot seem to you improbable, that I was convinced. Surely you could not suppose me capable of imagining for a moment that a being endued with the power of such a self-manifestation could *falsely* identify himself with Jesus of Nazareth. Incredible to me as was that identification, it was impossible for me not to accept it instantly for true. But perhaps the stress of improbability for you lies elsewhere?

Yes, we find it difficult, to the degree of impossible, to believe that such a voice out of such a light did really come to you. That is to us the chiefly, the supremely, improbable thing.

But, O my friends, from the point of view of true science, of the highest reason, and, I will say, even of common sense, that is not only not so improbable as it

seems to you, but, on the contrary, is inherently so probable that it may be declared a thing to have been expected
to occur—in some signal case, if not in mine. What can
be imagined more fit, more in accordance with transcendent *law*, than that a being who had walked among men,
unrecognized by them for what he was, his divinity
veiled, who had nevertheless foretold his own violent
death, and foretold besides his triumphant resurrection
soon to follow, and then his ascension to the glory that
he had with his Father before the world was—all this,
alike the humiliation and the exaltation, experienced by
him in order that he might save a race insanely unwill-
ing to be saved, a race set against him in an invincible
obstinacy of unbelief—what, I ask, more fit to the character of such a Saviour, better adapted to convince mankind and effect the purpose of ineffable grace for which
he came, what, in short, more antecedently *probable*,
than that, in some fashion wonderful to us, but *natural*
for him, he should show himself, as he showed himself
to me, no longer the despised Nazarene, but, indeed, as
he foretold would be the case, and as men were in
perishing need to believe, the possessor now of glory and
the wielder of power which could best be exhibited in
the selection of the maddest human foe to him that could
anywhere on earth be found, to be, in the very acme
of his madness, overwhelmed into belief, into obedience,
into adoration, into lifelong loyalty of service maintained
unshaken to the end in the teeth of every difficulty,
every discouragement, every earthly loss, every hardship,
every suffering? Oh, the depth of the riches both of the
wisdom and knowledge of God! If we mortals, in our
blindness, could not have foreseen the probability of some
such experience as mine, to occur once for all, as sufficient without repetition, it is at least easy in the sequel
to look back and see that nothing was more probable,
nothing more conformable to the *law* of grace which
reigns supreme in the kingdom of a God of wisdom, of

power, and of love. I do not feel that I am in the smallest degree unscientific to burst thus into a strain of doxology, in view of the miracle of which I was chosen to be the subject—chosen because I was of all men the least worthy to be chosen, so to glorify the sovereignty of the electing grace of God.

Yes, certainly, from your own individual point of view, it was, we can see, entirely becoming for you to raise such a note of exultation over the supposed circumstances that attended your happy change of mind— for a very happy change of mind it was indeed, we all feel, however it was produced. Yes, and given to science the wide range and high sweep that you suggest, it cannot but be admitted that your *carmen triumphale* was quite within the limits of the scientific even. We, however, we men of science, are accustomed to be carefully moderate in our way of thinking and speaking. We bound our claims for science to what can be observed by our senses, or what can thence be inferred logically by our reason.

But are you not thus in danger of unconsciously ignoring God? Him certainly you cannot apprehend by your senses. Are you sure you exercise your reason as much as you ought, with a view to apprehending him through reason from what your senses report? You would not be virtual atheists, I suppose?

No; "atheists" is a disagreeable word. We do not consider ourselves atheists. We simply do not regard God as a proper object of science. We neither affirm nor deny his existence. We might consent to be thought of, and to be described, as " agnostics "—in this particular regard. On the whole, however, we prefer not to confess even that purely neutral and negative attitude as to God. We are *evolutionists*. We mean by that term

H

to imply that all we know, or can know, about the universe is that it, with all its kinds and forms of being, animate and inanimate, has always been, is now, and always will be, engaged in a process of *becoming*. What we ourselves, for instance, now are, we have *become*, not within the moment of time since our birth, but through an indefinitely long, let us say, an eternal, series of changes, from stage to stage of slow, gradual, imperceptible growth and development.

Am I to understand that this evolution or development is eternal, in the sense of never having had a beginning, of never having had a cause? Does it escape the necessary, the otherwise omnipresent, omnipotent, law of cause and effect?

We do not say that. We simply say we find no beginning, and, as far as we can see, the process is its own sufficient cause. At any rate, in the presence of the mystery of the universe, we deem it wisest to be very modest and moderate in our pretensions, and to keep our language, as we keep our conceptions, quite sober, and, above all, taking no counsel of our desires, not to give way to our emotions which, as often as otherwise, we think, are likely to lead us astray. It will be no offense, we trust, if we take the liberty very respectfully to suggest that you perhaps were yourself led astray, on that great occasion, by your emotions. Understand, we entertain the very highest opinion of your personal character as a gentleman of truth and honor, with even a fine sentiment of holiness in your make-up, such that Voltaire's, for example, was not to be compared with it [ironic glance, the author's, at John Morley's surprising remark about Voltaire, " he missed the peculiar emotion of holiness, the soul and life alike of the words of Christ and Saint Paul."] Still, this our sincerely cordial and even admiring esteem for you does not prevent our apprehending that you were, quite honestly of course, deceived about that experience of yours. In the absence of all other hint as to the process, mental and spiritual, through which you passed to arrive at your new state of mind, and being scientifically unable to accept your own interpretation—perfectly honest, we must keep protesting our conviction that it was—of your experience on the way to Damascus, we have, nevertheless, our final theory of explanation. It was a case of what, for want of a better term to describe it, we call "suggestion."

Indeed! And what, pray, does "suggestion," in this somewhat novel, and, I must suppose, quasi-technical, use of the word, mean, may I ask?

It names that singular, but universal, tendency which possesses men to think and feel as the crowd about them think and feel—quite apart from any independent individual exercise of reason and judgment. This is a pregnant principle, of which it is only of late that psychological philosophers and scientific students of history—especially scientific students of biblical history—have made the surprisingly fruitful and satisfactory wide application that it has been found to admit. It is perhaps the very most effective of all available methods of exorcism for that haunting spirit of supernaturalism which, where it enters, so interferes with the proper clear vision of science. For instance, the principle of "suggestion" gives us at last the key to the true interpretation of the New Testament stories of the resurrection of Jesus, by enabling us to understand how those simple-minded first disciples could, with perfect truthfulness, report falsely what happened in sequel of the crucifixion. Some one got possessed with the notion that he, or she—it was likely to be a woman—actually saw the familiar form and face, actually heard the familiar voice, of his, or her, late crucified Master risen from the dead, as, it was

now recalled, or perhaps imagined, he had himself foretold he would rise.   This person communicated his, or
her, impression to another, and to another, and finally to
many, possibly even to no less a number than the five
hundred you refer to in one of your letters as having
together seen and heard the risen Master at one and the
same time.   All a matter of what advanced psychologists
have decided to call "suggestion."   The same principle
accounts for the mad multitudinous cry, "Crucify him!
Crucify him!" that a few days before had hooted Jesus
to the cross.   Of all that wild mob not one man really
wanted to have Jesus crucified.   They were all together
carried away by the principle of suggestion.

A master principle truly!   And so you will have it
that I, Paul, was the victim of suggestion, when I became
a believer in Jesus as the risen, the reascended, the glorified, Lord of all.   But does not suggestion also, great
principle as it is, obey some sort of law in its working?
Does it not have to have a start somewhere, in obedience
to the universal sway of cause and effect?   In the case
of the multitude that cried "Crucify him! Crucify him!"
it is well understood that the rulers of the Jews—my
own social class—set them on to that cry.   But, as to the
small number of persons who first, to their own surprise,
came to believe they had seen and heard their Master
risen from the dead—who was there to supply *them* the
false "suggestion"?   They were all alike sunk together
in bottomless depths of disbelief and despair, no one
of them so much as dreaming aught but that their beloved
Master was hopelessly lost to them forever.   But, most
wonderful of all, the idea that Paul—of all men, Paul—
should fall under the dominion of "suggestion," with no
source near, or assignable, whence the suggestion could
spring to him!   A truly curious case it would seem to
be, of freakish exception to the great law of cause and
effect.   And then, too, may I ask, Does Paul seem to

you to have been the kind of man to fall an easy prey of a sheer delusion, with no fact at hand to give it rise in his mind?

IV

The fiction of colloquy, with Paul for interlocutor, has become a pretense too glaringly transparent to be longer maintained. Indeed, I have been as well aware as my readers must all along have been, that I was expressing myself in my own character rather than in the character of Paul. Let me now bring this argument to a close with mention, little more than mere mention, of some material considerations bearing on the case here discussed.

In the first place, it is duly to be considered that in Paul we have a witness, differing from all the rest of the apostolic witnesses, to the great facts relating to the resurrection, the ascension, the resumed glory and power, of Jesus Christ—differing in the very important circumstance that he was an extraordinarily able man, and, besides, a man of thoroughly disciplined and exercised mind; a mind, moreover, richly furnished with wide-ranging information and knowledge.

In the second place, Paul, not having been a personal follower of Jesus while he lived in the flesh, and not probably having been a personal witness of any of his mighty works, was consequently exempt from what may, in "modern" parlance, be called the "hypnotic" influence supposably exerted by an exceptional personality incarnate in that Man of Nazareth.

In the third place, notwithstanding the fact of such exemption thus secured for Paul, he was so near, both in time and in place, to all the great transactions and events of those momentous years covering the public life of Jesus and covering the time immediately following his crucifixion, that he had every opportunity to inform himself fully concerning the facts, or alleged facts, involved in a case of such peculiarly critical and crucial importance, by eminence to *him*.

In the fourth place, Paul, while, by a certain quasi-poetic mystical quality in his temperament, fitted to conceive more adequately than any other of the apostles, even than John, of the transcending preexistent and eternal rank and glory of his Lord, and thereby peculiarly prepared to receive communication from that unseen and ineffable majesty—Paul, while thus gifted with capacity of sublime spiritual intuition, was at the same time a singularly practical man, a man of the sanest common sense, in short, an ideal level-headed man of affairs—the last man in the world to be carried away with groundless delusions, to become and to remain lifelong the subject of monomaniac mental obsessions.

In the fifth place, it is not to be overlooked that, in extant writings unquestionably his, Paul plainly alludes to signs of a miraculous nature attending his ministry— a fact here brought forward because it shows that Paul felt the necessity of grounding his claims of peculiar authority from the invisible Christ, on something besides his blank assertions and assumptions; namely, on sensible objective attestations, of a nature such that he could safely appeal to the personal knowledge, from observation, of those to whom he was writing.

I am framing now an *a priori* argument, an argument from antecedent probability. Of course, I do not forget that *a priori* arguments prove nothing; but they may, if sound, tend to forestall and countervail contrary *a priori* arguments. And that is what, I submit, the considerations now urged do effect. The antecedent probability of some such demonstration from heaven as that contained in the miraculous conversion of Paul is an antecedent probability so many-sided and so great that the antecedent improbability—which I fully admit because I keenly feel—lying against all miracle, is squarely met, in the present case, and triumphantly overcome.

I proceed to press other considerations reenforcing my *a priori* argument, and tending, I think, to show that Paul's conversion, taking some such exceptional form and method as, according to the narrative in the Acts, Paul's conversion did take, was an incident to have been looked for; it possesses all the marks of a divine wisdom, as well as of a divine power, working in it.

The human and earthly life of Jesus had been lived, and his death had been accomplished, as he foretold would be the case, in Jerusalem and not elsewhere. This life and this death, with the resurrection and the ascension following, were subjects of testimony from witnesses in all respects competent to fulfil the office of witnesses on those points. Now there was wanted a witness to attest the reality of the unseen and unspeakably glorious life into which Christ, after his humiliation as Redeemer, had entered as Conqueror and King. The witness needed, we, wise after the event, can see was precisely such a man, so qualified, not only by nature, but also by circumstance, as Paul. Some of the traits in Paul's equipment as witness for Christ have been noted, but not all.

In the sixth place, then, Paul, besides being intellectually and spiritually qualified, beyond almost any other man that ever lived, to know Christ truly and to sympathize with him deeply, was supremely endowed to be ethically a pattern and a teacher of Christ's doctrine and spirit. It may startle, but I do not hesitate to say that, as plain matter of fact, what is sometimes called the " essential " Christ—that is, the most intimate, most regnant, spirit of Christ—is more fully shown, more effectively reduced to practicability for human souls, in Paul's writings, than in all the four Gospels taken together. Paul is often, perhaps generally, misunderstood as predominantly a theologian. The truth is, Paul was the greatest ethical teacher, the greatest ethical force, that has ever lived and written himself into literature. Take for one example of his surpassing ethical height, and of a surpassing sweetness and tenderness in him adapted to commend his exhortations to acceptance, the twelfth chapter of Romans. That chapter is the noblest manual of sweet and beautiful human behavior to be found anywhere in literature—unless, indeed, the famous canticle of love in the thirteenth chapter of First Corinthians excels it. It was very essential to the fruitfulness in human conduct of the gospel of Christ, that it should be drawn out in manifold applications to life, as it is drawn out in Paul's Epistles; and the character in Paul which rendered him capable of doing this work increases indefinitely the antecedent probability that, if a supernatural demonstration of convincing force were to be vouchsafed from heaven in attestation of the truth of Christ's posthumous life in power and glory, that demonstration would, by divine wisdom in choice, of all men in the world light upon Paul.

In the seventh place, it needed that the one greatest apostle, that one apostle who should longest, most profoundly, most effectively, impress himself and his teaching upon the mind and the heart of mankind, should be conversant chiefly with the eternal Christ rather than with the temporal Jesus of Nazareth. By the necessary nature of things, the temporal Jesus was very imperfectly known, and very imperfectly represented in literature. The eternal Christ, who " came," to be Jesus of Nazareth for a season, and then went into the heaven of heavens, to be forever where he was before—that Being, who was " Son of God " in a unique, discriminated meaning of that expression, a meaning of it which made him coequal with his Father (just as a human son, though by filial relation subordinate, is by nature essentially equal to his human father)—*He* was Paul's Christ, and he, through Paul, has always been exerting his power to help us believers live, in a world of sense, a life of faith, as if, indeed, and in truth, our citizenship was not here, but in heaven. It was antecedently probable, therefore, that Paul's calling to be an apostle would be in a unique, remarkable manner, a calling impressively from heaven—from the unseen Christ, that is to say, rather than from that visible Jesus of Nazareth by whom all Paul's brother apostles had been called.

An important suggested remark, by the way. When we remember that Paul's transcendent Christ, according to Luke's report of Paul's testimony, identified himself to Paul, in express terms, with Jesus of Nazareth; when we remember also that Paul, as reported by Luke, makes one precious independent and additional contribution to the extant *memorabilia* of the living discourse that fell from the lips of Jesus of Nazareth, in his citation of those famous words, " It is more blessed to give than to receive "; when, still further, we remember that Paul enjoyed every opportunity of time and place for informing himself accurately as to the real facts concerning Jesus of Nazareth—then we perceive that, quite apart from the four Gospels, Paul individually stands forth an unimpeachable witness—witness in the ordinary sense of that word—for the " historicity " of Jesus. In view of this fact, there is no scientific possibility left for doubt or question on that point—a point, however, to which historical critics of the present day, seeming, all of them, to ignore Paul's testimony, a testimony by itself alone absolutely conclusive, are disposed to recur again and again, as if doubt and question had not been definitely precluded, had not been rendered scientifically impossible. It is, of course, quite true that it was Paul's prevailing habit to name his Master by his title " Christ," using that designation either alone, or with " Jesus " attached before or after; but he sometimes spoke of him simply as " Jesus." This is proof enough, if proof were needed, that Paul had not in mind an " Idea " simply, or an Ideal Person who never existed in the world of reality, but a true historical character, as living and literal as he was himself. It was natural, and it was most fit, that to Paul, his Master should be "the Christ," for he never knew his Master except as "the Christ." Those who believe in a divine Providence presiding over human history, and preeminently concerned for the continued existence of his Church and the consequent salvation of sinners, may well see, in the very peculiar relation of Paul to Jesus, a provision of evidence, foreseen to be needed at last, to meet the cunning, fatuously cunning, incredulity of science, respecting the actual appearing among men of such a personage as Jesus of Nazareth.

And, by the way, it is not to be regarded as a defect in the preparation of Paul for standing forth in witness of the truth of the gospel, the fact that he had no testimony to give derived from personal observation and knowledge of the historical Jesus. That fact is a qualification rather. For the transcendent Christ, the Pre-existent, the Ascended, the Glorified, the Reigning, needed —if perception on his part of our human need may be regarded as creating a need in himself—the transcendent Christ *needed* a witness of his being and power and glory, such as Paul. And Paul could perhaps even better be the witness needed, for *not* having had the opportunity, through personal contact with his Master during the days of his humiliation, of forming preconceptions to interfere with, embarrass, confuse, the abundance of revelations from Christ in heaven of which the last-chosen apostle was made the recipient.

v

The *a priori* argument that I have been incidentally and quite subordinately conducting, concerns only the question of the antecedent probability of such a phenomenon as the reported conversion of Paul, and it will have weight only for those who accept the presuppositions underlying it. Those presuppositions are:

1. The being of a God graciously disposed toward his creatures; 2. The possibility of the supernatural (God at least is supernatural!) ; 3. The " historicity " of Jesus; 4. His survival of death (not necessarily his literal bodily resurrection, though that is an article of my own unwavering personal faith) ; 5. His present exaltation to a throne of power and glory by the right hand of God.

Some professing Christians who accept the foregoing presuppositions are, nevertheless, strongly inclined to reduce to a minimum their admission of the supernatural into the providential scheme of human affairs. This is an inclination which I can understand and which I myself in some measure share. I submit, however, that, in view of the *a priori* considerations presented above, that man is at quite needless pains, who, obedient to his principle of parsimony in belief of miracle, seeks a so-called rational, that is, naturalistic, explanation of Paul's conversion. The accompaniments of that great event in no sense constituted an empty spectacular phenomenon, the product of delusion in the subject or of fictive fancy in the narrator. The whole incident in all its details was a counsel of Divine wisdom, in gracious condescension to human need of evidence supplied in yet one more illustrious epiphany, to show that Jesus was not dead, but risen, ascended, enthroned, still concerned for his disciples, their Lord and their Saviour forevermore.

Let me now in conclusion clinch my argument with a personal testimony. I herewith bear witness that as for me, when I might feel every other anchor drag in the stress of storm without and storm within, I feel this anchor holding me immovably safe to my moorings in the faith of the gospel—Paul, the historic problem that admits of but one only solution; Paul, the embodied testimony, that no critical skepticism can successfully gainsay.

To guard against the possible misunderstanding that there lurks some disparagement of the four Gospels concealed in certain expressions of mine preceding, let me add, by way of caveat, that nothing was farther from my thought. I have myself all confidence in those invaluable memorials of a brief, indescribably precious, and sacred past. To dispense with them would be like blotting out the sun from heaven. Still, such is the amazing providence of God our Saviour, that he has, as I undoubtingly hold, furnished us in the apostle Paul a guaranty of the essential validity of the claim of his Son to be Lord and Redeemer of the world—a guaranty sufficient in itself not only to warrant our unreserved faith, but also to create an overwhelming antecedent probability, almost amounting to demonstration, in favor of a heavenly precedent manifestation like that of which the four Gospels, with all their stories of miracle, constitute the self-evidencing noble and beautiful record—record, by its own confession, left eloquently so incomplete!

CHAPTER VII

SOME VOICES OF REVOLT

I

THE Apostle Paul, is, let it be said boldly, one of the most redoubtable figures in human history. There is, indeed, only one historic figure more redoubtable than he. (Startling as the assertion doubtless will be to many, it may yet truly, though paradoxically, be maintained, from the strictly critical rationalistic point of view, that, as, without Jesus Christ, Paul would never have been the redoubtable figure in history that he is, so, reciprocally, without Paul, Jesus Christ would never have been that *more* redoubtable figure in history that we behold him to-day. The two historical figures were necessary to each other, *equally* necessary both, the less as necessary as the greater. They will always continue thus to be linked together. The revolt against Paul may seek to separate them, but the attempt will forever be vain. The church will always need the heavenly Christ, and the heavenly Christ will always need his Apostle Paul. The " bond-slave " is safe, held in the right hand of his Master.)

Take into view the whole circle of Christendom and the whole period of the so-called Christian era, and you will agree that no other personage, with the one exception already noted, has been more talked of, written of, commented on, followed as master, than the Apostle Paul. Yet I believe it to be true to-day that of all men great in history, the Apostle Paul is the one man least understood, the one man most misunderstood. It is a vast pity that this should be so, and every sincere and intelligent effort ought to be welcomed and cheered that is directed toward having it otherwise. The hope is cherished that this volume may be accepted as such an effort loyally put forth by the present writer.

That there is on foot just now a widespread, strongly supported, very formidable, movement in revolt against the Apostle Paul, has already been herein abundantly implied. The revolt is against Paul the Apostle rather than against Paul the man. Paul the man is almost universally praised in the highest terms, even by those who most vehemently oppose Paul the Apostle. Apostle, in the sense of true representative of the historical Jesus, Paul, the insurrectionists say, was not. He thought he was, he loyally meant to be, but his intention failed, and he in fact misrepresented the Master whom he professed, and fully purposed, to serve. The simple gospel of Jesus, Paul's opponents say, was overlaid, until it came finally to be replaced, by what they call " Paulinism "; that is, by a scheme of Christology and of theology, originated by Paul, and by him developed into a wide divergence from the teachings of the true, the historical, Jesus of Nazareth. It is a curious cry that is raised, a compound paradoxical cry, ' Down with Paulinism! Hurrah for Paul! '

As was to have been expected, this new rationalism, the current revolt against Paul, finds its protagonists in Germany. It will be fair to them to let them state their case for the reader of this volume. It will also be fair to the reader. Indeed, it will be fair not less to Paul himself. Let us begin genially, with specimens of the praise bestowed by the insurrectionists upon Paul. Perhaps, however, these will be read with greater zest if we interpose beforehand one or two very exceptional expressions of an opposite tenor.

Weinel, in his late remarkable book, " Saint Paul the Man and His Work," quotes from Nietzsche the following expressions concerning Paul:

" One of the most ambitious of men, a passed master in importunacy, whose superstition was only equaled

by his cunning. . . This much-tortured, much-to-be-pitied
man, an exceedingly unpleasant personage both to himself and others. . . If it had not been for the aberrations
of his mind and the waves of emotion that passed over
his soul, there would be no Christianity."

Now another German (also quoted by Weinel), with
a half French-looking name, Lagarde:

" It is monstrous that men of any historical training
should attach any importance whatever to this Paul. . .
It was Paul who introduced the Old Testament into the
church, through the influence of which book the gospel
has perished as far as it could perish. . . The early
Christian church, Jewish as it was, was less Jewish
than Paul, in its opinions."

In contrast of such expressions, quoted by Weinel to
be by him dissented from, hear what he himself says:

" Few, very few, really know him [Paul]. . . But for
those that do know him, the form of the tent-maker
and divine looms ever higher and higher in the world's
history. . . Wonderful charm of the personality of the
great apostle. . . Saint Paul is a hero in the domain of
the will, a born leader of men. He is also a hero
in the domain of thought, . . he has impressed forever a whole series of fundamental ideas . . . on the
thought of the Western world. Millions of men to-day
think with his thoughts and speak with his words. . .
I have wanted to make our people understand and love
Paul. . . Most people still distrust Paul, the ' fanatic '
and the ' dogmatist '; and no wonder [so this sworn lover
of Paul goes on to say] he has become a bond and
a yoke." Weinel's praise and his revolt are thus uttered
in the same breath. But, as will presently be seen, his
revolt at length finds more distinct and positive expression.

From the " bond " and the " yoke " which, according to Weinel, Paul has " become," it is in Weinel's
friendly mind to free people and thus instate his beloved

Paul in their affectionate good will. He in effect flouts the *apostle* to make the *man* beloved. But it is always to be borne in mind that, as with others, so with Weinel, it is only against Paul as apostle of the ascended and glorified Christ, that is to say, against Paul as *authoritative* organ of his Master and of the Master of all human history, that the standard of revolt is raised.

Another important German author who deals with Paul in the way of revolt against him, is Wrede. Wrede says:

" He [Paul] remains not merely a great, but a noble character; a faithful steward, to his very depths an unselfish fighter, and a true hero. . . What enabled him to accomplish the task of his life was that, religiously, as well as intellectually and morally, he was an extraordinary personality; and no doubt this also, that he had not become a Christian in the normal way."

Wernle, in his " Beginnings of Christianity," says:

" Paul never knew Jesus during his lifetime, and nevertheless it was he who best understood him. . . As one surveys the whole of what he achieved, one stands in silent amazement at his greatness as a thinker. . . He himself, the man Paul, is one of the most inspiring and comforting characters in all history, one of those who are an unfailing source of courage and of joy to us a smaller breed of men."

Our American Prof. G. B. Foster must be counted in the anti-Paul ranks, or, as he would prefer to express it, in the ranks of anti-Paulinism. In his case, *revolt* it emphatically is, for he was, not so long ago, a loyal and even ardent evangelical. At that time an expression quoted to him of repudiation for Paul's doctrine of atonement by the Cross, " contradicted his experience," he said. It is a pity that he did not continue to trust his experience rather than to surrender himself into the hands of German rationalists. But he pays generous tribute to the personality of Paul, thus:

" A hero of powerful personality, trained in scholastic theology, mighty in word and pen, inflexible of will and lively of temperament, indefatigable in work, but yet as earnest and zealous for ' doctrines' as for souls. Won by Jesus whom he had not known, he became lifelong servant and missionary of the Christ throned in the heavens, and preached his apostolic gospel of the crucified and risen Son of God. It is an awe-inspiring tribute to the power of Paul that to this day the Gospels are read by most people in the light of the Pauline theology."

" Awe-inspiring ! " That is a happily true word, unhappily misapplied. " The ' awe' inspired should be awe toward the power that worked (and works) *through* Paul, not toward the " power *of* Paul." The " power of Paul," great as it was, could never have produced the result of which Professor Foster was speaking. To assume that it could, is to make a capital mistake in historical criticism.

The truth is that the Gospels *ought* to be read in the light that Paul throws upon them. Not to read them thus is to make another capital mistake, this time a mistake in literary criticism. Sound literary criticism requires that a given literary production should be studied in the light of literature contemporaneous with it, and especially in the light of contemporaneous literature, should such be available, produced by a master mind dealing with the same subject. The effort to escape Paul's influence in our study of the Gospels is effort to throw away the chief available aid for the right understanding of those Gospels.

Still, it is in fairness to be acknowledged that Professor Foster shows himself a sincere lover of truth. For example, at a certain place, in a footnote, he quotes at some length from a book a passage which, as he evidently, while quoting it, is fully aware, makes strongly against himself—I should be inclined to say, conclusively, against himself.

I

After being shown the preceding array of glowing testimonials to the character and the achievement of Paul, what, my reader will be ready to exclaim, what can this writer mean by representing these encomiasts as engaged in a revolt against the great Apostle? I hasten to explain, or rather to expand into something like fulness the explanation already suggested. The revolt is against Paul as wielder of authority, an authority received from a supernatural Christ. Hear Wernle:

"A *myth* [italics mine] from beginning to end, and cannot be termed anything else [said of Paul's 'heavenly Christ'] Here [that is, in Philippians, the great second chapter of that Epistle] the Jesus of history is completely smothered up by the *myth* of the heavenly Son of God."

In the same tenor, Wrede uses the following language:

"The thought that a divine being forsakes heaven, veils himself in humanity, and then dies in order to ascend again into heaven . . . is a *mythological* [italics mine] conception. . . He, Paul, has thrust that greater person, whom he meant only to serve, utterly into the background."

Now, let it be observed, the foregoing statements declaring the "heavenly Christ" of Paul to be a "myth," are blank, unsupported assertions. The writers who make them do not attempt to support them by argument. They simply make them. They throw them out as postulates, as self-evident truths, requiring therefore no proof; indeed, perhaps in their view, like the axioms of mathematics, admitting of none. The writers are apparently men of conscience, men of serious purpose, who have explored their "sources," who know well their facts, and who mean to treat their facts, with freedom indeed, but also with fairness and candor. As has been shown, they are well affected toward Paul, the man. They sincerely, they ardently, admire him. They, of course, do not question his truthfulness. His testimony on all points they unhesitatingly accept. They therefore accept his testimony as to his " heavenly Christ." But they *inter-pret* it. His " heavenly Christ " is a " myth." That is, there is no heavenly Christ. Paul's heavenly Christ is a figment of Paul's imagination; it is one, of course the chief one, of " the aberrations of his mind," a porten-tous fragment of the wreckage washed up on shore by " the waves of emotion that passed over his soul." It is well said by Nietzsche, from whom, on the authority of Weinel, the last-quoted phrases are taken, that, without such experiences on the part of Paul as his critic so de-scribes, " there would be no Christianity." I will venture, with all seriousness and solemnity, to add, There would not now be even any form, however empty, of Chris-tianity in the world, without the *reality,* the objective reality, answering to these subjective experiences of Paul. Furthermore, more seriously and more solemnly still, I am profoundly convinced that from the moment when the church of Christ surrenders its belief in the reality, the non-mythological character, of those experiences of Paul, from that moment, Christianity, as a religion of human redemption, will cease to exist under the sun. That profound conviction of mine is the reason why this book is written and published.

II

This book would perhaps not have been written and published, had I not met lately with certain unexpected and very surprising things in a book, a valuable book, from the pen of a writer who means to be, and who evi-dently believes himself to be, a thoroughly orthodox evangelical Christian, and who is an honored and in-fluential teacher in a theological seminary hitherto re-puted to be of the straitest sort of soundness in the faith of the gospel. This author attributes to Paul " a type of teaching so different from anything that we find in the words of Jesus as to be in effect a totally new gospel." He says, " Paul saved Christianity from perishing in the

cradle," by securing the differentiation of it from Judaism.
" It would have been," he says, " an incalculable disaster
if Paul had not won " in this matter. " But," so he goes
on to say, " it was an almost equal disaster that Paul did
win; for in becoming differentiated from Judaism, the
new faith became the Christianity of Paul rather than
the Christianity of Jesus."

It will at once be seen how exactly in the sense of
those German critics to whom we have just been listening,
this orthodox American author expresses himself. I
quote him here in evidence of the fact that the spirit
of revolt against Paul has got beyond the ranks of the
confessed rationalists, has in fact invaded the camp of
supposed orthodox Christian champions. It is certainly
time that a revolt against the revolt should be raised.

Unless, indeed, the current and increasing revolt be
justified in reason. Is it? Does the " divergence " openly
spoken of, with use of that very word, by our American
author, the alleged divergence, namely, of Paul from
Jesus—does this divergence in fact exist? I have sought
to find enumeration somewhere of the points of supposed divergence, but my quest, though assisted by citation of " sources," supplied to me in a friendly way by
leading members of the New Testament faculty in the
Divinity School of the University of Chicago, has been
without important fruit. The divergence alleged seems
in effect to reduce itself to this: That the Gospels give
us the Jesus of history, while Paul presents us almost exclusively with a Christ risen from the dead, ascended to
glory and to power in the heavens and thence reigning
supreme in the church and the world. Here certainly
is a difference, a wide difference; but is the difference a
divergence? Does Paul, dealing with his heavenly Christ,
oppose himself to the historical Jesus; or does he only
continue and advance, " produce," as geometers say, the
historical Jesus, setting him forward in that realm of
supramundane being of which the historical Jesus thought

when he said, " All authority is given unto me in heaven and in earth," also when he said: " I came forth from the Father, and have come into the world; again, I leave the world, and go to the Father "?

III

It was not my purpose in the preceding pages to criticize the critics of Paul. I quoted them simply to show what the current tendency is in the treatment of the great apostle. It is, however, difficult to refrain from criticism of writers who, with all their merits, lay themselves so open, as all these writers, do, to just objection on critical grounds. For instance, Wrede, in stating " what enabled him [Paul] to accomplish the task of his life," adds, as a kind of afterthought, not in his opinion very material, but necessary perhaps to fulness and fairness of treatment, " and no doubt this also that he had not become a Christian in the normal way "! In printing that, I could not forbear affecting it with an exclamation-point. What historical, what critical, what critico-historical, sense must be the man's who was capable of saying *that* in *that* way?

The point that Wrede dismisses in that shuffling negative manner, Weinel treats seriously. Seriously, but— soundly? Let us see. He accepts without a question or doubt the New Testament story of Paul's conversion, but, as a " modern " man, a man living in an age of " science," he supplies an explanation, an interpretation. Here is what he says:

" Paul *saw* [italics Weinel's own]. . . Men see in two ways. One way rests on retina pictures transmitted physically from without, the other on retina pictures communicated from within in states of extreme psychical emotion."

Weinel is a writer of acknowledged importance. He has exerted, probably is still exerting, great influence in the crucial contention now in progress in the theological world, on the subject of " Paulinism," so called, that is, on the subject of the right of Paul to maintain his long-held place of primacy as molder of Christian doctrine for the universal church. Weinel would unseat Paul from his throne of power. This he would do because he loves Paul and wishes to make people in general love him, which they cannot enjoy the inestimable privilege of doing, as long as Paul lords it unlawfully over their faith. I am saying this not in irony, but in all sincerity of meaning, and in a spirit of true loyalty toward Weinel, whom I recognize as not only an able and a thoroughly well-informed critic of Paul, but also a cordially sympathetic, even enthusiastic, and in most respects very discerning, evaluator of the great apostle.

If Weinel were *not* such a man as I have just now intimated that I esteem him to be, and a wielder of such influence, I should not think it worth while to devote the attention that I am about to devote, to the foregoing explanation from his pen of Paul's Damascus experience. I must ask thoughtful readers to consider that explanation at some length and with some care. It is not to be passed over negligently as simply a way on Weinel's part of saying that Paul's experience was a purely subjective experience, not answering to any objective reality. It would have been safer and wiser in Weinel to confine himself to the usual vague assertion offered by rationalistic critics that Paul's case belonged to a well-known class of such cases, all of them alike admitting of a perfectly satisfactory psychological explanation without recourse to any hypothesis of miracle.

But Weinel's candor made him more bold than prudent. He thought he had a little physical *science,* as well as psychological, that could advantageously be brought into play. So he lays down what he seems to think an unquestionable fact, even principle, in the science of vision: pictures are sometimes formed on the retina through "extreme psychical emotion," without the intervention

of any external objects to produce them, pictures therefore that represent nothing but subjective, self-begotten,
notions of the excited brain. Then he plainly implies
that a picture was so formed on the retina of Paul's eye
as he approached Damascus that memorable day. Not
only so; he plainly implies also that the picture thus
formed was a picture of Jesus the Nazarene. Yet more;
he plainly implies that Paul *identifies* the picture without
hint or help except from his own excited brain—this,
although there is no proof that Paul ever saw Jesus during
his earthly life. (To be sure, the New Testament account states that Paul asked, "Who art thou, Lord?"
and that the Lord replied, "I am Jesus of Nazareth";
but Weinel takes no notice of this; it is, according to
him, "Paul's *uneasy conscience*" that cries, "Saul, Saul,
why persecutest thou me?")

All the foregoing implications (and more) are contained in Weinel's explanation. My reason for enumera-
ting them is to say that every one of them all is pure
assumption, without the shadow of evidence for its
being true. Moreover, the alleged optical fact, or principle, namely, that images are sometimes formed on the
retina through psychical excitement, is a thing not only
not ascertained, but a thing incapable of being ascertained, even if true.

The quasi-scientific solution propounded, with such
sincere respect toward the apostle, as well as with such
serene self-confidence on the part of the propounder, by
Weinel, of that great problem, the crux of the historical
criticism of Christianity, the conversion of Paul—this
solution is so interesting and so curious that it deserves
the study here bestowed upon it. Futile and false as it
demonstrably is, it yet is the best attempt I have ever
met with to dispense with supernaturalism in connection
with the Damascus experience of Paul. Let readers observe, Weinel says, Paul "*saw*"—with emphasis placed
by him on that verb. 'Certainly,' we feel him saying,

' certainly Paul saw. He tells us he saw, and Paul is a truthful man, his word is not to be questioned.' Paul's critic then proceeds to tell *how* he saw. The explanation offered is apparently very simple, but it is really very complex. It contains assertions and implications as follows (I recapitulate):

No. 1. Images are sometimes imprinted on the retina solely through " extreme psychical emotion ": pure assumption, no proof, no possibility of proof.

No. 2. An image was thus produced on the retina of Paul's eye that great Damascus day: pure assumption, no proof, no possibility of proof.

No. 3. The image thus produced was a " picture " of Jesus the Nazarene: no proof, no possibility of proof; nothing whatever to make it probable.

No. 4. Paul recognized the picture, identified it as Jesus of Nazareth—this, though there is no proof that he had ever seen Jesus of Nazareth during Immanuel's earthly sojourn; therefore obviously no possibility of the assumption's being true that Paul *recognized* the picture, *unless* he recognized it through an intervention of the supernatural, the very thing by all means to be dispensed with.

No. 5. Paul " saw " a " picture," which we have no reason to think existed, on the retina of his eye; whereas, any retina picture, however produced, would be visible only to an outside observer, and not at all to the subject himself whose retina supposedly held it.

No. 6. Paul, at a given moment, *suddenly,* without preparation for it (as far as historical evidence exists), became the subject of " extreme psychical emotion," in such an overpowering access of it that the singular result followed, of his having a picture of a non-existent object vividly imprinted on the retina of his eye. Just why " extreme psychical emotion " should take the turn of so affecting the retina of his eye, does not readily appear. Indeed, when one gives the point a little thought, it really becomes very mysterious, that precisely *this* physical effect should be produced. In fine, Weinel's explanation is so many-sidedly preposterous that one wonders how it could ever have been propounded seriously by so able a man as its originator.

It will perhaps be satisfactory to those among my readers who may have experienced a shock of incredulity when they encountered the statement that images on the retina of the eye, however produced, are visible only to an outside observer (and, by the way, the observer must be equipped with an ophthalmoscope in order to make his observation), not being visible at all to the subject himself—it may, to such readers, be satisfactory to see a confirmation of the view, proceeding from a source more authoritative than the present writer can claim to be. I quote from a scientific authority, writing in the article, " Vision," in the " International Cyclopædia," edition of 1899:

" As has been shown by previous writers, the difficulty [the difficulty of accounting for our seeing objects right side up though the retinal images are inverted] has arisen solely from the assumption, contrary to fact, that we *see* the retinal pictures, whereas, considered as images, they are not even the means, but only the concomitants, of that operation of light by which we see. . . In a strict sense there is no *image* upon the retina, but only a concourse of rays, which, *to the eye of another person,* will undoubtedly give the perception of an image, but cannot be affirmed to exist, as an image, except in relation to this second observer." The italics shown in this quotation are the italics of the Cyclopædia writer. For my own purpose, I should like to have readers regard the three words above, " contrary to fact," as also italicized. I trust that Weinel's scientific explanation of the fact admitted by him that Paul " *saw,*" on that memorable day, will be acknowledged to have been scientifically disposed of. I may add that the " New International

Cyclopædia" has a different article on the subject of "Vision," which, however, has nothing contradictory to what has been quoted, but, on the contrary, is, in a form less full, confirmatory of it.

IV

The explanation of the curious fact of Weinel's explanation is very simple. The explainer's mind was completely occupied, usurped, tyrannized over, by a certain presupposition which he assumed to be impregnably scientific, but which, I submit, is in fact the reverse, the contradiction, of the scientific. This last point will come up for discussion in subsequent pages. For the moment let me content myself with proposing, as universally applicable, a postulate submitted to all true lovers of science.

I am myself, though not professionally a scientific man, nevertheless of a decidedly scientific turn of mind. I have been pleased with believing that if I had addicted myself to scientific pursuits I might have had as good prospects of success in that line of life as in any other that I could have chosen. One prime natural qualification for scientific research and discovery is, I take it, an ever-present, ever-wakeful, spirit of skepticism, a disposition to refuse belief until adequate evidence is supplied. At any rate, that is my own instinct and habit of mind, always alert and active, whatever may be the particular subject that engages my interest. I am therefore heartily in sympathy with the open-minded, inquiring, investigating, scientific temper held to be characteristic of the current age of the civilized world. But I apply my tests even to this temper, with which all the time I heartily sympathize. I doubt, and I ask, The reigning scientific tendency of the times—is it certainly altogether on the right track? In other words, is it soundly, safely scientific? In the posture of mind thus indicated I have evolved for myself a prime postulate for universal application, which I now submit for criticism and correction, invited from whatever source:

The true, the scientific, prime attitude toward any alleged fact, historical or other, demanding consideration, is simply and strictly this, Does the fact exist? Is it a fact? What is the evidence?

This postulate forbids our meeting any alleged fact with a dead wall of presupposition against it. We must not say of some alleged fact in history, This alleged fact cannot be a fact, for if it were it would be a miracle, or would involve miracle, and miracles do not occur. To classify an alleged historic fact as a miracle and consider it in that way satisfactorily disposed of, is not, I submit, a genuinely scientific procedure. Our question ought not to be, *Can* this have occurred? It ought to be, *Did* it occur?—let us weigh the evidence.

I hold therefore that void and vain is all discussion of the subject of Paul's conversion that starts and persists with the obstinate, invincible presupposition in the mind of the person discussing it, that nothing supernatural can have been involved in the event—void and vain, because hopelessly unscientific. Let us be truly scientific and our results must stand, whatever they may turn out to be.

Here is an historical phenomenon to be accounted for, an historical problem to be solved, the historical phenomenon, the historical problem, of Paul. For my own part, I am such a believer in science, in the science of historical criticism particularly, that I pledge myself beforehand, without qualification, without reserve, to accept for true and final whatever finding may be reached in the forum of historical criticism. I only insist that the historical criticism applied shall be sound historical criticism, conducted in accordance with sound scientific principles, and in pursuance of sound scientific methods. The historical phenomenon of Paul is itself a thing undisputed, indisputable. The problem is, How came that phenomenon to be? The New Testament story of the conversion, so called, of Paul—that is, of his change from being Saul the persecutor, to become Paul the apostle—

is a story that all the world knows. On the face of it,
nothing could be simpler than the solution, furnished
in the New Testament story, of the historical problem
of Paul. A cause, an alleged cause, one evidently, self-
evidently, *adequate* to produce the unquestioned, unquestionable effect—such a cause, according to the story, in-
tervened. Why, then, is not the historical problem of
Paul thus at once solved? No reason why not, unless
we doubt the fact of the *alleged intervention*. But why
should we doubt it? Here is a remarkable, a truly astonishing, *effect,* obvious to everybody and quite beyond
the possibility of question; and here, to match it, is a
correspondingly remarkable, astonishing, *cause.* The two
things, the effect and the cause, fit each other perfectly.
Apparently, therefore, the problem of Paul is solved.

But is it really? Let us beware of a too hasty conclusion. Will it not be well to do a little analyzing? There
are various elements involved in the case. I propose that
we consider these elements separately. Our problem is
not the problem simply of the conversion, so called, of
Paul; it is, likewise, the problem of the sequel to that
conversion, namely, Paul's subsequent lifelong career,
the immense, that is, unmeasured, immeasurable, historic influence exerted by him and by his work. This
influence demands, by the way, to be considered not only
with respect to its volume, immense, as I have just said,
but also and equally with respect to its character or quality.
This latter particular point will be treated in pages to
follow; I merely invite here, in passing, needful attention
to its very great importance. We must find a cause
adequate at once to producing at the start the conversion
of Paul, and adequate to producing the stupendous historic influence ostensibly exerted by him.

The cause that would bring about in the man the
change from Saul to Paul, must be a very potent cause;
especially very potent must be the cause that would
bring about that change, at a most unlikely moment, and

bring it about *instantly, in the twinkling of an eye.* The required cause must furthermore be equal to making the change unchangeable, fixed and permanent forever. This demand we, in order to be soundly scientific, must meet; there is absolutely no possible escape from the necessity that is upon us—if we would be truly scientific.

As to the abruptness, the instantaneousness, of the conversion, of course it is open to the historical critic to say: It is contrary to psychological probability that such a change as Paul's conversion should have taken place altogether suddenly; there must have been previous preparation for it. This *can* be said, and this, in fact, *has* been said. But in the total absence, the absolutely total blank absence, of any hint in the historic literature of the subject suggesting that such a process of preparation preceded the change, is it scientific to assume it as a fact?—is it not, scientifically considered, a vicious *a priori* procedure to assume it? Is it not, rather, true historical criticism to say, No, had there been such precedent preparation, history would assuredly have given us a hint of it. Paul would assuredly himself have supplied us with some allusion from which it might at least be inferred.

By some authors of conjecture in this baffling mystery, Saul's part at the stoning of Stephen has been suggested as having perhaps occasioned a degree of shame and remorse in the breast of the persecutor, predisposing him to the change that so abruptly supervened. This, let it not for a moment be forgotten, is pure conjecture, having not the shadow of support in any recorded fact. Besides, it is conjecture in a very high degree improbable, since, after Stephen's martyrdom, the persecutor went on persecuting, with increased rather than diminished ferocity, at the same time with a ferocity not frenzied, not precipitate, a ferocity that took its measures coolly, deliberately, *in the legal form. Subsequently,* Paul does indeed reproach himself for his persecuting course, but he makes no allusion to Stephen, and all the grief he

expresses is grief that he persecuted his Lord. Thus unlikely does it appear that there can be discovered, in the
facts of the history, any least hint of a predisposition on
the part of Saul preparing him to become the subject of
such a conversion as was his.

Rationalizing criticism of Scripture (let me explain that
here and elsewhere I employ the terms, "rationalizing,"
etc., in no invidious sense; I am a rationalist myself, as
one fond of using my reason—within exactly the right
bounds—that is, scientifically!)—rationalizing criticism of
Scripture is very full of resource. Its fund of expedients seems never exhausted. For instance, at the
point of which we have just been treating, the suggestion
is sometimes made that Paul does indeed furnish hint of
previous preparation on his part for the great experience
which was his that day near Damascus. In a famous
passage of his Epistle to the Romans he speaks of a tor-
menting warfare going on within the unregenerate human
soul, between the spirit and the flesh. Here he, no doubt,
it is claimed, was describing his own experience. And
was not this experience a preparation for his conversion?
it is asked. I reply: If, to use Wrede's expression, he
had "become a Christian in the normal way," then the
answer to that question might be, Yes. But I submit
that *no* "experience of the disappointing, self-defeating
character of life under legalism," would tend in the least
to prepare its subject for the particular experience described in the history as Paul's. If, for instance, an in-
terview could be imagined as occurring between Peter and
Paul before the latter's conversion, in which Paul should
confess and deplore the wretchedness of his spiritual condition, and Peter should point out that there was a way
of relief for him in owning the lordship and saviourship
of Jesus as Christ, and should support this assurance of
his with convincing argument, then Paul, convinced and
submitting, would "become a Christian in the normal
way" (or in *a* normal way), and that normal way would

consist in part (an important part) in the preparation
supposed of spiritual distress. But, I repeat, such a precedent condition would not constitute in the least degree
preparation for the solemn spectacular conversion that
Paul actually underwent.

V

The whole case for supernatural Christianity—that is,
for Christianity, as I hold—hinges ultimately on Paul.
We cannot be wrong in looking at the problem of Paul
from every possible point of view.

That problem admits of being stated in a quasi-mathe-
matical, logical, form: Given certain effects, required the
cause. This suggests an order of procedure which it may
be wise for us provisionally to pursue. The effects in
the case under consideration are known; they are not in
any dispute, for they are notorious and indisputable—not
indeed *all* the effects involved, but all that we need for
the present to consider. The outstanding great effect is
of course the conversion of Paul. We shall pursue a just
scientific method if, from this effect, we reason backward
in quest of the cause. We have already made some very
inadequate attempt to show the prodigious character, both
in quantity and in quality, of this effect. In subsequent
pages this point will be recurred to; but it is difficult
to dismiss it here without some further insistence upon a
point so important, and a point hitherto in general so
strangely neglected. I mean now the suddenness, the instantaneousness, the catastrophic character, of the conversion that occurred. With this extraordinary abruptness
in the change, there is to be conjoined the remarkable-
ness of the particular *moment* of its occurrence. Altogether, the conversion of Paul constitutes an effect so
stupendous, so incalculably great, that, considered from
the strictly scientific point of view, it demands a cause,
I will not say infinitely great, but I will say indefinitely
great. This I think it is strict science to maintain. What

cause commensurate with the effect can be verifiably assigned?

The effect in question is made up of so many elements that it is extremely difficult, indeed it is sheerly impossible, to embrace them all satisfactorily in one view— this, even in thought, much more in expression. Let us make a throw at it nevertheless. Here is a man in the heyday of his youthful maturity; a man of native mental and moral power truly magnificent; a man of unbounded ambition; a man of zeal and tenacity of purpose never surpassed, perhaps never equaled, among the sons of men; a man whose pride, whose self-reliance, mounted to an overweening degree that gave him, in the face of obstacle or opposition, an attitude as of habitual, perpetual scorn; a man who had chosen his part and was fixed in it not only by his inborn obstinacy, but alike by the antecedents of his past, by the aims and hopes of his future, and by the decisive activities in which he was that moment with all his energies engaged—this man, who had drawn upon himself the admiring and expectant gaze of his whole nation, as if inviting them to look and see him, with bloody stroke upon stroke of unsparing persecution, make an end of the execrable cause of a crucified Messiah— this man, now at the very culmination and climax of his spectacular career, is to be changed, *suddenly, instantly, utterly, forever,* from a despiser, into an adorer, of that very crucified Nazarene. Such is the *effect* which unimpeachable historic testimony compels us to contemplate as having been somehow actually produced, and the problem is to find for it a competent producing *cause*.

The " scientific " historical criticism that underlies and animates the current revolt against Paul, seems to me not sufficiently aware of the seriousness of the problem with which it has to deal. For it faces the *effect,* the stupendous effect, to be accounted for, which, if at too great length, still very inadequately, I have just been describing—this effect it calmly faces with the proposal of a certain inward subjective *experience* on Paul's part, answering to no outward objective reality, for a supposedly competent producing *cause*. The proposal strikes me as so nearly approaching the absurd, in its inadequacy, that I find it difficult to treat it with decorous respect, in pointing out its futility. Granted for the moment that any such experience could produce the effect in question, what in turn produced the experience? The historical records existing supply absolutely nothing whatever for " scien-tific " historical criticism to use in framing its conjecture in reply to this question. That criticism must exercise itself much after the manner of a man attempting to live and breathe *in vacuo* under an exhausted receiver. The simple scientific fact is that the conversion of Paul we can satisfactorily account for in only one way, and that way is by accepting at its face value, without strained " interpretation," the story of the conversion as told in the New Testament.

If what I have said be true with reference to Paul's conversion, considered strictly and solely by itself, much more is it true with reference to the immense historic sequel of influence flowing from the conversion. Inadvertently and incautiously, I have used a word that misrepresents both the fact and my own thought of the fact. The historic influence of which I speak did not " flow " from the conversion of Paul. It followed that conversion, but it cannot properly be said to have " flowed " from it. It was, and it is, *created* continuously, by the continuous putting forth of the power that worked in Paul's conversion. " Scientific " historical criticism will strive in vain to account for it in any other way.

This element in the historical problem of Paul, namely, the long-continuing posthumous influence exerted—let us not say *by* him but *through* him—is far more important, far more difficult to account for, on purely naturalistic principles, than is the element of his conversion, important and " scientifically " unmanageable as

K

that is. Critics of the naturalistic school in their struggles with this particular element of their problem have,
unawares to themselves, brought out into clearer light the
difficulties that for them encompass the case.   Revolting against Paul, and undertaking a reclamation from him
on behalf of Jesus, under the rallying cry, " Back to
Christ!" they have unwittingly made more plain than
ever it was before how commanding, how all-overshadow-
ing, how tremendous, has been the world-historical posthumous power of Paul, or, to insist on expressing it more
truly, the power exerted not *by* him but *through* him.
These historical critics have, some of them, gone so far
as to erect Paul into the author of Christianity to the re-
placement of Jesus Christ.   And as a matter of apparent
ecclesiastical or theological history, it cannot be denied
that, on the face of things, regarded and interpreted by
the light of mere rationalism, their contention herein,
however startling to some it may seem, is in a very high
degree plausible, nay, let us candidly and fearlessly say,
is, viewed in that light alone, not only plausible, but
actually convincing.

But these critics have, without being awake to what
they were doing, created for themselves a new problem
more irresoluble on their principles than the one they
were attempting to solve.   Paul, they point out, has
foisted upon the pure and extremely simple teaching of
Jesus a whole system of elaborate theology of which,
they assert, that simple teaching of Jesus has not a trace.
We need not concern ourselves to deny this assertion
of theirs or to disprove it.   Indeed, if there *were* nothing
in the teaching of Paul different from the teaching of
Jesus as given us in the Gospels, if there were nothing
new, nothing additional, nothing supplemental, comple-
mental, that lack rather would be a matter of surprise,
of misgiving.   For Jesus, according to the Gospels, foreshadowed communications of truth to be delivered to his
disciples, his apostles in particular, after his own personal

withdrawal from them. But even if there had not sur-
vived any intimations from his living lips that such
would be the case, still it would remain a thing reasonably to be expected that the ascended Christ Jesus should
manifest himself to his disciples, in his own chosen way,
from the heaven into which he had returned after his
earthly sojourn. The reassurance on this point which
our human weakness of faith so greatly needed, he
graciously granted in the one overpowering spectacular
Christophany vouchsafed that day near Damascus to
Paul. And then we have it on Paul's solemn attestation that, afterward, such communications as were promised by Jesus in the days of his flesh, were, in fact, given
abundantly to him. Let then the unconscious fellow help-
ers of the truth enlisted in the revolt against Paul, among
the skeptical critics of the apostle and his work—let them
go on accumulating their allegations of his differences
from the historical Jesus. They are, it is true, thereby
increasing the difficulty under which they labor to account, on their " scientific " principles, for the age-long
ecumenical spread and prevalence of a Pauline gospel
held by them to be a gospel perverted and corrupted from
the gospel of the historical Jesus; but they are at the
same time thereby showing the need there has always
been, the need there still is, of Paul, to make good the pre-
dictions and promises of that historical Jesus concerning the " many things " remaining to be disclosed beyond
what they could bear while he was present before them
in the flesh.

That Paul should be by eminence the chosen recipient
and trustee of such disclosures from his Lord, was only
what was naturally and reasonably to be expected, after
the transcendent and extraordinary manner (the not
" normal " manner!) of his call to his apostleship. What
occurred in sequel to the conversion was exactly what
should have occurred—if Paul's supernatural Christ was
not a " myth," but an adorable divine reality. Let that

once be frankly and humbly and gratefully admitted, and
all in the historical problem that was dark as night before
instantly blazes with heavenly day.   On the contrary,
if Paul's supernatural Christ was a " myth," then nothing is explained and nothing can be explained.   Paul's
conversion becomes more a miracle than ever—resolved
into the effect of an " experience " on his part that there
was nothing whatever to produce—an " experience " itself therefore indeed a " myth," begotten upon an absolute historical vacuum by the brooding brain of the
" scientific " critic.

It is no question of a merely academic interest, this
question of Paul in his relation to Jesus.   It is a question of the most vital concern both to the church at large
and to every individual Christian.   For, be it understood,
let the revolt against Paul succeed, let it be supposed
triumphantly shown that, in this age of science, the
notion of a heavenly Christ cannot survive, that the
" heavenly Christ " is indeed a " myth," then there is
only an historical Jesus, an earthly historical Jesus, reduced to the measure of a man, left for us to trust in as
the almighty Saviour that we need.   It is a result of destructive historical criticism not to be characterized adequately as, in conception merely, anything less than
appalling.   And the result of a revolt against Paul undertaken ostensibly on behalf of the honor of Jesus!   I
do not charge conscious treachery toward Jesus upon
those who join actively or passively in this revolt against
Paul; but virtual treachery it is that they commit, however unconscious.   I call aloud to the fundamentally
faithful among them, the Abdiels in the revolting host,
to be aware of the true character, the true significance,
of what they are, though perhaps only by silence, abetting.

VI

The interest at stake is so momentous, so vital, and the
passing moment seems to me so critical, that I find the

temptation well-nigh irresistible to recur to points already presented and, committing the logico-rhetorical mistake of "too much," present those points again, and still again, from somewhat varying angles of vision. May I beg readers to gird up the loins of their minds, and engage themselves in my company somewhat seriously with the problem of historical criticism which necessarily confronts and challenges those historical critics who either openly or covertly refuse to admit any element of the supernatural into their discussion of the phenomenon of Paul. As already pointed out, these critics all have their postulate, their presupposition: Nothing miraculous is scientifically admissible in a world like ours, presided over by universal, invariable, inviolable law; this is a first principle omnipresent and sovereign in all their reasoning. "Scientific" historical criticism, therefore, accepting for true, as it does, the New Testament story of Paul's conversion, must go about to *interpret* that story, since, on the face of it, there *appears* to enter an element of what is called miraculous. Here is their interpretation: Paul thought he saw a great light, he thought he heard a great voice. In reality he saw—nothing. In reality he heard—nothing. He simply *thought*.

That word "thought," by the way, implies an activity of the mind too definite, too clearly self-conscious, in short, too "normal," to suit the facts in the case. Paul hardly "thought" at all, according to the interpretation we are considering. His brain was too much dazed for thinking. In truth, it is difficult to choose a word that will nicely fit the need. Paul *dreamed,* shall we say? No, for Paul was very wide awake. There is no single word that will quite answer our purpose, to describe what, in the naturalistic critical view, went on in Paul's mind. Let us say, Paul had an hallucination. This is really the one interpretation, under whatever form presented, that the naturalistic critics, all of them, arrive at.

It is fair to acknowledge that the rationalizing historical critics of the New Testament do in general treat the documents they handle with much decent respect—a sentiment no doubt sincere, though perhaps inspired not less by complaisant regard for the conventional estimate of sacredness which is still popularly current concerning these documents, than by any genuine conviction, either religious or scientific, of their exceptional character and value. I do not remember having met in their literature with any instance of the employment of the word " hallucination " to describe Paul's mental activity, experienced, whether at the moment of his conversion or subsequently. Still, in effect " hallucination " is what these critics all attribute to Paul. The same " interpretation " is applied by them to the Gospel stories of the resurrection of Jesus. The first witnesses of the risen Jesus were subjects of an hallucination. Like Paul, they " thought " they saw, they " thought " they heard.

This method of dealing with the New Testament narratives seems to work very smoothly and satisfactorily— as long as it is left in the vague—a general, wide, indefinite statement. My own sense of what is truly scientific requires me to try running out the " interpretation " now under consideration into a little specific detail, and when I do this the result reached seems to me far less conclusive.

In juridical procedures the formal process of cross-examination is found sometimes of the greatest use in sifting statements and enucleating the really material, really determinative, points in a mass of testimony. Can we not to advantage employ a somewhat analogous method here? Let me suppose that our rationalistic critics of Paul will magnanimously consent to answer a few questions that I will respectfully propose to them, thus:

You say that Paul simply " thought " that day near Damascus. What made him " think "?

Why, " extreme psychical emotion."

How do you know he had " extreme psychical emotion"?

Why, the facts show it.

What facts?

Why, the fact that he thought he saw that great light and the fact that he thought he heard that great voice. He could not have thought those things *without* " extreme psychical emotion."

You are quite sure he could have thought, would have thought, just those very things *with* extreme psychical emotion? Is this scientifically demonstrable?

Well, yes, we may say that it is. Such a fact belongs to a well-known, familiar class of psychological facts.

Now, let us understand each other. Do you mean that there is a well-known, familiar class of cases in which " extreme psychical emotion" causes the subject to think he sees a great light, which does not exist, and to think he hears a great voice pronouncing words which, in fact, are not spoken?

Why, no, hardly that. We only mean that " extreme psychical emotion" is well known to produce illusions of various sorts in the mind or imagination of the subject.

This you think scientifically accounts for Paul's experience when he was nearing Damascus that day?

We have no other scientific explanation to offer.

Let us, then, for the sake of perfect clearness, put this explanation into statement at once as simple and as complete as possible: Because persons of a certain character, in states of " extreme psychical emotion," are sometimes subject to hallucinations, therefore Paul, though not known to be then in a state of " extreme psychical emotion," was, at a particular moment, the victim of an hallucination leading him to think he saw Jesus of Nazareth in a stupendous blaze of light and to think he heard a great voice from above pronouncing his name in challenge, and rebuking him for the course of conduct on which he was

embarked. And this seems to you historical critics to
be an unquestionably sound scientific conclusion arrived
at by the use of unquestionably sound scientific methods?
What sort of man, may I ask, do you take this Paul to
have been?

We may answer in our own printed words about him:
"A hero in the domain of the will, a born leader of men;
also a hero in the domain of thought; looms ever higher
and higher in the world's history;" "Not merely a great,
but a noble character;" "One of the most inspiring and
comforting characters in all history;" "As one surveys
the whole of what he achieved, one stands in silent amazement at his greatness as a thinker."

Such in your opinion was Paul, and yet you think him
to have been, his life long, the victim of a craze, an
hallucination, that held him bond-slave to a "myth,"
the figment of his own disordered imagination! You
must admit that Paul's hallucination, if hallucination it
was, presents an extraordinary case of the phenomenon?

Yes, that we cannot deny—quite extraordinary.

Is there, let me ask, a whole class of well-recognized,
scientifically verified, parallel cases of such hallucination?

We cannot say that there is.

Is Paul's case in fact unique?

We have always preferred to put it in a class of
psychological phenomena easily explained on scientific
principles.

But does the class in truth exist in which you would
wish to put it?

'Class' is an elastic term capable of including either
few or many according to the varying need.

Well, there should be at least *two* cases in order to
constitute a class, should there not? Do you know of
one case, other than Paul's own, scientifically suitable
to be classified with his?

At this moment we cannot recall any other.

Your argument then reduces itself to this, does it not? There are hallucinations, *therefore* Paul's experience was an hallucination.

Put in that short way, our view does not look so scientific as we should like to have it. Ah, the word 'therefore' is not good logic. Change that and say simply, There are hallucinations and Paul's case was one.

May we not cut it still shorter and say, Paul's experience was a case of hallucination?

That looks bare and unsupported, stated so, but really that is our view.

Your view then consists of a naked *assertion?*

The assertion looks naked, but it is in fact supported by the whole strength of the basis on which science rests. There is silently implied an absolutely inexpugnable argument, which, put into expression, would run on this wise: Paul's case was one of hallucination, because, if it was not, there would be a miracle involved, and the miraculous never occurs.

Such, put under fair cross-examination, " scientific " historical criticism, exercising itself upon the case of Paul's conversion, turns out to be. Surprising truly! In the imagined personal presence of the sponsors for such criticism, I limit myself respectfully to that simple expression of surprise.

But I confess I should have more respect for a rationalistic historical criticism that held a different language, that said, for example, something like this: I " stand in silent amazement " before the phenomenon of Paul and his work. I cannot understand, cannot construe, him. He is inscrutable, inexplicable. There is indeed a very simple key offered to my hand for unlocking the mystery of him. I have only to accept the New Testament story contained in the Acts and in his Epistles. That would make everything delightfully clear. But alas, to do that without applying " interpretation " full of doubtful conjecture,

I should have to admit an element of the supernatural, which for me, "modern" as I am, and nothing if not "scientific," is not to be thought of. I am shut up to say simply: I am baffled; the problem is insoluble. I will not stultify myself by employing a hermeneutic, applying an interpretation, which, employed elsewhere theologically, after the manner of the old-fashioned Biblical scholars, I should laugh to scorn. Let me emphasize the adjective, and let my "amazement" be "silent"!

To be sure, admitting a little, a very, very little, of the supernatural involves stupendous consequences. As Wernle well says, the "roots" of "Saint Paul's theology are to be found in the experience of the vision of Christ." "Paulinism" cannot be made away with, if Paul's conversion was really such as the New Testament represents it to have been. The "heavenly Christ" of Paul, that "myth" of the "scientific" historical critics, is, logically and indissolubly, continuous and one with the Being who identified himself to Paul as Jesus of Nazareth, and it is not true, as Jülicher asserts it to be, that "not a single element in this extraordinary system of Pauline Christology [underlying and supporting the Pauline theology] can be derived from the words of Jesus." To make that assertion, Jülicher of course has to ignore the Gospel of John, which begins with affirming one element at least of Paul's Christology, the preexistence of Christ, not to say his equality, his identity, with God. That affirmation does not indeed purport to be in "the words of Jesus." But, "Before Abraham was, I am," does purport so to be; likewise, "I and my Father are one"; and, "Now, O Father, glorify thou me with thine own self, with the glory which I had with thee before the world was."

VII

Let me imagine that the historical critics with whom I have been dealing, have overheard the foregoing asides

of mine spoken in the ear of the public.   They catch at the
citations made by me from the Gospel of John, and say
to themselves, ' This writer seems not to know that John's
Gospel is not an accredited " source " concerning Jesus,
while, at any rate, the whole production known by that
name is manifestly Paul's work at bottom, and therefore
of no weight to give collateral support to his extraordinary Christology.   Turn and turn about is fair play;
this writer has been cross-examining us, now suppose we
take a turn at cross-examining him.'   With pardonable
abruptness, they begin:

You have dealt very freely with us, and we are not sure
that it has not been *infra dignitatem* in us to permit it.
Who and what, pray, are you?

I am simply a plain common man, deeply interested in
the subject under discussion.

Are you an expert in historical criticism?

I do not claim to be.

We suspected as much from the course of your questions.   Now we are recognized experts in this business,
and it ill becomes us to cross swords with any not our
peers.   Can you understand our feeling in the matter,
and will you pardon our frankness?

I can indeed, and do, understand how you feel, and I
am honored that you have condescended so far.   I should
be pleased if I were able to salve any natural mortifica-
tion experienced by you, by appearing, if I could, a foe-
man in your eyes less unworthy of your steel.   Pardon
the ignoble figure of speech that I use.

Well, you confess yourself an amateur, and——

Not exactly that, but not a professional—in the full
sense of the word.

Ah, then, in some sense you are professional?   Have
you ever been, for instance, a college professor?

I see, I see; it may be a certain relief to you to know
that I did once enjoy that dignity.

Possibly even a university professor?

Yes, that too.

But never one of a theological faculty?

Why, yes, I have had even that experience.

We begin to feel more like recognizing you in the quality of peer. If, now, you could say that you had held a professorship in the department of New Testament literature?

There I have to disappoint you. I never did hold such a professorship. But cheer up, gentlemen, I was once talked of for exactly that position. The learned president of a certain theological seminary of high rank had seen, he thought, in published work from my pen, signs of fitness in me for filling a New Testament chair just fallen vacant in his institution. I never quite realized how near I came to being an " expert " in historical criticism as applied to the New Testament. If I had only taken the chair in question!

Before accepting our final dismission from hearing, we should like—so our complaisant friends, the historical critics, may be supposed to say—we should like to make a certain correction or modification of one of our previous statements.

Certainly, I reply, that will be quite in accordance with the usage of the courts of law whose order of procedure we have been after a sort imitating.

Well, we were perhaps overhasty when, in reply to your challenge of us to produce a single instance of a case parallel to that of Paul in his conversion, we said, " We do not at this moment think of one." Do you know, may we ask, Matthew Arnold's " Saint Paul and Protestantism "?

I do. You are probably thinking of the instance that he brings forward in that book of his.

Yes, what have you to say to that?

Why, this—that I have not been in the habit of numbering Matthew Arnold among the really qualified professional critics of the New Testament. I was fully aware that he, being properly, quasi-professionally, a critic of general literature, had done some amateur work in the way of criticizing the Bible religiously. Now I do not rate Matthew Arnold very highly as a critic, in whatever sphere, and I once gave myself the pleasure of examining his claims somewhat carefully in a paper of length, which I included in a book lately published [" Some New Literary Valuations "]. Incidentally, I made the parallel instance to which you refer one of the topics that I treated in exhibition of Arnold's quality as a critic in general. With your permission I will quote from what I said in that paper of mine, bearing on the pertinency and validity of his ostensible parallel instance.

VIII

Arnold says:

" The conversion of Paul is in itself an incident of precisely the same order as the conversion of Sampson Staniforth, a Methodist soldier in the campaign of Fontenoy. Staniforth himself relates his conversion as follows, in words which bear plainly marked on them the very stamp of good faith: ' From twelve at night till two it was my turn to stand sentinel at a dangerous post. I had a fellow sentinel, but I desired him to go away, which he willingly did. As soon as I was alone I knelt down and determined not to rise, but to continue crying and wrestling with God till he had mercy on me. How long I was in that agony I cannot tell; but as I looked up to heaven I saw the clouds open exceeding bright, and I saw Jesus hanging on the cross. At the same moment these words were applied to my heart, Thy sins are forgiven thee. All guilt was gone, and my soul was filled with unutterable peace; the fear of death and hell was vanished away. I was filled with wonder and astonishment. I closed my eyes, but the impression was still the same; and for about ten weeks, while I was awake, let me be where I would, the same appearance was still before my eyes, and the same impression upon my heart, Thy sins are forgiven thee.' "

" An incident of precisely the same order " as the one
thus related, Arnold pronounces the conversion of Paul
to be.   A truly extraordinary judgment for a man to
make who takes himself seriously as a critic.   The simple
fact is that the two incidents have nothing in common,
nothing in approach to mutual resemblance, except that
in both cases a " conversion " occurred.   Instead of being
incidents of " precisely the same order," they are incidents separated from each other, save in the one respect
named, as widely as possible; they differ by the whole
heaven.   Note:

First, as to the outward or objective features of the
two cases:

1. The time, in Paul's case, was midday; the time, in
Staniforth's case, was midnight.

2. Paul was journeying on urgent business; Staniforth
was, until he knelt, standing on watch.

3. Paul was traveling, with companionship; Staniforth
was alone, had taken pains to be alone.

4. Paul, unexpectedly to himself, was suddenly smitten
helpless to the ground; Staniforth deliberately, of set
purpose, and of his own accord, assumed a kneeling
posture.

Secondly, as to the inward or subjective features of
the two cases:

1. Paul was a self-righteous Pharisee, complacently
persuaded that he was at the moment doing God service;
Staniforth was a convicted and penitent sinner, casting
himself humbly on the mercy of Christ for salvation.

2. Paul hated Jesus Christ; Staniforth adored Jesus
Christ.

3. Paul thought of Jesus Christ as a deceiver; Staniforth thought of Jesus Christ as a Saviour.

4. Paul was breathing out threatening and slaughter;
Staniforth was praying, " wrestling with God."

5. Paul felt in no need of forgiveness; Staniforth felt
in perishing need of forgiveness.

6. Paul was in a state of mind such that, had the idea of his own conversion once occurred to him, he would have flouted it with measureless scorn; Staniforth was eagerly, earnestly, agonizingly, desirous of conversion.

So much for the points of difference existing, to start with, between the two cases—as far as those points admit of being arranged under heads of outward and inward conditions. Another point of antecedent difference, at once outward and inward, may be mentioned. Paul's environment, the atmosphere in which he lived and moved, was one of intense hostility to Christ; Staniforth's environment, the atmosphere in which he lived and moved— that is, the spiritual atmosphere and environment—was one of worship toward Christ, and of trust in him for salvation through his suffering on the cross.

Now for the points of difference between the two cases in what *happened* to Paul and Staniforth severally:

1. As already said, Paul was struck to the ground, blinded by an insufferable light from above; Staniforth voluntarily knelt to pray.

2. Paul's eyes suffered a physical effect, which perhaps continued his whole life long, but which, at any rate, when sight was restored to him after three days' blindness, yielded as it were scales from his eyeballs.

3. Paul heard a voice uttering words from on high, and even answering a question that he asked; Staniforth simply felt certain familiar words ' applied to his heart,' " Thy sins are forgiven thee."

4. Paul, though now convicted of sin, and rendered obedient in heart, yet had apparently no immediate sense of forgiveness; Staniforth felt at once that " all guilt was gone."

5. What Paul saw was for an instant only, and for that instant it was simply an intolerable light; Staniforth " saw Jesus hanging on the cross "—this, whether his eyes were open or closed, and the " impression " lasted the same " for about ten weeks."

Now I think true criticism would say that not even Staniforth himself for a moment supposed himself to be seeing, in the way of normal vision, " Jesus hanging on the cross." It could not be, for the " impression," he says, was the same when his eyes were closed. He evidently meant nothing more than that he had a vivid imagination of the spectacle of the crucifixion of Jesus. John Newton was in the prime of his manhood at about the same time with Staniforth, and he wrote a hymn, which it is not unlikely Staniforth had often heard sung, with this stanza in it:

> I saw One hanging on a tree
> In agonies and blood;
> He fixed his languid eyes on me
> As near his cross I stood.

Staniforth's experience may have been in a sort colored and controlled by that very hymn; he, probably no more than Newton, meant that he " saw " that spectacle, in the sense of normal outward vision. One feels sure, from the narrative itself, carefully read, that Staniforth, if he had been asked closely, would have testified that he simply had a vivid imaginative view of Jesus hanging on the cross. Paul, on the other hand, as Arnold admits, thought that what happened to him happened indeed, happened objectively. Paul could hardly have doubted this—at least while that three days' blindness lasted, and then at the moment when those scales dropped from his eyes!

Jam satis, I seem to hear my supposed inquisitors say. I was well inclined to make respectfully full my answer to their inquiry as to what I thought of Matthew Arnold's attempted paralleling of Paul's experience. This I have perhaps already now made sufficiently plain. The discussion is pursued at considerably greater length, pp. 120-128, in the volume here quoted from, " Some New Literary Valuations." But I cannot suppose that my esteemed friends, the expert professional critics of New Testament history, would care for further attention from me to the amateur incursion of Matthew Arnold into their critico-historical province.

IX

My raillery of our friends, the men of science in historical criticism of the New Testament, especially of Paul—which I hope they will take in good part—is meant only as a pleasant way of signifying how little in my opinion it matters whether or not the person who meddles here be a professional, if he only be an intelligent, candid, open-minded lover and seeker of the truth. I have not written in these pages with lively hope of convincing even so much as one rationalistic critic of Paul, that his wish, sincere no doubt, to be, cost what it may, *scientific* at any rate, has in reality made him fundamentally unscientific. The obsession of that overmastering wish of his, supported as it is by the omnipresent spirit of the age pressing upon him on all sides like an unescapable atmosphere—an atmosphere in which he perforce, but with full consent of his mind, lives and moves and has his being—that obsession is far too strict and stringent to be breached by any force except one that should work from within instead of from without. (Would I might have even a little of such hope as is that which I thus regretfully deny to myself!) But I do hope to stay in steadfastness here and there an endangered fellow believer shaken in the confidence of his faith by the sapping and mining now going on all round him, underneath the very foundations on which he had previously rested.

For myself, I must bear this testimony: Paul, with that "heavenly Christ" of his, is ever, in the last extremity of storm, the sheet-anchor of my faith, my hope, my strength, my courage, my joy. I should like to help make him such to any soul that I may reach with these words of mine.

L

X

It will perhaps seem late, too late, in the order of treatment here pursued, for the discussion of my subject, but I wish, even though logically too late, to introduce at this point for submission to readers certain additional evidences which have confirmed me in believing that, in the current revolt against Paul, the Christian church is caught in a solemn crisis of its history. Our institutions of higher education are, I am convinced, in at least a considerable number of cases, to be reckoned as passively, if not actively, enlisted in this revolt. This judgment of mine does not except even those institutions which are nominally evangelical, and therefore supposedly sound in the traditional faith of the Christian church of nineteen finished centuries.

A passage or two of conversation held by me a few years ago (which I may report anonymously without any violation of confidence—there was no injunction of secrecy, either express or implicit, nor did there lie any such injunction involved in the nature of the things that I have to report) will serve to indicate what I believe to be the prevailing tendency of theologic thought at most of the seats of higher education in the land, perhaps then also in the world. It will be recognized as a trend that could not establish itself save in defiance of the teaching and authority of the apostle Paul. It is part, therefore, and a very important part, of the current revolt against him.

I met casually a valued friend of mine (a distinguished university professor, who was likewise a preacher, member of a presumably orthodox evangelical church), and in all simplicity I sought from him sympathy and support in the concern I felt for the suffering cause of Christian truth. I said abruptly: "Do you feel, as I do, the tremendous set of tendency current now toward reducing the Lord Jesus Christ to strictly human terms of measurement?" (This, as nearly as I can fix the date, was some ten years ago.) "I know what you mean," was his reply, "and I recognize the tendency, but I do not feel about it as you do." I was dashed and disappointed, but I said, "How do *you* feel about it?" "Why," said he, "to me it seems more like a tendency to exalt man to equality with Jesus Christ." "But you believe, do you not, in the divinity of Christ?" "I do not think Christ was divine in any other sense than that in which I think you are divine," he said.

I was amazed and shocked, but as soon as I could ease sufficiently the painful tension in my mind, I said with all earnestness, even with solemnity: "You recognize, do you not, the fact that if *Paul* had thought as you do about Christ, we should not be talking on this subject to-day." My friend had a very alert mind, and it took him but an instant of pause to see the implication contained in my words, that but for Paul's different view of Christ there would not now be any such thing as Christianity in the world. "Yes," he said, "I suppose that is true. It was necessary, for the time, that Paul should misconceive of Christ as he did, but it is no longer necessary for us." He spoke with imperturbable assurance, and he used an illustration from history. "It was necessary," he said, "for the preservation of the American Union that Webster's wrong view of the Constitution should prevail. But for that, we should not now be a nation." "You think Webster's view was wrong?" I said, dissenting interrogatively. "Yes, Webster's doctrine was what ought to have been, but not what really was," he said. Not following up this line of historical disputation, I appealed to my friend's presumed religious experience. "Don't you feel your personal need of a Saviour; in short, of a Christ exalted in the heavens, and there wielding power to save?" "I do not see what such a Christ can do for me," he said. My interlocutor was, I knew, in peculiarly intimate personal touch with the president of the institution, which led me subsequently to ask him: "Do you think your views were the views also of the president?" "Yes," he said, without hesitation.

I repeated this conversation not very long after, naming no name, if I remember right (but indicating the academic rank and standing of my interlocutor), to a divinity professor, whom I judged to be representative of what I may call the coming school of theologic thought and belief, at even the supposedly evangelical among our seats of higher education. "What I have now reported to you," I said, "as the view of that friend of mine, is virtual Unitarianism." (By the way, that friend of mine did indeed, in a later conversation, with characteristic clear-headed frankness, fairly confess himself to me a Unitarian, not repudiating that definite word.) The second professor said: "Yes, and that is now the general trend of opinion in university circles everywhere." He spoke, I thought, as if himself yielding to the general trend, or, at least, not protesting against it or deploring it.

Of course neither of these two university men can have accepted, in a straightforward way as literally true, not calling for any strained interpretations, the New Testament narrative of Paul's conversion. They were, that is to say, both virtually enlisted in the revolt against Paul. Neither probably of these two gentlemen would acknowledge this—in that form of expression. But they would no doubt unite in declaring themselves opposed to " Paulinism "; that is, to the view that Paul is rightfully *authoritative* in the realm of Christian doctrine. They are therefore, in my sense of the expression, engaged in the revolt against Paul.

A third university teacher I met one day and, in distress of mind, said: "I see Dr. A. B. Bruce quoted as teaching that Christ's sufferings in the garden and on the cross were discipline for him and not atonement for us." "That," was this third gentleman's reply, " is the present prevailing trend of theologic thought." I was disappointed, for I had expected, and I had reason to expect, from this university man a response sympathetic with my own recoil from the sentiment reported. " But what is *your* attitude toward that view?" I asked. " It contradicts my personal religious experience," he replied. No long subsequent interval of time had elapsed, when this gentleman had committed himself in print to views far more violently opposed to Paul's theology than was Doctor Bruce's alleged teaching.

I may add that a fourth member of the teaching body of the same university so responded to request from an important periodical for an expression of personal view as to the doctrine of the divinity of Christ, that the editor, whose wish was to set in formidable array a great host of witnesses *for* the doctrine in question, did not see fit to publish the expression he had invoked.

I narrate these incidents of my personal experience to show why I think there is need of a very positive stand to be taken in support of the Christian church's long-held allegiance to Jesus Christ in that view of his person, of his lordship, and of his atoning work, which is presented in the writings of his chosen chief apostle, the apostle Paul. Yet another incident, an incident as I think of pregnant significance, which however I cannot relate without bringing matters home more closely than naturally I should wish to do, to a particular institution. Even so, I shall not need to name individual names.

Some years ago, an undergraduate student of the University of Chicago, a bright young fellow whom I had come to know, although he had never been a pupil of mine, made a call on me at my house and surprised me with the question abruptly proposed: " What do you think of the Divinity School of the University of Chicago?" He had evidently come for the express purpose of asking that question. I " hedged," and retorted the question, " What do *you* think of the Divinity School of the University of Chicago?" My young friend did *not* hedge in replying: "I think it is a Unitarian institution." "What do you mean by that?" I said; "you do not mean that the divinity of Christ is assailed, do you?" "No, but the teaching is in general such as you would expect to find in a Unitarian school." I asked him what opportunities he had had to form such an opinion. He said he had become acquainted with some of the leading Divinity students, and had learned from talks with them what ideas and beliefs were current and controlling among them. Besides, he said he boarded where Divinity students sat at table with him, and he overheard much of the talk in which they engaged.

All this time I had said almost nothing myself, but now I remarked to the young man (who, by the way, was unusually intelligent and well informed on matters in general—he had had some practical experience in city journalism): "You seem to be concerned about the doctrinal complexion of the Divinity School; I did not suppose you were yourself very strictly orthodox." "I am not, as you are, and as my father is [he was son of a Baptist minister], but "—and he shook his head and shrugged his shoulders—"I can't go Unitarianism!"

Knowing that this young man had passed one or two of his undergraduate years at a certain denominational college in a State farther west, I propounded this question to him: "You have had personal experience as student at two different seats of learning; what, in your opinion, would be the comparative probabilities of conversion for a student taking his college course at the institution where you began yours, and that same student taking his college course here in the University of Chicago?" "Why," said he, warming up with a glow of conviction, "in the former college that student would almost certainly be converted; in the University of Chicago it would be a miracle if he were."

"As I understand it, your purpose," I said, "is to

resume your journalistic career after your graduation?"
"Yes," was his reply; but a few weeks later he called
again, and announced a very serious change of purpose;
he was going to devote himself to the work of the Christian ministry. "But first a theological course, I suppose?" "Yes." "Where? Here?" "No, not in this
Divinity School."

It may be said that this young man may have mistaken the state of things that he undertook to represent,
or that he may have inherited a blind unreasonable prejudice against Unitarianism. At any rate, I should myself, as matter of courtesy, wish to avoid the *odium theo-
logicum* likely to be evoked by the use of that word, and
certainly I do not quote the young man's testimony as
final and conclusive; but it is, I think, at least indicative
of an existing apparent tendency at one great university to drift toward anti-Paulinism—that is, to exert an
influence felt by students favorable to revolt against Paul.

"The Biblical World," a University of Chicago periodical holding justly a high rank and exerting great influence, had in June last, an interesting article from the
pen of a professor teaching Old Testament in the Divinity
School of the institution, in which the writer says:
"The Hebrews were given no extraordinary or abnormal aids or advantages not within the reach of other
men, then as now. . . The Hebrew prophets and saints,
having the same opportunities, were possessed of the same
faculties as other men, no more and no less"—language
which of course has the effect of denying special divine inspiration to these "prophets and saints," and seems flatly
to contradict Paul: "What, then, is the advantage of the
Jew? . . Much every way; first indeed that they were
intrusted with the oracles of God; . . Israelites whose is
the adoption, and the glory, and the covenants, and the
giving of the law, and the service, and the promises." The
article reads as if it might have served as a classroom

lecture to ministerial students. At any rate, it unquestionably indicates the trend of the Old Testament teaching given by this professor—a teaching obviously opposed
at a vital point to the teaching of Paul, and obviously
irreconcilable with belief in his right to rule, as representative of Christ, in the realm of Christian doctrine. Such
teaching belongs therefore to the literature of revolt
against Paul.

All the university men anonymously quoted from by
me are personal friends of mine, brethren esteemed and
beloved. Am I lodging accusation against them? Far
be it! I am simply bringing out certain facts tending
to show that I do not contend with shadows when I
appear in arms against the disposition to discredit Paul,
and to discredit the doctrine he was inspired to impart to
the church. I have disclosed no facts which in the
nature of things ought to be regarded as privileged from
disclosure. I recognize the absolute right (as before
men—as before God, this I dare not affirm) of these
university men to exert their influence in favor of what
they hold, even if mistakenly, to be truth.

Whether they have a right so to exert that influence,
while still occupying their present positions, is another
question. That is a question into which I do not enter.
It is a question not so easy as it might seem to decide
offhand. I might for myself decide it offhand, but I
should then decide it only for myself. At all events,
what I wish here is to make it plain that the things I
have stated, have not been stated as accusations anonymously lodged against my brethren. If I thought as they
do, I should certainly, unless it might seem to me to be
kinder to refrain, try *somewhere,* as they try where they
are placed, to make those views prevail. Where they are
placed, is doubtless the very best vantage-ground from
which to work toward that end, to be found anywhere in
the world. If evangelical Christianity ought to be " liberalized " and is to be " liberalized," no other agency

existing, or likely hereafter to exist, will more than the University of Chicago have deserved the credit of that achievement. If, on the other hand, disaster impends— that is to say, if the liberalizing process is to go on unchecked until a new generation, not far off, of mankind shall have arisen who must live face to face with the rigorous alternative, "scientific" agnosticism or Roman Catholicism—then for *that* result a full measure of responsibility will have been incurred by the University of Chicago.

From the point thus reached, the transition will be natural and easy to the discussion dramatically conducted in the next chapter.

CHAPTER VIII

IS THE UNIVERSITY OF CHICAGO [1] SUCH A VOICE?

IF it is, however softly it may speak, it will be heard afar. Indeed, if I were asked, What, in your opinion, is the most potent of the forces at present in revolt against Paul? I should ask myself, before answering, Is it the University of Chicago? A serious question. I raise it, I consider it—I hold my answer in suspense. This chapter is to be simply a frank, but carefully guarded, setting forth of the situation as I believe it exists at the University of Chicago, with respect to the historic ascendency of Paul hitherto maintained in his capacity of authorized and accredited representative of that heavenly Christ, by whom and in whom the Christian church has lived through nineteen completed centuries of its life in the past, and by whom and in whom, I am fully persuaded, it is to live, if it lives at all, in the unknown centuries yet to come.

If Paul ought to be, and is to be, dislodged from his seat of vicarious rule for Christ, if the great doctrines of the divinity of Christ, of Christ's literal bodily resurrection from the dead, of Christ's ascension to glory and to power in the heaven of heavens, of Christ's

[1] It hardly seems needful, but it may nevertheless be advisable, to say that no one except the author himself is in the smallest degree responsible for what is contained in this chapter—least of all are the publishers responsible. They, indeed, have faithfully forewarned me of a result likely, they think, to follow the publication, namely, that readers will be found to misconceive the author as making an "attack" upon the University of Chicago—this, notwithstanding the disclaimer, with all sincerity made, as will be seen, in the body of the text, and, for emphasis, repeated thus in a footnote.

A kind friend of the author, the weight of whose name, if it were proper to reveal it, would be generally recognized, in pronouncing his sentence upon the present chapter, submitted to him in manuscript for his criticism, having used these words, "Very telling and very true," added significantly a deterrent "but." In short, various wise counselors have in effect bidden me beware—the University of Chicago is very formidable. Formidable? Yes, I well knew that, and that is the reason why this chapter was written.

intercession for us at the right hand of God—if these great doctrines, the prevalence of which has been chiefly due to the supposedly inspired and assisted influence of Paul, are, in fact, mere figments of a human brain, creating a superstitious intellectual bondage, from which now, in a truly "scientific" age, the church and the world should be, and are destined soon to be, freed, then the present chapter, so far from being an attack on the University of Chicago, might with much more fairness be taken as in effect a vindication for that great institution of the preeminent part it will have played in the work of such a needed and beneficent emancipation, long delayed, but happily triumphant at last. I write certainly not in the spirit of attack, but in the spirit of an arduous service undertaken on behalf of beleaguered, I will not say imperiled, vital truth.

There are special reasons why I am specially concerned about the policy and the consequent influence of the University of Chicago. These reasons are of such a personal nature that in order to give them, I shall be obliged to obtrude myself in a manner and to a degree that will ask the indulgence of the reader so to pardon it, as not to let it operate in his mind to the defeat of the object with which I write.

Circumstances ordered it so that I was peculiarly related to the founding of the University of Chicago. It was on this wise: In the spring of 1887 I was on my way to attend what I may call the "Baptist Anniversaries," held that year in Minneapolis. In the Pullman car with me were others having the same goal in view, among them the Corresponding Secretary of one of the great societies whose anniversaries were about to be observed. This gentleman's mind was teeming with a great idea, the idea of an "American Baptist Education Society." He had cast the idea tentatively into written form. This sketch he placed in my hands, with the request that I would examine it and form an opinion as to the merits of the plan proposed. He added that he had not yet decided whether to broach the plan at the Anniversaries, but, if I thought well of it, and if he did broach it, he would be glad to have me say something publicly in its favor. I did think well of the plan, and I promised to give it, if broached, my support in the manner suggested.

The plan was duly broached, and in fulfilment of my promise I made a short speech approving it, in which I said I believed I knew where there was large wealth ready to flow in educational channels, whenever there could be provided in some form satisfactory guaranty that such gifts would be wisely used. The proposed Education Society would, I thought, provide the necessary guaranty. I expressly explained that I ventured on saying what I did, without the shadow of anything like authority from any one for saying it, but added that I was not speaking at random, that I had in mind a particular man when I spoke as I did. That particular man, I may now confide to the reader, was John D. Rockefeller, who, in private conversation with me at his table, had, not very long before, asked questions of me bearing on the subject of higher education, which I thought plainly enough indicated a fruitful practical interest on his part in the matter. That was the hint, not intended by him as a hint, on which I acted in making my venturesome public remark.

That remark was taken, by one man at least, to be significant, significant enough in his case to call out from him a letter addressed to me urgently requesting, almost demanding (for he repeated his request in a second letter), that I tell him who was the person anonymously referred to in what I said. I of course declined to disclose the name, although he claimed to have an educational project in contemplation, which he thought should appeal to just such a man of means. I told him, however, that unless I had first satisfied myself by personal investigation that a given educational project was such that, in the improbable case of my man's asking me, Would you advise my investing here? I could answer unreservedly, Yes, I should not deem myself at liberty to set a force of solicitation at work upon him, even by furnishing simply his name to an applicant for it. When, however, a year or two later Mr. Rockefeller offered to the American Baptist Education Society to contribute $600,000 toward the founding somewhere of a new educational plant, if, within a reasonable time, named, I think, by him in his offer, the Baptist denomination would bring about the rounding out of his gift to a full million of dollars— when, I say, this offer was made by Mr. Rockefeller, he did approximately what I thought he would do, under the guaranty supplied in the administration of a responsible society, such as had been meantime created.

The canvass for the raising of the supplementary $400,000 needed was immediately begun, and pushed with great vigor and great skill. The Corresponding Secretary of the new society was naturally the directing and inspiring head of the forces set at work in the canvass. This gentleman knew that I was enlisted with all my heart for the campaign. I made my modest subscription in money, and I secured other subscriptions in money through personal solicitation among my neighbors at home.

I did more, much more, than this. For, at the suggestion and request of the Secretary, I prepared an editorial article designed to promote the movement and to convince Mr. Rockefeller that the hosts of educational progress were with him. This editorial article was originally destined for the great Baptist organ, " The Examiner," in New York. I had previously done editorial work for " The Examiner," and it was supposed that the editor-in-chief of the paper would accept such an article from my pen without question. Unexpectedly he declined it, very courteously explaining that he thought the influence of his editorial columns should be exerted on behalf of Baptist interests belonging to the State of New York, rather than on behalf of an enterprise, however worthy, having Chicago for its center. By this time, the *place* for the new institution, it had been pretty well decided, was to be Chicago. And, by the way, for this decision my assistance had been invoked by the enterprising Secretary, who arranged to have a broadside of supposedly influential opinion on the subject of location, displayed conspicuously in the pages of the Chicago Baptist newspaper, and I was invited to contribute an expression, with reasons assigned—which I did. There seemed to be some need of this, for a quasi-rival movement was on foot, with apparently powerful support, favoring New York City as the seat of a great new university to be under the auspices of the Baptists.

Up to the moment of the writing of the rejected editorial, the idea of the proposed new institution was to make it simply a college, not a university. It was fortunate that " The Examiner " declined that contribution. The result proved to be that a much better place for it was found. With characteristic, broad-minded generosity, " The Independent " opened its editorial columns to give it the hospitality it needed. The day of its publication it happened that Mr. Rockefeller set out for a journey from New York to some point in the West, and the alert originator of the American Baptist Education Society, who had somehow got wind of this movement of Mr. Rockefeller's, placed in his hands just as the train started a copy of " The Independent " of that date fresh from the press. The article boldly threw out the hint that the modest proposal of a new college might, if properly welcomed and supported by the denomination to which it was tendered, expand ultimately into the prospect of a great university, munificently endowed.

The seed-thought of such a university, the writer knew, had before been planted in Mr. Rockefeller's mind. This was in the truly imposing form of an elaborate and masterly sketch, in print, of plans for an institution of university grade to be located in the city of New York, and calling for an initial outlay of at least $20,000,000. A copy of this outline sketch was placed under Mr. Rockefeller's eye. It was, as I had the opportunity to judge—for the accomplished author of it submitted a copy also to me, with the suggestion that, if I approved the idea, I write in favor of it to Mr. Rockefeller, or, "better yet," go and see him—it was, I say, so at least I judged, prepared with a view to have it commend itself to a man of Mr. Rockefeller's known moral and religious principles. To the suggestion that I use any supposed possible influence of mine with Mr. Rockefeller in aid of the enterprise, I replied that if he should seek counsel from me I would freely give him my opinion on the subject; but that I thought I had better not volunteer an expression unasked. It is fair, I think, to set it down to the credit of the author of that plan, that the University of Chicago perhaps owes its existence to the far-sighted pioneer initiative which this projector took in the field of foundation for advanced higher education in this country. If his proposal had been the one to pass into realization, instead of that later proposal which his led to, the history of higher education on this continent might have been surprisingly different; for a man of very different controlling ideas in religion, namely, the real originator of the Baptist university plan, would naturally have been the first head of the new institution; and, as first head, he would almost necessarily have impressed upon it for permanency the character that it would bear. *Sic vos non vobis!* Those famous words of Virgil are irresistibly called to mind.

Well, the full million of dollars was secured, and a great feast of felicitation over the result was to be celebrated at the Anniversaries in Chicago. I sentimentally much desired to be present, and witness and share the joy. In an hour of weakness, I told the Secretary that if I could have known that my little contribution would simply do so much toward swelling the excess above the amount required, I should even have reserved the half of it to help pay the expense of a trip for myself and my wife from Tarrytown to Chicago. The responsive Secretary promptly " rebated " to me the half, and made it easier for me to accept it by declaring that my counsel, if I could be present, would be worth much more than the sum rebated!

Those Anniversaries were a memorable occasion—a veritable riot of rejoicing beneficence. It was moving, even to tears, to witness the beautiful, but half-pathetic, eagerness with which Baptists from all over the land— I might almost say from all over the world—country pastors, missionaries from the frontier, missionaries from distant foreign countries at home on furlough, contended with one another to be foremost in getting their offered contributions accepted and recorded. The offers came in faster than they could be caught and recorded. The enthusiasm of giving was almost uncontrollable. This is literally true. But it had to be controlled, and at length it was controlled; for the time was more precious than were even these popular tributes of love and devotion. I make a note of these things because they show what a stake the world-wide dispersion of Baptists thought they had in the future University of Chicago. The afternoon was so far spent when I was called on to say my say, that I rose and simply begged to be excused from detaining the great congregation to hear me speak. For this, the Secretary of the Education Society gently, but seriously, upbraided me, for he wished, he said, to have my remarks go into the record which was to be printed and, as he hoped, to be read.

The culmination and climax of the great occasion took place in the form of an assembly, addressed by various speakers, in the thronged Auditorium. The Secretary, whose originant and constructive mind had conceived the idea of the American Baptist Education Society, made the great address of the evening, and a great address it truly was. He rose fully to the height of the occasion. The other Secretary, the one who had led the canvass for the million to its brilliantly successful conclusion, would have me sit that evening by his side on the platform. I was inspired with a whisper to plant in his ear. I said: " I believe Mr. Rockefeller will be so pleased with this result that he will promptly give your Society another million of dollars." This Mr. Rockefeller did; and with that fulfilment of my prognostics the spirit of prophecy in me ceased.

Least of all things did the prophetic spirit in me whisper hint of my some time becoming myself professor in the University of Chicago. All that I have thus far related was anterior to any thought or dream on my part of such a possibility. The organization of the university proceeded, without my having aught to do with it, except to wish it well and to watch the progress from afar—until one winter evening, or early spring it may have been, I remember only that there was some depth of snow on the ground—as sudden and as unlooked for as would be a thunderbolt falling out of a clear sky—an unannounced call at my house in Tarrytown from the university President accompanied by the Secretary of the Education Society. They came to propose a professorship for me in the forming university. I at once said that I thought it would be a mistake, both for the university and for me. This attitude on my part seemed to take the President by surprise. In first broaching the proposal, he assumed (diplomatically perhaps) a somewhat indifferent air. It was a very informal overture, he said, was not to be taken as officially made. Nevertheless he entered into an argument to overcome my disinclination.

This argument the Secretary interrupted, saying:

M

"Now please let me do the talking; I know Doctor Wilkinson as you do not." The President folded his hands and sat silent (save for one remark interjected), while the Secretary presented the case in a way adapted, as he not unwisely thought, to make the desired impression on my mind. It was deemed advisable, he said, to have conservative views in the matter of biblical criticism represented in the faculty. It had proved difficult to find young men of the conservative type, and there was the President belonging to the opposite camp. "I am a conservative," the President interposed to say. "The President belonging to the opposite camp," the Secretary imperturbably repeated, and pressed the necessity of a conservative element to redress the balance in the University faculty.

I at length yielded far enough to say that I would take the matter into serious consideration. The President now put off his indifferent air, and acknowledged outright that, in spite of what he had said about the non-official nature of his call, it was really quite serious in its purpose. My callers left me with only the rather unsatisfactory assurance to take away with them, that I would consider the matter and report my final decision within a week. At the end of the week, I surprised myself by reporting that, under certain conditions, which I stated, I would accept a position as professor of rhetoric and criticism, if elected as such. The conditions were assented to, the President personally assured me, and I accordingly became from the start a member of the faculty of the University of Chicago.

I have been more than full enough, the reader will perhaps, and not unnaturally, think, in detailing the circumstances of my election to my professorship; but I have suppressed one circumstance which very seriously affected my mind, predisposing me to apprehension concerning what was likely to be the character, and the consequent influence, of the great institution of which I was now to be an inconsiderable part. I knew that the part I was to be would certainly be inconsiderable; but that did not lessen my sense of responsibility for the little measure of influence on its future that I might exert. I could furnish a list, and it would not be a short one, of the efforts put forth by me to help keep the University true to the original great idea in which it was founded. These efforts were none of them productive of any apparently valuable result, but they continued nevertheless to be made. I tried meantime to be loyal, not only to the institution, but to its head. It may be accepted as evidence of success on my part in this endeavor, that the Secretary who had acted so influentially in getting me placed where I was, wrote to me that the President expressed himself warmly, I think he said "affectionately," in appreciation of the services I was rendering. But it was a difficult office that I undertook, the office of suggesting criticism of the conduct of affairs.

Instead of specification in detail of the evidences that fell under my observation of the drift toward divergence from evangelical orthodoxy that has marked the course of the University from the beginning, I may sum all up at once in a single sentence, by saying that, in my opinion, if the purpose of the administration had been to "liberalize" the orthodox Christian denominations, and to emancipate them from the authoritative dominance of Paul as apostle of the heavenly Christ, that purpose could in no other way have been more effectively prosecuted than in the way actually pursued by the University of Chicago. I do not charge that the administration had such a purpose. I think rather that the policy adopted and carried out had simply for its motive the ambition and the aim to build a great university. Everything appeared to be directed, everything subordinated, to that sole end. And, assuredly, the imposing monumental result already achieved, conspicuous in all men's eyes, sufficiently attests the worldly wisdom of the course of policy pursued.

Might a different course of policy, one having a different ambition and aim for its motive, namely, the purpose to be absolutely loyal to the great original idea in which the University was founded—might such a different course of policy, firmly, unfalteringly, pursued, have issued in an equal success, a success that would have made up in ethical value what it possibly might by contrast lack, in splendid impression on the imagination?

This is a question brought under discussion in the present chapter—a chapter in which, as the reader will perceive, I make use of that freedom of speech about the University, which it has been from the beginning one of the cardinal principles of the University itself to assert and maintain for all its professors. The question to be discussed is virtually an ethical question. It might fairly enough be stated in the following form: Could the University of Chicago become the greatest force in revolt against Paul and still remain constantly true to the highest ethical standard? This is a very grave question, and I am fully conscious of its great gravity in raising it. In order to discuss it candidly, and in a manner to give consideration to as many as possible of its various bearings, I adopt the plan of supposing a discussion of the question to arise in a meeting of the Board of Trustees of the University. I desire the reader to bear constantly in mind, as he reads, that the discussion is one *that never took place*.

It is a literal fact, however, that the President of the University of Chicago had authorized newspaper publication of the following statement, which was made by him in view of a certain case of alleged theological aberration on the part of a professor in the institution:

" I shall never recommend to the trustees of the University of Chicago the removal of any professor on

account of his theological opinions. Theological conformity may, under some circumstances, be desirable in
a denominational college. To require such conformity in
a university would be intolerable. Moreover, the charter
of the University of Chicago is broadly non-sectarian.
It is a charter requirement that two-thirds of the trustees
and the president shall be Baptists. But it is also a
charter requirement that no sectarian test or particular
religious profession shall ever be held as a condition
precedent to the election of any professor. Obviously
the same principles apply to the tenure of any professor.
Members of the University faculties are of many religious
faiths, a minority being Baptists. The trustees and the
president are in entire accord in regarding this policy of
religious freedom as the only one which can be followed
by a university worthy of the name. The policy will
continue to be that of the University of Chicago."

The publication of the foregoing statement may be
supposed to have been followed by an unintended and
unlooked-for result—taking the form of a very unusual
discussion arising in the course of a University trustee
meeting—that never was held. To report that discussion (which never occurred), is the object of the present
chapter.

The reporter in the case has done his work with every
possible advantage in his favor. He knows personally a
few only of the members of the Board of Trustees, and
those few, barring one or two exceptions, not at all
intimately. With no one of them had he ever, before
preparing this report, talked on the subject treated in
it; nor had he ever heard any one of them even allude to
the subject. Moreover, he had never had reported to
him, either directly or indirectly, any expression of
opinion on the subject from any one of them all. This
is true as to the President of the University, no less than
as to the other members of the Board of Trustees. As

will be seen, the reporter could thus do his work unembarrassed by inconvenient private knowledge, which it might seem a breach of confidence to divulge.

There could not therefore be, as there is not, any attempt here on his part to reflect individual characters or individual views, under a more or less transparent mask of anonymity; and any attempt accordingly on the part of any reader to identify any one of the *dramatis personæ* will obviously be futile, since such an identification is sheerly impossible; there are no portraits in the account. The President of the University is the sole recognizable personality in the whole representation, and what is attributed to him in the way of sentiment or purpose is, as already said, thus attributed without pretense to any knowledge of his views and his policies, except knowledge derivable from his own openly published statements concerning them.

How, then, did the reporter of this exceptional discussion (which never took place) obtain the information that furnished him the material of his report? Well, he obtained his information in a way of which he could not even to himself give any very intelligible account; he got it from the air—that is, from the University atmosphere in which he lived and moved and had his being; it came to him by a process of what may best perhaps be conceived of as a kind of wireless conduction in the realm of thought, as mysterious as anything of the sort known in the physical realm. He has, however, the utmost confidence in the clairvoyant veracity of the medium of transmission that has served him.

The word "Baptist" will be found frequently occurring in the pages to follow. This is because that word occupies a very important place in the "charter," popularly so called, of the University of Chicago, with which the present chapter has to do.

Here is perhaps the proper point at which to explain, as I am able to do on the authority of a man who knew what he affirmed, that, in the constituting of the University there was no denominational, much less was there any sectarian, purpose intended in the legal requirement that the Board of Trustees should always be predominantly Baptist. The main purpose of the original, responsible framers of the charter would have been just as well satisfied to have the word " Presbyterian " in the charter instead of the word " Baptist." The inspiring idea was only to keep the institution safely and soundly orthodox and evangelical in spirit—acknowledgment of Paul's authority as source from Christ of Christian doctrine being, of course, presupposed. Baptists had long enjoyed the reputation of being singularly true to that orthodox and evangelical spirit; and, besides that, Baptists had, in fact, been the real founders of the institution. It seemed doubly fit therefore that " Baptist " should be the keyword of the charter, as it was accordingly made.

But all evangelical Christians, of whatever denomination, have precisely the same stake as have the Baptists, in the character and the influence of the University of Chicago. That stake is vital, so vital, in the estimation of the vast majority of all evangelical Christians, that it is safe to make this affirmation: *Could it have been clearly foreseen that the institution would prove to be other than faithful and friendly to evangelical Christianity*—pure hypothesis, no implication here as to what is the existing fact in the case—*the institution would never have been founded.* A guaranty that, from the first, it should be, and that it should always thereafter remain, thus faithful and friendly, was supposed to be lodged in the constitutive provision that, to the end of time, a commanding majority of the trustees should be members of regular Baptist churches—this, as already intimated, not in order to make the institution a propagandist of the *distinctive* Baptist beliefs, but to have it stand fast forever for the truth of the gospel as that gospel was preached and taught by Paul, and as it is understood and accepted and rejoiced in by all evangelical Christians throughout the length and breadth of Protestant Christendom.

So much it seemed necessary to premise in the way of accounting to the reader for his being confronted here with what, in the absence of explanation, might seem to him like the obtrusion of a needless sectarianism.

To one taking only a hasty, superficial view of the matter discussed in this trustee meeting (which never was held), it might very naturally seem that the interest and importance of the subject were as ephemeral as the immediate occasion was that gave rise to the supposed discussion. Such, however, is by no means the case. The subject is one of widely-extended interest and of lasting importance. The conditions still exist that rendered possible that remarkable departure from orthodoxy in teaching, on the part of a University professor, to which the University gave what had the public effect of sympathy and support. An acute symptom has, after a sort, settled into a chronic condition. Nothing contained in the discussion here reported is without its just application to the actually existing order of affairs at the University of Chicago. The professor whose heterodox teaching, in a *book,* a book bearing the imprint of the University of Chicago Press, was the occasion of such outcry in protest, still teaches the " Philosophy of Religion " in the University, and he from time to time is the " University Preacher " on Sundays. (He is held to preach eloquently; " sublime," a cultivated lady who heard him at the University on a very recent occasion, pronounced his discourse.) Many other like indications might easily be mentioned of what is the religious attitude assumed, and of what must be the religious influence exerted, by this great institution of learning. Nothing can be clearer than that the Christianity which Christ gave distinctively to the apostle Paul to teach—" Paulinism," that is to say, to call it by the ill name its opponents are fond of using—must overcome the influence of the University of Chicago if it is to survive and have a long future in the world.

The Board of Trustees of the University of Chicago is to be imagined in session, the President of the University being present in his capacity of trustee. A certain member of the Board, not of the required Baptist majority, not a professedly religious man, but a man of recognized high character, and carrying with him the weight of reputation for a commanding business success honorably achieved—such a member of the Board has brought into the meeting a certain printed document with which he has just previously become acquainted. He waits until what seems to him the fit moment, a moment of apparent pause and leisure in the proceedings of the Board, when he rises respectfully and addresses the Chair:

"Mr. Chairman, I wish to make a confession. I confess that I accepted the honor of trusteeship here without knowing, except in a vague general way, what the responsibilities were that I thus was assuming. I ought to apologize for saying that it would be a relief to me to know that I am not alone in this respect. Will my colleagues permit me to ask most respectfully that they clear my mind on this point by letting me know, through mere show of hands, how many are in like case with myself, as not having read carefully the charter of this University before entering upon the duties of trusteeship to it. . . Thank you, gentlemen. As I said, it affords me some relief to know, as now I do, that I am not the only member of this Board that neglected that preliminary formality.

"Well, I have myself now read the charter, and I have done so, I acknowledge, not only with interest, but also at some points with a degree of surprise. I knew, or supposed I knew, that the institution was in some sense

Baptist in character, but in exactly what sense, it had never troubled my mind to consider or to inquire. The daily newspapers, however, have of late been making so much noise about things with us here that I have felt bound to inform myself somewhat on the subject involved. The honored President of the University [with a decorous inclination of the head toward that important functionary, present as trustee], in an admirably brief and dignified statement, which he wisely allowed to appear printed in one of our daily newspapers, touched on the point brought lately into controversy, and in doing so spoke of the 'charter' under which our institution was established. This led me to look up the charter and examine it carefully.

" I was struck with the fact that our President, referring, without emphasis, to that provision in the instrument which makes the University a denominational school, laid the chief stress on that other charter provision which makes it, to use his own language, 'broadly non-sectarian.' Somehow the denominational, the *Baptist,* character stamped indelibly upon the school by the language of the charter, made more impression on my mind than did the language forbidding the application of a religious test in the election of professors. The denominational provision is stated in terms peculiarly impressive, and, besides that, a *reason* for its being introduced is assigned, assigned in such a way, and apparently with such a purpose, as to give that particular provision very much the nature of a contract obligation binding on the University and binding on us as trustees in control of the University. [Here the speaker produces from his pocket the printed document referred to above, and reads from the charter as follows:]

" 'At all times two-thirds of the Trustees, and also the President of the University and of the said college, shall be members of regular Baptist churches; that is to say, members of churches of that denomination of Protestant Christians now usually known and recognized under the name of the regular Baptist denomination; and, as contributions of money and property have been and are being solicited, and have been and are being made, upon the conditions last named, this charter shall not be amended or changed at any time hereafter so as to abrogate or modify the qualifications of two-thirds of the Trustees and the President above mentioned, but in this particular this charter shall be forever unalterable.

" ' No other religious test or particular religious profession shall ever be held as a requisite for election to said Board, or for admission to said University, or to any department belonging thereto, or which shall be under the supervision or control of this corporation, or for election to any professorship, or any place of honor or emolument, in said corporation, or any of its departments or institutions of learning.'

" That language in the charter seems to me, Mr. Chairman, to put the University under a virtual covenant; it makes us, as representing the University, virtual parties to a *contract*. I for my part would not be found wanting to my proper share in the responsibility thus created for us all. As my fellow members in this Board all know, I am myself no Baptist; I do not make any profession whatever of religion, but my sense of honor obliges me as much, I think, as it would if I were a Baptist of the strictest sort, to do my part toward fulfilling the manifest purpose of the charter in keeping the University perfectly loyal to the denominational idea in which it was founded. In this, I make no doubt my colleagues are all of one mind with me.

" Really, I am making a very unexpectedly—to me very unexpectedly, to you, I fear, it will be seeming a most unconscionably—long speech, but I must say before stopping that I am afraid I think our Baptist two-thirds (begging their pardon for the frankness) have been all too modest in asserting and vindicating their denominational title to this University. I have heard much said about the importance of keeping the University broad and free—in which idea I naturally sympathize with all my heart—but I do not remember ever to have heard spoken one word about the importance of keeping the University true to the Baptist denomination."

As may well be supposed, an interval of silence follows on this, which, at length, the President of the University breaks, by saying:

"Mr. Chairman, I think we should all like to have our highly esteemed colleague make his speech still longer by telling us, somewhat specifically, what he would wish to have us do in the way of being faithful to our denominational obligations."

The first speaker resumes:

"I should hardly be willing, Mr. Chairman, to respond to this challenge, if it had proceeded from any other than the honored head of the University. For to him belong, as I suppose, the right and duty of initiative in the matter of policies to be pursued in the conduct of our University affairs. But, assuming that I may be frank without offense, I will venture to say that I was surprised to read this [referring now to a newspaper clipping held in his hand], purporting, and I had no reason to doubt, truly purporting, to be our President's own language: 'I shall never recommend to the trustees of the University of Chicago the removal of any professor on account of his theological opinions.'

"I was surprised, I say, not of course at the purpose thus firmly announced, for it was a purpose that would at once approve itself to everybody as wise. No one, I take it, would wish a professor removed for his 'opinions,' theological or other. The question is a question, not at all of 'opinions,' but of *teaching*. The purpose expressed by our President was so obviously self-justifying, that it hardly needed to be expressed.

"Was there not then, I asked myself, underlying the purpose *expressed* a purpose *implied*. I could not help thinking there was; and it was this implied purpose that surprised me.

"If I could have understood that expression from our President as simply a discreet, quasi-diplomatic, form of statement, indicating only that some other way of ridding the University of improper instruction and influence, from a professor holding and *teaching* views not consistent with Baptist beliefs—that some other way to this end would be adopted, less open to objection on grounds of comity, of expediency, than the drastic method of recommendation to the trustees that they formally ' remove' such professor, why, I could understand that, and I should approve the wisdom of it. But I felt forbidden to suppose applicable any interpretation like that of our President's announcement. The announcement was not an abstract, general indication of policy. It was an announcement made in distinct view, expressly *acknowledged* view, of a particular case which had become notorious, a case of the very widest divergence in a professor's teaching—in his teaching, and not simply in his privately held ' opinions '—the very widest divergence possible from the theological beliefs deemed most vital, and cherished as most sacred, by Baptists. And the implication seemed unmistakably to be, that no initiative of any sort would ever be taken by the responsible head of our institution, to put an end to what seems to many minds, and, I need not say, to my own mind among them, the open scandal of such antagonism, or at least disrespect, from the University to the religious denomination that founded it and that had bound it fast, as was supposed, to be forever true to its solemnly entrusted treasure of religious belief.

"Our honored President went beyond the mere expression of his own individual and official purpose of abstaining from interference to prevent antagonism on the part of the University to Baptist theological beliefs. He announced, as by authority, that his own policy of non-interference would ' continue to be that of the University of Chicago.' The view that I felt obliged to take of the purport and intent of our President's declaration seemed to me the more certainly the true view, from the fact that the declaration was made by him in consequence of a letter he had received from a Baptist divine of prominence, remonstrating against the University's attitude toward that particular notorious case of the erratic professor's heretical teaching. The declaration was therefore equivalent to a notice served on the protesting divine, and through him on all men, that protests were of no use, that the University would always in future permit any professor to teach, without let or hindrance, any notions of his, however antagonistic to Baptist beliefs, that he, the professor, might take to be true notions.

" I am bound to say that, in the face of this attitude on our part, I do not wonder, and I cannot wonder, that some earnest Baptists, feeling themselves to be comparatively powerless against the well-nigh omnipotent influence of a great University, supported by uncounted millions of money, and having now an incalculable headway of momentum in its chosen path of policy, gained by twenty years and more of steady, unchecked, triumphant advance in it—it is no wonder, I say, if some Baptists are more indignant than wise in uttering exclamations of protest. Mr. Chairman, perhaps I have myself become more indignant in their behalf than wise. I am sure you will all believe me sincere when I beg to disclaim any intention of personal offense in what I have said."

The chairman of the board, discerning, as he thinks, signs of some slight discomposure, well veiled, in the

President—whether from vexation, or from a momentary perplexity of mind, seemed uncertain—interposes with a rally of half-pleasantry, having an agreeable effect of complaisance in his manner of making it:

"It will not, I trust, be deemed obtrusive if the Chair begs to remind our knightly defender of the Baptists that, in the generous enthusiasm of his sympathy on their behalf, he has been eloquent indeed, but has quite failed to respond to our President's suggestion that he tell us somewhat specifically what he would have us do in fulfilment of our denominational obligations."

"Why, yes; I confess judgment there," the speaker replies; "and indeed for me to improvise a schedule of proper presidential expedients in administration, would be a presumption on my part, that I ought not to have put myself into a position to be fairly called upon to be guilty of. But I must now even be guilty of it, or cry, *Peccavi*. Well, I should say, to begin with, that the case is one in which prevention would be easier, wiser, and more effective, than remedy. In my own individual business I have certain principles in some respects a little different perhaps from those generally prevailing. When I employ a new man in a position of importance, I begin by explaining these principles to him, and my reasons for adopting them. 'Have I made these points clear to you, and are you willing to be governed accordingly?' I ask. If he says, Yes, I seldom have subsequent occasion to complain of any departure from the course marked out. Now—but really I am ashamed to be thus, as it were, acting the part of an instructor to those much wiser in all University matters than I am."

The speaker pauses embarrassed, and the President very handsomely comes to his support:

"I beg, Mr. Chairman, to assure our colleague that I am greatly interested, as I feel confident we all are, to have him proceed to any length on this line with the utmost freedom. The conduct of a University is business, and our colleague's experience in business, and his well-known brilliant business success, entitle him to speak on all these topics as full peer of any one in this Board, and certainly of the President of the University."

"Very gracious, very reassuring, and very characteristically so, are such words from our President," the speaker responds, and proceeds: "Well, in the case of a professorial candidate, why should it not be a rule, an invariable rule, for him to be shown a copy of our charter, and to have his particular attention directed to the denominational features of it? 'You see'—thus it would be natural to state the case to him—'that this is a Baptist institution, and as such it asks and expects from everybody officially connected with it, a proper regard for its denominational character. This regard simply means that in the conduct of the University nothing is to be done inconsistent with the principles of Baptists, nothing that could justly be construed as antagonistic to those principles. You are not asked to adopt them. You may, in fact, utterly reject them. But, as professor, you are to abstain from teaching anything, from throwing out anything by the way, contrary to them.' Any course other than this would clearly be unfaithfulness on our part to our covenant obligations."

At this point a member of the Board, well known to all and by all deservedly esteemed as an intelligent, conscientious, consistent Baptist, though one by no means aggressive in his denominational spirit—such a Baptist trustee, with evident effort to be outspoken this time, and faithful, begs to be heard a moment as a matter of personal privilege. "Mr. Chairman," he says, "not undertaking to represent my fellow Baptists in this Board, but speaking solely for myself, I desire to say that, for my own part, I felt hit, fairly hit, by my colleague's good-natured rally and rebuke to us of the Baptist majority in our number. Mindful of the fact expressed in the French proverb, *Qui s'excuse s'accuse,* I am disposed to enter an apology for my failure, or at least an explanation of it. The simple truth is, I have been, or have felt myself to be, hopelessly overborne into silence and inaction, when I ought to have spoken and to have acted. I have been conscious of yielding too passively to a dominating will outside of myself. I think all will understand what I mean, for all must, with me, have felt the presence, the pressure, the push, of an overpowering personality, always exerting itself, in the first President of our University. It was not easy to withstand the tremendous momentum of purpose which made a kind of animated projectile of that man. ["A live human catapult, I called him," ejaculates a concurrent individual voice from the body.]

"All this personal power was exercised in the direction of vindicating absolute freedom for the University from any restraint that might seem to hinder success. I will not accuse his memory by saying that he consciously, intentionally, disregarded the religious conditions of our charter, but he did in effect disregard them. They seemed never to be present to his mind, unless it were in the effort to put an interpretation upon them that would leave academic freedom intact, unhampered. To say the least, his personal interest and sympathy were all, and always, in favor of academic freedom, rather than in favor of religious or denominational loyalty. This no one of us could help feeling. And this spirit in him, constantly alert, was bold, was aggressive. An atmosphere was thus created in and about the University in which considerations of simple good faith, of straightforward denominational loyalty, were made to seem narrow, petty, not at all in keeping with the breadth, the largeness, which should characterize a university.

"Well, there was, and there is, something too in the

N

spirit of the times in which we live, that powerfully reenforced, that still, and ever increasingly, reenforces this
sentiment of freedom.   The condition I have been trying
to describe, as a method of explaining at least, if not
justifying, my own denominational inertness, established
itself at once in the University, and it has been steadily
growing more and more stable, more and more fixed,
by simply continuing to exist unchallenged, until now it
wears the aspect of a law of nature, it looks immemorial,
immutable.   I confess I had not the strength, the courage, to challenge its right to be.   If any one, for instance
a Baptist living outside of University influence, should
say now to me: ' Have you not yourself been in some
degree affected—not to use the word *in*fected—by this
pervasive modern spirit raised to its highest power in the
life of the University of Chicago? '—I should not be able
to reply with a prompt, round, full-hearted, No, I have
not.   The hypnotism, active here, especially in the time
of the first President, was too subtle, too powerful, for
an individual personality no stronger than mine, to resist
it successfully.

"But the very unexpected rally of our non-Baptist
friend, with his production of those charter clauses, has
roused me.   I have blindly felt all the time that there
was an obligation resting on us as an institution that
we were not fulfilling.   I was in at the birth, in fact
before the birth, of the University of Chicago, and I
know, I am qualified to bear witness, that the institution
was born Baptist.   That means born to be free in
thought, free in speech, free in action, in all that concerns religion, *but* free with that freedom which springs
alone from a certain bondage, namely, the bondage of
obedience to the Lord Jesus Christ.   Obedience to Christ
is the one all-inclusive Baptist principle."

This good Baptist ceases speaking, with the air of one
conscious that he had at length delivered his soul, that
now at any rate he had witnessed a good confession.

The non-Baptist who had preceded, the one who had opened the discussion, now says:

"That principle may govern my colleague. It is a principle that I respect, though I do not profess adhesion to it. My own sense of honor, my plain, every-day, worldly conscience, is what actuates me in this matter. I feel bound by my trusteeship here to do my part toward carrying out in good faith the denominational idea of our charter—not at all because I am a denominationalist, for a denominationalist I am not, but simply because I believe in living up to my engagements. In accepting a place on this Board, I find out—a little too tardily, I confess—that I entered into a virtual engagement to see to it, so far as in me individually lies, that the University of Chicago is kept true to Baptist theological beliefs—not of course in the sense of openly propagating them, but in the sense of not antagonizing them, of not treating them with the smallest disrespect. I may secretly wish that there were no denominational conditions of any sort affecting our charter. I may have the opinion that the ideal university would be without such a condition. But I am trustee, not of an ideal university— such as never existed—but of an actual university founded in a certain way and having certain unescapable relations to a certain religious body. The simple question for me is: What is the upright, the honorable, course of conduct for me, as trustee of the existing University of Chicago, to adopt? Those of our number who are Baptists may act as Baptists; I for my part will try to act simply as a straightforward, honest man."

As this speaker pauses, a different member of the Board, a liberal-minded Baptist, speaks up informally from his seat, and says: "Our colleague has made his own individual position very clear, and no one will say that it is not a position that does him honor. But I am a practical man, and I plainly see that there are prac-

tical difficulties to be encountered, and very nice lines
of discrimination to be drawn. Our friend did us the
favor to outline a method of dealing with a professorial
candidate, which he thought would tend to forestall and
prevent unfortunate results; but [and now voice is given
to a thought that had before spontaneously occurred to
all] supposing the candidate says, perhaps a trifle im-
patiently: ' I know nothing about Baptist principles, what
they are, and I might, without intention and quite unawares, be saying something inconsistent with them. It
would be very uncomfortable for me to be haunted
by a fear that I was trespassing. I like a sense of
freedom.' "

"Yes," responds the chief speaker, " I had myself
thought of that as something not at all unlikely to
happen. I had even supposed an extreme case. I had
supposed the case of a candidate of great distinction, a
man enjoying an international fame, we will say, in his
particular department of knowledge and research. He
would be a *scientist*—of course, in these days of the
dominance of science. Not improbably, he might be
a foreigner, a German for example—conceivably the
acknowledged head of the world's authorities in his line
—a man, in short, with eminence enough, and consciousness enough of eminence, to feel the University to be
a candidate to him, quite as much as himself to be candidate to the University.

" The situation would not, I admit, be without its difficulty for our resourceful President. But I think he
would be equal to it. I can imagine him saying blandly
to the candidate: ' I have thought it only fair that you
should know the existing state of facts with us. But
really there would, I am sure, be no such embarrassment
to you in your teaching as it is natural for you to apprehend. Your subject is biology. You deal with it
purely as a matter of science. You have nothing whatever to do with religion. You have your own intimate

individual convictions on that subject, but these need not appear in your teaching. Indeed, they will not, if you keep yourself, as of course you would keep yourself, strictly, rigidly, within the bounds prescribed by pure science. As long as you do this, there is no danger whatever of your being betrayed into any expressions inconsistent with the principles of Baptists.

" ' The Baptists, by the way,' our President may be conceived as going on to say, ' are a highly respectable body of people. They are numerically important, numbering in this country millions, perhaps well toward half a score of millions, of adherents. They have an honorable history, illustrated with many great names, and with at least one great civic achievement, for they contributed the first example in history of a State in which absolute religious liberty was guaranteed in its institutions of government. [This, I believe, Mr. Chairman, is sheer undisputed record. All honor to them for it! I do not know but there may be some Baptist in my blood! I must look up my ecclesiastical pedigree!] I need not say that they are important by the possession of great wealth, for the very existence of this University is evidence of that.

" ' It might be interesting to you to acquaint yourself a little with their principles. That is not necessary, but it might interest you to add so much to your stock of general knowledge. It would not be a serious task. It may summarily be said that, apart from their views, which accord with the most enlightened scholarship of all time, on the subject of baptism—with which, of course, it is inconceivable that you should ever come into collision—Baptists agree substantially in faith with almost all Christians, the world over, of whatever name. There is therefore practically no abridgment whatever of academic freedom created by our charter, that can in the least affect the proper teaching of science in any of its departments. If a teacher of science does not go out of his way to attack theism, if he does not let slip any gratuitous expression implying doubt or disbelief of the doctrine of the divinity of Jesus Christ, he will be in no danger of trespassing, to use your own word.'"

The liberal-minded Baptist speaks again, with the manifest concurrence of most of his colleagues indicated in their approving looks:

"We have had it strongly impressed upon our minds from the start, and we have come to regard it as a first principle of administration here, that there is a broad distinction between a college and a university. Our President succinctly said in that printed expression of his to which reference has been made, 'theological conformity may under some circumstances be desirable in a denominational college. To require such conformity in a university would be intolerable.' Does not our colleague agree?"

The chief speaker replies:

"I neither agree nor disagree. I do not need to do either, for there is here, as I understand it, no question of 'theological conformity.' Nobody in our Board, nobody in our faculty, is asked to 'conform.' We are simply asked, and this only by our individual consciences, to be true to the trust committed to our keeping by our charter. By the way, I have made some effort to inform myself on the point, and I have not found any example of a denominational *college* that exacts theological conformity in its professors. But, since here certainly there is no theological conformity demanded, and since this institution, though a university, is as much a denominational institution as is any college, more so indeed than any college that I can hear of, I do not see that there is need of emphasizing the distinction between college and university at this particular point—since at this particular point there is no distinction between college and university. I think, with our President, and with no doubt every member of this Board, that the enforcement of theological conformity would be intolerable in a university. And so, for my part, I think it would be intolerable in a college.

" As might be inferred from things that I say, I have had some communication with Baptists outside of this Board. I thought this a wise course to pursue, in order to be the better acquainted with the prevailing Baptist sentiment on the subject of the particular individual case of alleged professional vagary that has of late been making such stir in the newspapers and elsewhere. As to the alleged vagaries themselves, there need be no doubt, no difference of opinion, for the professor has put them into a book, two books in fact, both of them bearing the imprint of our University Press. Our responsibility as trustees of the University is peculiarly clear therefore, and it certainly is very great.

" A stalwart Baptist of my acquaintance, an intelligent, a reasonable, man, who knew something of both books by reading them, talked freely in my hearing on the subject. He had noted our President's use of the word ' intolerable,' to characterize his sense of the condition that would be created if theological conformity were required in a university. ' I will tell you,' said this gentleman, ' of something else that would be, no, not *would be,* but *is,* intolerable. It is intolerable that Baptists, not a few Baptists, but hundreds, I might almost say thousands, of Baptists, not Baptists of this city and vicinity alone, but Baptists from all over the world, from foreign missionary fields even, should found a university, and pledge it sacredly for all time to the guardianship of truths which they deem vital, which they hold infinitely dear, and then should see that university employing and paying professors whose teaching is openly, flagrantly, defiant and subversive of those very truths; should see that university giving rank and standing to such professors; should see that university not only furnishing classroom accommodations for them in which to promulgate infidel doctrine, but furnishing them students, in large measure probably drawn from Baptist homes, to whom to impart their infidel doctrine; and, crowning offense, should see that university stamping its *imprimatur* on books that may carry that infidel doctrine far and wide to the ends of the earth—that, that, my dear sirs,' this stalwart Baptist waxing very warm, very vehement, exclaimed—' that, exactly that, is the spectacle now presented to the world by the University of Chicago, and that, I protest, is well worthy of the President's strong descriptive word, *that* is indeed truly " intolerable." It is a monstrous breach of faith. It is a colossal perfidy.' "

It was easy to see that the trustee speaking had himself been carried away by the torrent of indignation that he thus reported. He hardly restrains an apparent expression of his own vicarious sympathy with it. Presently the President rallies, and says:

" We have found, Mr. Chairman, we are all conscious— I, naturally, more so perhaps than the rest—but we are all together vividly conscious of having found an advantage in the reputation for perfect academic freedom reigning here, that the University everywhere enjoys. A late brilliant convocation address from one of our family of professors celebrated this with contagious enthusiasm, heralding it proudly for all the world to hear. Now I confess we should not need to part, to any serious extent, with this advantage, *if* the simple denominational condition that affects us could only come to be properly understood by the public, in both its restriction and its broad liberality.

" In the fear that this denominational condition would be misunderstood to imply more restriction than it really does imply, we may have made a mistake in keeping our denominational obligation too much in abeyance. As to the particular case that has brought on the present acute stage in denominational feeling, it is of course an extreme case. I have not myself read carefully the books in question, but the cursory glances at them that my occupation with affairs has permitted me to take, has satisfied me that they are at least liable to be understood in a sense hostile to Baptist religious beliefs, and hostile as well to the religious beliefs of all evangelical Christians. So much I am obliged to admit, and it is no doubt regrettable. But since members of our teaching body, better versed in theology than I can pretend to be, have seemed favorable to allowing such teachings to take their chance with our students, I have been disposed—and here perhaps has been a mistake on my part [at this point the reporter must have nodded, and dreamily attributed to the President a half-confession, which he thought would be becoming in him, instead of limiting himself strictly to what was actually said; at least, the present editor cannot recall any presidential expression implying such an admission of possible error in administration]—to regard this case as one which would serve admirably, without real harm to anybody, though possibly with accompaniment of uneasiness to some minds, as advertisement to all mankind that the University of Chicago is an institution in which there is to be enjoyed absolute freedom in the quest and the proclamation of truth, in whatever department of thought.

"We have taken our stand accordingly, and it is certainly very difficult now to yield it, and recede. Still, what ought to be must be, if it is within our power. Embarrassing as it may be to do our duty, our duty must be done."

Here the President pauses, seeming lost for the moment in a mood of groping solicitous thought. A member of the Board, who has sat silent till now, sees his opportunity and seizes it. He is a gentleman with some modest pretensions, courteously acknowledged on all sides, to literary culture, and he has ideas on the subject of

pedagogy, as having perhaps in his day been himself a
teacher, or, if not, as having been a thoughtful observer
of teaching. Besides, he is one apt to qualify his talk
with a dash of good-natured humor. This gentleman
says:

"I recall the fact that some time ago the professor
who has been the cause of so much talk was trans-
ferred from a chair in the Divinity School to his present
chair in the University proper. This was generally
understood to be for the reason that his teaching was
already then theologically objectionable—that is, antagonistic to Baptist doctrines—and it seemed more fit to have
it given elsewhere than in the Divinity School."

"Yes, so it might *seem*. [This is an irrepressible
obiter dictum interjected by a legal member of the
Board, who had been strongly impressed by those charter
provisions read in the meeting.] But in reality it was less
fit, for, outside of the Divinity School (which has a
charter of its own, I believe), all departments of the
University are under the restraints of the general University charter—restraints which were manifestly meant
forever to prohibit teaching not consistent with Baptist
religious views."

The interrupted speaker resumes and proceeds:

"That point, I mean the point just raised, Mr. Chairman, however well taken, does not bear on what I was
going to say. I was going to say that a plan, a tentative
toward a plan, this moment occurs to me, which I beg
to submit for our President's consideration. The books
that have stirred up all this tumult seem to me, from the
examination that I have made of them, to possess a character, in mode of presentation, unfitting them for general
comprehension. If I may express myself in a quasi-
confidential way here, I will say that, however valuable
may be the guesses at truth that they contain, they betray
a mental idiosyncrasy in the author that tends to disqualify him, that perhaps does disqualify him, to be a

really effective teacher. At least I do not see how young men and young women can possibly profit intellectually by such instruction as he must be giving. They may think that they are profited, but that makes matters worse, if they are not really profited.

" Take, for example, the sentence I will ask permission to read from the professor's book. I had the curiosity to copy it out that I might carry it with me for study in moments of leisure, and for submission to my ' cultured ' friends as an exercise in interpretation—take, I say, this sentence, and estimate the amount of educative value likely to be lodged in the instructions of the author of it, for students, male and female, still in their intellectual gristle, as of course most university students are. Pardon me, listen, while I read this specimen sentence, in my best interpretative manner:

" ' Granted that, as tradition in history, so mechanism in nature, are alike derivative, not ends in themselves, but means to an end, the static precipitate of dynamic purposive force, ministrant to the ends of the latter—I care not how organically and intimately this dynamic and this static are related to each other, so unitary that as I look at the static only I am materialist, at the dynamic only I am idealist—yet grant the primacy of the dynamic as original and active, who shall limit its freedom and power of self-expression in the forms of the historical life?'

" In my opinion, few more injurious intellectual influences can be brought to bear on young minds than the influence of instruction that makes the impression on them of being profound, while, in fact, it is only unintelligible. Perhaps a chair could be found, or could be created, for this professor, that will virtually compel him to leave the German cloudland in which he loves to dwell, and come out into the white, dry light, dear to the American mind, of clear thought and clear expression. His subject now, I believe, is the Philosophy of Religion. That word

'Philosophy' takes him off his feet. He struggles vainly in mid-air, 'embracing cloud, Ixion-like.' Suppose he be translated to a different, sublunary, sphere. If, in order to be happy, he must needs have 'Philosophy' in it, let it be Philosophy in no way connected with Religion. It might do to establish a chair to be entitled, say, 'The Philosophy of Logic and Rhetoric.' In such a chair he could disport himself in 'Philosophy' as much as he pleased, while the Logic and the Rhetoric would serve as intellectual ballast, and tend to keep his feet firmly on the ground. He would, so to speak, against his instinct, be compelled to be fairly intelligible.

"By the way, while it may in fairness be admitted that the specimen sentence I quoted from him means something, still the meaning, whatever it was, swelled so large in the writer's mind that he could not get it out without doing violence to an elementary rule of simple grammar. Possibly then it might be salutary for our professor himself to extend the bounds of his subject, tentatively proposed by me, so as to have it include grammar as well as logic and rhetoric; 'The Philosophy of Grammar, Logic, and Rhetoric' would make a well-sounding designation of his chair." [A ripple of smile at this running round the circle of the Board, the speaker adds]:

"I would not have my remarks taken to imply any lack of respect for the professor's engaging personal qualities, which every one that comes in contact with him delightfully feels. And I will say, besides, that I caught here and there in his books glints and glimpses of what seemed to me truly charming in literary manner. He might perhaps make for himself a name in literature —if he could only escape the snare of 'philosophy.'"

As soon as this is added, another gentleman, who, being an evangelical Christian, though not a Baptist, is intelligently in sympathy with Baptists as to the religious interests concerned, speaks, in a tone of grave sincerity which at once commands respectful attention, and says:

" I wish, Mr. Chairman, our honored President would quite seriously consider this last practical suggestion so pleasingly made. It perhaps hints at the true solution of our problem. Such a proposal of transfer for the professor to some perfectly neutral department of instruction he would of course assume to be an indication that we do not wish to continue any longer the strained relations he has brought upon us, not only with our Baptist founders, but with all evangelical Christians as well; and the concession thus made by us to these serious-minded people they would doubtless accept in a good spirit, as a sign that we were going in the future to pay more regard than we have paid in the past to the religious pledges of our charter. This certainly it will well become us to do, remembering that, without those pledges the University of Chicago would never have been founded.

" That Baptist whom we by eminence designate in all our University public documents as ' Founder,' Mr. Rockefeller, it is no secret, wished the institution to which his munificence gave birth, to be an exceptionally, a peculiarly, religious institution—very ' peculiarly ' religious [the speaker, dropping his voice to a parenthetical undertone and smiling pleasantly, permits himself a passing somewhat solemn play upon the ambiguous word]— very ' peculiarly ' religious, our critics would insist, the University certainly has been from the start, and still is; and, that sense of the word being taken, the Founder's hope and aim have been abundantly fulfilled!

" Seriously, I suppose, from what I have heard, it is not too much to say that if Mr. Rockefeller could have foreseen, at the time of his great initial gifts, such a state of things as has of late existed here, those gifts would never have been bestowed. His extraordinary modest forbearance has kept him, during all these years, from making his influence felt in the way of checking our progress in a path that assuredly he would never have chosen for us. It may be that what we call the time-spirit, the *zeitgeist,* as our friends the Germans call it, tremendously reenforced by the influence of this University, has moved the chief Founder, together with some among the subordinate founders, farther along in the direction of religious liberalism than either he or they would once have believed it possible for them to go. That may be, and it therefore may be that he does not look on the present attitude of our University with as much concern as far-sighted observers, or observers who think themselves far-sighted, believe that he would, if he really knew the innermost truth of what is going on here. But whether or not this is so, certain it is that too many earnest Christians deplore what they feel to be our jaunty gait of advance along perilous ways, for us to ignore them, for us not to pay them respectful heed.

"By the way, it is a consideration worthy to be taken into account, especially by those who nervously fret against the idea of being hampered by our charter, and who sincerely believe that it is a great misfortune for any institution, or any individual, to be bound by checks, that, however wise and good for one generation, are not suited to the needs of the generation following—I say, it is well to remember that the safeguarding religious provision solemnly inserted in our charter, is such in its nature as to admit progressive adjustments applied perpetually to perpetually changing needs. For, the provision is not compulsory subscription to an unchangeable form of creed; the provision consists simply in a particular constitution of our Board of Trustees. If, for example, succeeding generations of Baptists believe differently, from one generation to another, such differences in belief will necessarily be represented in the Board of Trustees, since these have to be elected each time out of the Baptist generation then living. Our charter, though Baptist, that is, evangelically Christian, pronouncedly so, is really a remarkably liberal instrument. We may safely, as in duty bound we must, live up to it."

" Well, Mr. Chairman," the President now intervenes to say, " I think we owe thanks to the member of this Board who has brought on the present discussion. He has set us to thinking, and I am sure good will come of it."

The Chair takes the hint thus conveyed that the discussion might be regarded as closed for the present, and, after a suitable pause, says: " A motion to adjourn would now be in order "; but before the suggested motion for adjournment is made, the session is unexpectedly prolonged, as the result of a question modestly interjected by a certain mild-spoken, quietly persistent member of the Board, who has hitherto been silent, but who, considerately mindful to have impartial circumspect regard paid to *all* the various interests involved, now asks:

" Is it not true, Mr. Chairman, that contributions were solicited, and in some instances obtained, from persons other than Baptists, and should not these non-Baptist contributors be fairly considered? These questions of course answer themselves in being asked. It is notorious that such contributions were sought and were secured. What I wished was, simply to bring this rather important fact, with its important bearings, clearly to present attention. Now, with your permission, Mr. Chairman, I will assume general consent on the part of the Board, and venture to address a few pertinent questions to an individual colleague of ours, here present, who may be supposed to be exceptionally well informed in just this matter—that is, if he will kindly indulge me in a freedom of the sort " [with a deferential bow of inquiry to the gentleman intended, responded to by him with a silent sign of acquiescence].

Question: " Was the denominational condition, incorporated in the charter, brought to the knowledge of persons not Baptist who were approached with a view to the securing of subscriptions from them?"

Answer: " I of course cannot pretend to know the details of what occurred in every particular such case; but the Baptist character proposed of the institution to be founded was a matter of such pronounced and general publicity that those engaged in soliciting subscriptions may be supposed to have thought that no emphasis on the point was required by fairness. Concealment of the denominational feature, I am sure, was not practised."

Question: " Some large subscriptions were made by persons not only not Baptist, but not Christian, indeed by persons who would be not unfairly described as antichristian; I refer to certain of our Jewish fellow citizens. These subscribers, being very intelligent men, and being devotedly Jewish in faith, would naturally, before subscribing, have informed themselves with some care as to what might be the effect on the fortunes of their own religious body, of the distinctly Christian character of the institution, guaranteed by its charter. What assurances were given them as to this? Were any assurances given; were any assurances asked?"

Answer: " I recognize the crucial nature of the inquiries you now propound. It would be almost impossible that doubts and scruples should *not* be raised by conscientious and sagacious Jews touching the influence to be looked for from the projected institution, exerted possibly in antagonism to their own belief and practice. Would the institution be administered in a broadly liberal spirit? That would be a natural form for the question to take, and evidently that form is capable of being variously interpreted. The Baptist, on the one hand, might, in all good conscience, say: The institution, you may be sure, will not undertake, indeed will not permit, in its conduct, any propagandism of peculiar denominational views; and the Jew, on the other hand, might thence infer that, while *religion* would be favored and fostered in the

University, it would be *religion,* and not Christianity—
religion in a very broadly inclusive sense, hospitable,
alike and equally, to every religion that simply takes to
itself the name, Religion. It would be a great temptation
certainly, in a case in which a large possible subscription
hung trembling in the balance, for the solicitor not to
make the denominational condition gratuitously offensive. I really cannot say what kind, and what degree,
of diplomacy, was applied in such cases."

At this point, that alert-minded gentleman, whose very
unlooked-for initiative early in the session had brought
on the discussion in progress, could not resist the impulse
to interpose a relevant remark or two:
" That word, ' diplomacy,' Mr. Chairman, if our col-
loquists will allow the interruption that word, ' diplomacy,'
is very suggestive. Whatever may have been the diplomacy practised to satisfy considering Jewish investors
in this great University, the assurances given, whether
by direct expression or by pregnant hint, to the effect
that Jewish interests would be protected in the course of
administration, might, I should say, be considered to have
been abundantly made good. I have been informed that,
at the very beginning of things, whether or not in order
to forestall the promptly forming Young Men's Christian
Association is a matter of conjecture, a movement was
set on foot, originated at headquarters, and thence
guided and controlled, to organize a truly comprehensive
religious society, embracing the entire University body,
students and teachers alike. This movement, I have
been told, encountered at once a peculiar difficulty. What
should the organization be called? ' The Christian
Union ' was the name finally adopted, not however without a struggle to have it more inclusive than that adjective, ' Christian,' seemed to permit.
" Opposition to that descriptive word speedily came out
in a striking manner. A Jewish member of one of the

o

faculties, having early been invited to give a Sunday-evening address in the chapel, concluded his discourse (which consisted of a labored argument to prove that it was no matter what form religion took, that one religious creed was as good as another) with the very significant expression of a 'hope' that the time would soon come, in the quest of a 'union' embracing *all* religion, for the 'adjective' [Christian] to be 'dispensed with.' From this it should seem that the very elastically liberal administration which permitted a Jewish rabbi to undermine Christianity, in the chapel of an institution founded by Christians, before an audience furnished by Christians, on a day of the week held sacred by Christians—that an administration elastic enough for that, was yet not elastic enough to satisfy fully the Jewish appetite for unlimited comprehension. I beg pardon for thus interrupting the course of question-and-answer going on between my two highly esteemed colleagues. I will only add that money, from whatever source received, has a very persistent habit of getting itself effectively represented."

This energetic interruption had the effect to close the incident of the colloquy, and it was promising to end that session of the Board of Trustees, when a keenly observant, brisk-spoken, highly practical member, with a suspicion of tartness in his manner, rather than in his spirit, breaks in and says:

"I do not wish to prolong further this meeting, but I beg, Mr. Chairman, to raise a question appearing to me to be of some moment, to which I would be glad to have a word of reply from the President of the University. It is, of course, all very well for us here, in the privacy of our Board meeting, to criticize ourselves freely, even to the extent of seeming now and then to criticize one another. But how if, for example, some forthputting member of one of our various faculties should take it into his head to bring public opinion to bear on the administration of the University, by putting his ideas on the subject into print for all men to see?

"It is not to be doubted that wide-awake professors, knowing, as they cannot help knowing, what the trend is of our policies, have thoughts about the matter which they consider important; and it might very naturally happen that some one of them, big with a sense of responsibility for things in general, should conceive the notion of taking the outside community into the confidence of his views, in the hope that thus a pressure of public opinion might help bring the University administration round to his own way of thinking. I should like to know from our President whether he thinks this ought to be permitted. Is our great principle of free thought and free speech broad enough to cover such a demonstration from a professor?"

The President of the University, thus challenged, smiles easily as he says in reply:

"Well, Mr. Chairman, there are such things as considerations of propriety, of decorum, involved, and I might advise a particular professor in a particular case—provided he sought my advice—a prudent course, which, however, he might not see fit to pursue!—I might, I say, advise the supposed professor to abstain, for reasons of comity, from printing his views; while, if he did not abstain, I should be decidedly in favor of letting him free his mind, and that without the least prejudice to his standing as professor. If he made a bad thing of his demonstration, the reaction against it in public opinion would sufficiently admonish him; and if, on the contrary, he made a good thing of it, why should we not profit by it? All, I think, or nearly all, would depend on the way in which the thing was done. I should certainly not consider myself called upon to reprimand, as offender, a member of our teaching force who publicly criticized the administration of the University, however strongly I might feel that in doing so he had committed an error of judgment or of taste. Such a thing would, I am convinced, in practice take care of itself. At all events," the President adds, with happy self-recollection, exciting a responsive smile of mutual intelligence all around the Board, " I shall never recommend to the Trustees of the University of Chicago the removal of any professor on account of his use of the freedom of the press."

On this from the President, the meeting is in due form adjourned.

There needs to be subjoined an addendum to the foregoing imperfect report, or it would be left too glaringly incomplete. At one point, the reporter is not clear at what point, he was too much interested, not to say startled, to place the incident accurately—in truth, the incident came in out of any perceivable logical relation to the course of the discussion—at some point, up spoke a member of the Board who had till then sat silent, detached in mood, in fact, apparently wool-gathering, up spoke this gentleman, and said abruptly:

" Here we are, twenty of us, more or less, wise men, tangling our fingers together in the effort to untie a Gordian knot that we shall never succeed in untying. I propose that we *cut* it and have done. I have an Alexandrian sword that I think will do the business with neatness and despatch, and set us quite free to do hereafter exactly as we have been doing all along in the past.

" We are bound to be loyal to fundamental Baptist principles. Agreed. What Baptist principle is there *more* fundamental than the principle of religious liberty? Did not that great primitive Baptist, Roger Williams, found the State of Rhode Island on purpose to guarantee to every citizen in it absolute freedom to think and speak and act precisely as he felt in conscience bound to do, in matters of religion? We here have all along been consistently, however unconsciously, conducting this great University on just this principle, historically the formative principle of the Baptist denomination in America. We have felt, and rightly felt, that we should be recreant to our trust if we put a muzzle on the mouth of any one under our control who felt himself moved to speak out his mind, in whatever way, on the subject of religion. I submit the question: Does not this sword of Alexander cut for us at a stroke our Gordian knot with all its tangles? If not, why not? Perhaps our esteemed colleague, Mr. [he named a distinguished member of the Board who had earned a reputation for a certain slow-paced, sure-footed, quasi-judicial turn of mind] can tell us why not? He can, I am sure, if anybody can."

The gentleman thus challenged cleared his throat, in much the manner of a warship clearing her deck for action, and began deliberately:

"Yes, religious liberty is undoubtedly a principle of prime importance with us Baptists. It is, however, in strictness to be held not so much a *fundamental* principle, as an *essential,* a *vital* principle. *Fundamental* it is not, for it rests on another principle which accordingly, since it underlies this, is the really fundamental principle for Baptists. Religious liberty means for Baptists liberty to obey Christ. Obedience to Christ as supreme Lord of all human souls is the one true *fundamental* principle of Baptists. We quite misunderstand the Baptist doctrine of "soul-liberty," unless we understand its connection with the far more fundamental doctrine of obligation to obey Christ—obligation binding on each man for himself alone, by no means involving right on his part, much less duty, to enforce obedience on anybody else.

"Roger Williams established a commonwealth dedicated to the idea of universal religious liberty. He did this in order that Christ might be freely obeyed. If the example of Roger Williams's commonwealth is to be adduced here as a proper precedent and parallel for us, let us take care that we institute the comparison properly. Roger Williams, in establishing his commonwealth, did *not* proclaim: ' Come hither and here enjoy unlimited religious liberty. We are Baptists, and we believe in obeying Christ. But we make you free to disobey Christ, if you choose to do so, and not only this, we will tax ourselves in money to support you and pay you salaries for teaching the contrary of this, our most cherished belief.'

" Roger Williams did not in effect make any such proclamation. He was a man of good sound common sense, as well as of controlling religious convictions. He held, and he applied, his great doctrine of soul-liberty under the sway of sane common sense. We must not flatter ourselves that we are following the lead of Roger Williams, as the great historic champion of soul-liberty, in paying our professors salaries to teach the contrary of what our Baptist founders most ardently and most profoundly believe. To do this is to prove false to our trust, and no illusion on our part to the effect that so we are practising ' soul-liberty ' will acquit us at the bar of conscience and of common sense.

" Imagine Roger Williams, on the ground of religious liberty, paying salaries levied on his brother Baptists, for the support and encouragement of men devoting themselves to the inculcation of the doctrine of union of Church and State, the doctrine of the divine right of kings, nay, perhaps even the doctrine of persecution to ensure religious orthodoxy, the doctrine of the duty of the State to abolish religious liberty as tending to unbounded license and consequent ruin of souls. Imagine that, if you please, and then you will have imagined a state of things analogous to what we have allowed to establish itself here.

" Baptists believe in the deity of Jesus Christ—this not as Baptists, but simply as evangelical Christians ; our professor teaches that Jesus Christ was a mere man, very good and all that, but a child of his race and of his time. Baptists believe in a Christ such as Paul preached, a Christ exalted in the heaven of heavens, and there and thence now reigning supreme over human history; our professor teaches that such a Christ does not exist, that the idea is a pure 'myth,' using that very word to express his meaning. Baptists believe in a Christ risen from the dead and ascended into heaven; our professor teaches that the crucified Jesus never left the grave in which he was buried. And our University, presided over by a Baptist President, controlled and conducted by Baptist trustees, pays him a salary for doing this; nor only so, furnishes him classroom accommodations for doing this, then invites students out of the bosoms of Baptist families to imbibe the instruction from his lips, and, climax to the inconsistency, puts the *imprimatur* of our University Press upon his books, and sends them forth to do their unsettling work in the world —all in the sacred name, forsooth, of religious liberty!

"I do not generally, as you all know, allow myself to become heated in the statement of my views, and I beg you to believe that my present heat is a purely intellectual generation. Really, the absurdity of our course seems to me so preposterous, that it has stirred up a perhaps too lively ferment in my mind, whence the heat with which I have spoken. Graciously pardon it, I pray."

It cannot be supposed that after an adjournment closing such a discussion, there would not follow considerable activity of private reflection on the part of the Trustees, and considerable quasi-confidential exchange of ideas between one and another of the number. "If a new order of administration leading to repressive *counsel,* such as that hypothetically foreshadowed very mildly by our President, is to be instituted here, what will become of our boasted freedom of thought?" says one trustee to a colleague of his who happens to be a next-door neighbor. The neighbor replies:

" I do not see that there need be any less freedom of thought than there has been heretofore; somewhat less freedom of expression perhaps. If any one of our professors suffers from gathering fulness of thought denied vent in expression in a classroom, or in a book with the University imprint on it, he has only to seek his relief elsewhere. The world is wide, and, thanks largely to these Baptists of a former generation, absolute religious freedom, both in thought and in expression, is now the heritage of every American. But it by no means follows that Baptists are under obligation to furnish facilities—salary, classroom, audience, press privileges—for the propagation of ideas at war with their own dearest religious convictions. By refusal to admit such obligation, freedom of thought will not be imperiled, nor will any proper freedom of expression."

Another trustee, not the liberal-minded Baptist referred to previously, but a Baptist whose liberal-mindedness is not checked by serious religious conviction of any sort, says within himself, with a satisfaction that might also be described as a kind of intellectual chuckle:

" I liked what was said in the Board about the self-adjusting ease and elasticity of our denominational restriction. With more and more enlightenment, Baptist ideas will expand and accommodate themselves to the spirit of the times. We Baptists now in the Board are simply anticipating the enlightenment, which is sure to come soon to the whole denomination and to all Christian denominations. We are anticipating that period of enlightenment; and not only so, we are helping it along, hastening its arrival. We are the vanguards of a multitudinous forward march toward a completely emancipated future. If we have indiscreetly rushed on too fast ahead of the ranks, we can afford to slow up for a while to let the ranks close in behind us. We must watch the coming elections to our Board, and make sure of not getting in any reactionaries.

"There are plenty of Baptists in good and regular standing, who will not block progress through ill-timed obstinate adhesion to old-fashioned, worn-out religious ideas. Where is the Baptist church, at least in the enlightened northern part of our country, that would deprive any man of membership in its body, who was prominent enough to be a candidate for position as University of Chicago trustee, no matter how advanced his views might be in the direction of sympathy with the ideas set forth by the accused professor? Why, the accused professor himself would be eligible to our Board, for he is, I believe, a member in good and regular standing of an important Baptist church—yes, and, so I am told, he is from time to time an acceptable occupant of that church's pulpit. The simple fact is, that these zealot, clamant Baptist ministers wish us at the University to be more strict in matters of religious discipline than they dare to be themselves as pastors of churches. Who ever hears of one single pastor of them all urging his church to exclude a member of prominence for aberration in theologic belief? It is unreasoning, unreasonable clamor that is now rife in certain ministerial circles. Let it wear itself out and die, as it soon will, of exhaustion."

While such a course of reflection is going on in one trustee's breast, another trustee, distinguished among his fellows as the deepest theologian of them all, meditates as follows:

"As for me, I am a man of peace. I deprecate this tumult. The teachings that have stirred it up I abhor, while the teacher himself I love as a brother. It may be as some urge, that his amiable character, his suasive manner, only makes him more dangerous as a teacher of false doctrine. Yes, that must be so. Still, this great University simply cannot afford to stop his mouth, to muzzle him. It would be a reproach to us throughout the whole academic world. Besides, it would be *generally* unpopular. The secular press would be unanimous in charging poltroonery upon us. Well, it is a keen question, Is it not poltroonery *rather,* not to face this double opposition, and stand fast for *truth,* instead of standing fast for destructive error, not new, but imposing upon itself to think itself new and true? Can I at least, who profoundly believe these teachings to be not only false, but pernicious, pernicious in the extreme, can I as trustee lend my vote and my countenance to apparent endorsement of them—endorsement involved in their being inculcated in our classrooms and published by our University Press? Really, really, it is a very trying case. If I were a salaried officer of the University, I should suspect myself, I am afraid I should suspect myself, of being unduly influenced in my judgment, and in my consequent attitude and conduct, by that fact.

"I have not been able wholly to banish suspicions—for I seem to myself to have seen, or felt rather, reasons for entertaining them—that college and university professors not of our own body—yes, even theological professors, some of them, too—who like to be invited here to give lectures in the summer, or to serve as occasional University preachers, are more or less unconsciously bribed to seem, and through seeming at length to become perhaps in fact, less pronouncedly orthodox, in the old-fashioned sense of the word, than they would wish to be thought at home—bribed, yes, I may say *bribed,* through their unconfessed fondness for the honor and emolument of such invitations from the University of Chicago.

"For good or for ill, our tentacles reach out widely on every side to lay hold of and subsidize religious opinion into conformity with the standards that are known to prevail with us. Happily I have in that respect the advantage of those connected with the University whose income seems to depend upon their loyalty to the institution. Of course, personal interests far more important than income are at stake for all of us—unless our belief in a future judgment and a final award made according to deeds done in the body, is a superstitious delusion—and a fearsome doctrine that is, which, I admit, latter-day 'science,' with 'the passing of apocalypticism,'[1] tends (am I glad, I wonder?) to render more and more difficult for me to entertain with full and effective faith. At any rate, that serious consideration of 'something after death' is a remote and uncertain consideration, and the matter of current income is very nigh at hand and very pressing. On the whole, I am rather sorry for those under salary from the University who have to make up their mind on these momentous practical issues."

The discussion with its sequel took a wide range, but not range wide enough to include all the matter that might pertinently have been included. The reporter perhaps was at fault, he may have nodded, and so have lost something from the course of the discussion that better vigilance on his part would have secured. For instance, it seems impossible that the original speaker of them all should not have raised and pressed the point of the absurdity of assuming that there could be any good sense in the University's contenting itself with keeping the letter of the charter and ignoring the spirit. This speaker must, in fact, have said something like this: 'Do we fairly observe the terms of our charter when we merely keep Baptist the required two-thirds of the Board, and pay no attention to what was necessarily implied in that requirement, namely, that we should be watchful and faithful to have the University "at all times," to

---

[1] Allusion to a leading editorial article, in one of the University publications, bearing this title—which virtually, if not expressly, does away with Christ's solemn prediction of a future general judgment, and with Paul's circumstantial description of the second coming of the Lord and of the resurrection attending it.

use the words of the charter, absolutely true to Baptist beliefs? And yet have we not actually proceeded hitherto in just that absurd way?'

So much for the hypothetical trustee meeting, and for the hypothetical sequel of it enacting itself in talk and in reflection.

Now the reporter of that meeting, acting in his capacity as editor, begs to pass for a final moment from hypothesis to reality. He has in his possession a letter, lately received, from a gentleman of the highest character, who permits to be shown here the following extracts from his communication, although he wrote simply for the private eye of his correspondent. This letter, conceived, as, from its tone and tenor, will be self-evident, in the kindest spirit, though in a spirit deeply disappointed and grieved, will be found to possess a certain genuinely pathetic human interest. It puts into mild regretful expression a sentiment that is common to many faithful hearts. Could not the University of Chicago have been as successfully administered as it has been, without giving just occasion for such a sentiment as that of the letter now to be quoted from, in any heart?

And ought it not to have been?

The letter now to be quoted from was written in reply to the question why he, the writer, withdrew from his very important place as trustee of the University:

" The subject causes me to feel sad. Early in my " Chicago life I became interested in both Seminary " and University, when both needed friends and help. I " was invited to pronounce the banns, when in the Bap- " tist church building at Morgan Park the union of the " two institutions was formally effected, and the Semi- " nary became the Divinity School of the University. " A collation in Blake Hall followed; by request, I said " a few words there. In both places I was *cautious in* " *congratulations,* differing from other speakers, express-

" ing deepest regret if any departure from the Baptist
" polity and practice should be the result. I told Doctor
" Harper in the summer of 1890, while I was president
" of the Board of Trustees of the University, that I was
" afraid of him, of his loyalty. He laughed at my fears,
" saying he was all right. When I think of the positions
" held by [here follow four representative names of pro-
" fessors, the first name being that of the professor whose
" boldness and *naïveté* had brought on the current public
" outcry and discussion] etc., *I am very sorry that I ever*
" *contributed the little that I did to the institutions*
" [italics mine]—although in those earlier days, in the
" '70s, and '80s, both were conservative, compared with
" their present condition. *Frequently* the treasurer came
" to me lacking from $300 to $800 to make up professors'
" monthly salaries. I always gave him my check to make
" up the deficiency. I gave $30,000 toward the $400,000
" required by Mr. Rockefeller at the time of his first
" gift. I was *never* able to give what I have given.
" Like David at his temple contribution, I can say, ' In
" my trouble (poverty) I have given,' etc. I did it while
" I was in active business. I did it cheerfully as unto the
" Lord. If the institutions had remained loyal to their
" early faith under their first professors and instructors,
" I should rejoice to-day that I had been even a little
" help in their early struggles. I removed to my present
" place of residence early in 1890, but returned to Chicago
" to aid what I could in the restoration or reconstruction
" of the (old) University. I could not be a figurehead
" simply on the Board. I presume I should have remained
" on the Board longer than I did, had I not removed
" from Chicago, but I was *not satisfied,* even in those
" early days. I told Doctor Harper, ' Your *learned*
" doubts only *waken* and *strengthen my natural doubts.' "

If a census of expressions could be obtained from the
very wide dispersion of contributors to that first sum of

$400,000 which, under the conditions of Mr. Rockefeller's original munificent offer, it was necessary to raise, through what was virtually a popular subscription by Baptists, in order to secure his proposed great gift of $600,000 (and, as was speedily shown, the subsequent immense, almost perennial, flow of bounty from the same inexhaustible source)—if, I say, a census of expressions were obtainable from these much more humble, but not less generous, fellow founders of the University of Chicago, there can be little doubt that an emphatic majority of such expressions would be, each one, an echo of the pathetic and mournful sentiment italicized above: " I am very sorry that I ever contributed the little that I did to the institution."

It is an infinite pity that the conditions should ever have been permitted to establish themselves which have inspired, and which do now inspire, such a sentiment of keen and unavailing regret. All the more is it to be deplored, that it never was, and that it is not now, in the least degree necessary. To prevent the unfortunate result, it only required that the ethics of trusteeship should be more thoughtfully, more vigilantly, observed.

With reluctance overcome only with a great struggle, I have at length expressed myself as I have in these final words. I inculpate no individual, I leave it open to be assumed that every individual concerned has acted with absolute fidelity to conscientious conviction; but, for good or for ill, the great University of Chicago has, I fully believe, always been, and I fully believe it is now, the chief organized force existing anywhere on the planet at work, I do not say formally, but virtually, in aid of the movement against Paul.

Only those who have thought deeply on the subject, and have thought with the advantage of intimately knowing, from close-at-hand observation, or, better yet, experience of practical responsibility for administration, the conditions necessarily existing in the case—only such persons can adequately conceive the extraordinary difficulties with which the conduct of a great university has to deal, especially a great university bound by its charter to a certain fiduciary fidelity in the matter of religion. The public should be slow in judging, and very slow in censuring, the board of control. Obviously, in the case of the University of Chicago, the original make-up of the body of trustees, since this was to be a self-perpetuating body, needed to be very choice. The denominational provision of the charter could be fully met without being fairly met. Candidates for trustees could always be found that were indeed, in accordance with the requirement of the charter, members of regular Baptist churches, but members in form merely, not members in spirit. The Board might thus come to be anything but truly representative of the Baptist denomination.

This is a long chapter, and a serious; but I feel constrained to make it longer, and perhaps more serious, by adding a postscript.

POSTSCRIPT

"The American Journal of Theology" is a quarterly periodical published by the "University of Chicago Press" and "edited by the Divinity Faculty of the University of Chicago and colleagues in allied departments." These items of information are given on the outside of the front cover to the quarterly. On the inside of the same cover is printed a list of all the editors, numbering twenty-one names. Of these, three are designated as "Managing Editors."

It will be seen therefore that "The American Journal of Theology" is, in an important sense, very broadly representative of the University of Chicago as a whole, while of course especially of its Divinity School. Not that the University becomes responsible for the truth of everything set forth in the pages of its quarterly; but it is manifestly responsible for letting appear whatever does in fact appear in its pages. It is in the nature of things impossible that the opinions and beliefs of the numerous editorship should not, on the whole, tend to impress a character of its own upon their periodical, and to make its resultant influence felt in favor of what they hold to be true. The quarterly is conducted with ability, and, it need not be doubted, and for myself I do not doubt, with sincere desire and purpose on the part of the editors to have it always loyal to the truth as they see the truth.

What particularly concerns us, in the present discussion, is to determine, if we can, the attitude of the quarterly on the question of the apostle Paul's right to continue to hold his age-long position of divinely accredited authority as theologian and doctor of the Christian church. It happens that we have just now been furnished valuable aids for the prosecution of our quest. While, as has been intimated, the numerous and widely representative editorship of "The American Journal of Theology" are in general responsible for the appearing of what appears in its pages, they are in particular responsible for the appearing of matter that has been editorially asked for from the writer. This is the character of an important paper in the number of the quarterly for July, 1913, entitled "The Significance of Paul for Modern Christians." The writer is Johannes Weiss, of Heidelberg University in Germany. Professor Weiss had written and published on the subject of Paul previously to his being editorially invited to furnish this article. The editors therefore knew, or had the opportunity of knowing, what would undoubtedly be the trend of his invited contribution.

That my readers also may know, in part at least, what it may be assumed as certain that the inviting editors knew beforehand, I show a few suggestive brief excerpts from Weiss's work entitled " Paul and Jesus." This work has been translated into admirably readable English, and it is published in this country by Harper and Brothers. It is a serious book, written in a spirit of most decorous respect for both Paul and Jesus. It impresses one as sincerely religious, even devout, in tone, and the author has made himself, by thorough study, master of his subject—so far as real mastery was possible to a man obsessed with the invincible prepossession that nothing supernatural is credible.

For Weiss is a thoroughgoing rationalist. By this adjective, ' thoroughgoing,' I do not mean that he is a reckless, irreverent, irreligious, iconoclastic rationalist. He is indeed far from being such. On the contrary, he seems as seriously devout as was the great leader and protagonist of American Unitarianism, Doctor Channing. But Channing was a loyal believer in Scripture as inspired and authoritative. Weiss, in contrast of Channing, rejects such a view of Scripture. He is *more* a Unitarian than was Channing. His rationalism may perhaps best be described as a calmly, candidly " scientific " attitude of mind. To be scientific, as Weiss conceives the matter, he must—to begin with, to continue with, to end with—absolutely ignore, or, more positive, absolutely repudiate, the idea that anything happens, or ever has happened, not conformable to natural law. Paul's conversion therefore to Weiss had nothing supernatural about it, nothing not reducible to the order of nature, nothing not explicable on the principles of " modern " psychology. He sets cheerfully about the task of demonstrating this. As was shown to be the case with Weinel, the " retina " plays a part in his explanation. He is quite frankly outspoken. Here are his *ipsissima verba,* or their equivalents in English translation: " Modern criticism . . . considers that the experience on the way to Damascus was simply a vision or hallucina-

P

tion. . . The picture formed upon his [Paul's] retina was evoked by mental excitement."

As a sane and sensible historian, Weiss accepts, apparently without question, the New Testament story of Paul's conversion, and then proceeds to interpret it psychologically. The performance is really extraordinary, regarded as a performance in "scientific" gymnastics. Weiss evolves his explanation purely out of his own subjective consciousness, without pretense of any objective historic data to work with, depending wholly on what he holds *must* have been the psychologic process that went on in Paul's mind. It is, I confess, to my way of thinking, a fairly ludicrous exercise of the "scientific" imagination.

But now for the promised excerpts from the text of Weiss's book, "Paul and Jesus." After describing very suavely, almost sympathetically, what, briefly, we may call orthodox evangelical Christianity, remarking that "for centuries this form of religion has been regarded as Christianity proper," he goes on to describe what, briefly again, we may call a pious Socinianism, remarking that "these two forms of religious life exist side by side in our churches [he speaks of course for churches in Germany, but if current tendencies prevail the same might be said of our American churches—I know an instance in which an avowed Unitarian is not only a member, but an office-bearer, in a nominally orthodox evangelical church] and it is very desirable that they should coexist in mutual toleration, and that the preaching of the gospel should do no violence to either of them [that is, no preacher that believes in Paul should preach as if he did so believe]. I freely admit," so Weiss proceeds to say, "that I myself, with the majority of modern theologians, prefer the second form [Socinianism or Unitarianism], and I hope that it may gradually become predominant in our church. But, as a historian, I feel bound to assert that it is *a conception widely*

removed from the early Christian or the Pauline view.
[Italics mine.] On the other hand, I feel no less bound
to assert that the Jesus [not 'the Christ,' observe] of
history, so far as we know him, regarded himself as
sent to draw his followers into immediate experience
of the life of sonship, without requiring any place for
himself in their religious aspirations."

Weiss, it may be seen (from what is shown above in
italics, which are mine), is consciously and confessedly
in revolt against Paulinism; that is, against Paul. My
readers will note the agreement between this German
theologian's view as to the trend toward Unitarianism
of current theologic thought and the view expressed by
that theologian whose remark to the same effect made
in conversation with me was quoted some pages back.
The average man, conversant with the Gospels, may be
surprised at Weiss's assertion that Jesus required no
place for himself in the religious aspirations of his disciples. The average man will recall Christ's: "Without me ye can do nothing"; "I am the vine, ye are the
branches"; "One is your Master, even Christ"; "No
man cometh unto the Father but by me"; "I am the
way and the truth and the life"; "This do in remem-
brance of me"; and many another similarly requiring expression from Christ's lips, and will wonder what Weiss
could mean by saying that "Jesus required no place for
himself." The explanation is: As to some of these expressions, "interpretation" disposes of them, and as
to the rest, they are lacking in "historicity." "Scientificism" is a great matter! "I hope," says Weiss,
"that it [the Socinian or Unitarian "form of religion"]
may gradually become predominant in our church." Do
the ascendent powers in the Divinity School of the University of Chicago indulge the same hope? If they do,
the editors of the quarterly struck a fine stroke for them
toward the fufilment of that hope in publishing the invited
paper of Weiss.

But this paper will be followed with one invited from a soundly evangelical theologian? Perhaps, but hardly. Such a paper would necessarily not be " scientific "; and " scientific," at all hazards, a truly " modern " journal of theology must be. The paper supposed would not be scientific, for it would admit a miraculous, a supernatural, element in the conversion of Paul.

I cannot resist the temptation to show how this Unitarian German proves that Paul, contrary to the general belief, knew Jesus of Nazareth in the flesh. This is how: " Paul's vision and conversion are psychologically inconceivable except upon the supposition that he had been actually and vividly impressed by the human personality of Jesus." Therefore Paul knew Jesus, indeed knew him exceptionally well. Why? Because otherwise he could not have been converted as he was. How, then, *was* he converted? By the remembered " personality " of Jesus. But why did this remembered personality attack him just then, dash him to the ground, turn him stone blind? Weiss discreetly leaves these incidents of the great occasion unconsidered. To what straits is " scientific " method reduced in dealing with the simple story of the conversion of Paul!

The temptation is strong, but I must resist it, to pursue this criticism of Weiss. My true purpose is not to criticize him, but simply to exhibit him, in order that it may be seen what sort of man he is whom the editors of the quarterly thought fit to invite to teach their readers " the significance of Paul for modern Christians." What turned out to be the fruit of their invitation? Exactly such as might have been expected; this a few citations will show.

Weiss's first sentence is: " The title of this article has been formulated for me by the editors." He would himself have stated his problem differently. For our present purpose, no matter. Weiss soon proceeds to give certain specifications of difference between Paul and the "modern" man, tending to divest Paul of *any* "significance" for the "modern" man; these he numbers in order; they will be found to include nearly *all* that is vital in the teaching of Paul.

Number " 1 " reads: " The entire outline of his [Paul's] conception of the world, and of *his scheme of redemption* [italics mine] appears to us moderns *mythological*" [italics Weiss's].

" 2 ": " Paul's entire teaching consists of a theology of *evangelization* and *conversion* [italics Weiss's]. . . In the case of Paul sonship [to God] is regarded as the specific act of adoption of men who previously were not the children of God. We, however, are conscious of our sonship to God—in Jesus' sense of the term—as we are of the all-embracing and ever-present sunshine, to which we owe life and happiness, so that we have only to make use of it."

" 3 ": " The greatest difference is to be found in connection with the conception of the *divine spirit*" [italics Weiss's, who uses no capital letters in printing the term]. The paragraph following repeatedly speaks of the "spirit," always without a capital initial letter, and always in a way to indicate that Weiss's theology has no place for the Holy Spirit as a person. " On the whole," Weiss says, " the modern Christian will be inclined to give up prayer to Christ for prayer to the heavenly Father." Altogether, Weiss concludes that " for the whole of Paul's religion, it can continue to be vital for the modern Christian only in a very modified form."

Weiss seems conscious that he has thus vacated Paul of all vital " significance for modern Christians." He says: " It may fairly be asked whether a religious attitude [namely, Paul's] which originated so many centuries ago, and is expressed in such unfamiliar forms of thought can to-day lay any inspiring claims on men." Weiss then, whether out of complaisance to a still very widely

prevailing " form of religion," to wit, " Paulinism "—that
is, evangelical Christianity—or from a sense of fitness requiring him to make some concession in contributing
to a supposedly orthodox American journal of theology—
Weiss then girds up the loins of his audacity in affirmation, to say: " This question we venture to answer in the
affirmative." " In certain respects," he qualifies his boldness by saying. Those " certain respects " he specifies as
follows: " Namely, in Paul's conception of God, in his
teaching of the fundamental religious relation to God,
in his Christ-mysticism, and in his ethics." Obviously
these specifications well enough define Socinianism, indeed
define the religion of Jesus (of Jesus, note, as distinguished from Christ), according to the interpretation of
all Socinians, including Weiss—except that " Christ-
mysticism " seems a notion in Weiss's thought queerly
out of place for him to introduce as part of *his* view of
Paul's " significance for modern Christians."

Weiss's spirit of revolt against Paul expresses itself
still more strongly in his " Paul and Jesus." There he
says, with suppressed impatience: " No one would attempt
to depreciate the weight of the dogmatic burden [im-
posed by Paul] under which we labor at the present day."
How completely Weiss eases *himself* of this " dogmatic
burden," the following expressions from him somewhat
startlingly show: " One [any preacher, for example] who
is concerned with the awakening of religious experience
[this almost calls up the idea of a revivalist trying to
" arouse " sinners] *should not be so narrow-minded as
to condition this awakening on the affirmation of the doctrine of a personal God* [italics mine]. Pantheism may
indeed have its limitations and its defects, yet without
doubt it lies very near to our time, inspired as it is by
both scientific and artistic ideas. Why should we not
recognize this form of religion [pantheism] alongside of
other forms? "

In fine, Weiss very well exemplifies the inevitable

tendency of the revolt against Paul. That tendency is first toward Socinianism (I use that term rather than Unitarianism, because Socinianism is more definitely, more decisively, than Unitarianism, a "form of religion" that reduces Jesus Christ to strictly human measure; how freely Weiss conceives of Jesus appears in an incidental remark of his, parenthetically introduced, namely, "When Jesus unceremoniously denied the fundamental postulates of the whole system ['the official Jewish system']— *perhaps without fully realizing the radical consequences of his action*" [italics mine])—the tendency, I say, of the current revolt against Paul is, first, toward "liberalism"; then, toward Unitarianism; then, toward blank Socinianism; then, toward deism; then, toward pantheism; then, toward agnosticism; finally, toward atheism. There is no logical stopping-place in the fearful decline, till you reach atheism (or agnosticism, which is but a softer negative name for what in effect is the same thing as atheism). 'Pure alarmist extravagance!' some readers may self-defensively exclaim. Vainly—for atheism, as well as pantheism, "lies very near to our time."

It will serve further to indicate fairly the attitude toward Paul of the University of Chicago in its Divinity School, if I show here a few specimen expressions from several of the editors of "The American Journal of Theology" given out publicly under their own individual names.

In the "Biblical World," a monthly periodical issued by the University of Chicago Press, one of these "Journal" editors says (January, 1911): "Yet their cause [the cause of certain malcontent Jewish revolutionists, and even of John the Baptist] failed, while his [the cause of Jesus] succeeded—a significant testimony to the vital impress his personality left upon his disciples." Christ's "forceful personality," it is intimated by the writer, was "a very essential factor in the genesis of the resurrection faith"! (The writer might almost as well have said frankly, 'the resurrection *myth.*') "The exceptional manner in which he [Christ] awakened the deepest elements of religious faith gave the new religion a stimulus *through which it conquered even so stubborn a foe as Saul of Tarsus*" [italics mine]. This writer is, I think, entitled to the credit of originality in his idea that "the new religion" "conquered" Saul by means of a "*stimulus*"! Nothing like scientificism to account for Paul! "The disciples must have felt," the writer says, "that Jesus' superiority rested upon the force of his own character"! These expressions about the "personality" of Jesus sound like echoes of Weiss. I do not know who was first to make so much of the impressive "personality" of Jesus as a means of exorcising the haunting spirit of supernaturalism. The loose thought, well matched by the loose expression, in the foregoing extracts, should, but it probably will not, be its own sufficient antidote in the minds of the immature young ministers-in-the-making who listen to such teaching. "Elements of religious faith"—what are those elements? "The deepest elements." Has this Divinity professor analyzed "religious faith" into its "elements"; and, discriminating among those "elements," found out what are the "deepest"?

A second member of the editorial corps, teaching, as professor, the subject of Old Testament literature, had in the "Biblical World" for June, 1913, an interesting article, in the course of which he says: "The Hebrews were given no extraordinary or abnormal aids or advantages not within the reach of other men, then as now... The Hebrew prophets and saints having the same opportunities, were possessed of the same faculties as other men, no more and no less"—language which of course has the effect of denying special divine inspiration to these "prophets and saints," and seems flatly to contradict Paul: "What, then, is the advantage of the

Jews? . . Much every way; first, indeed, that they were intrusted with the oracles of God; . . Israelites, whose is the adoption [as children], and the glory [the visible glorious theophany] and the covenants [concluded by God with the patriarchs], and the giving of the law [on Sinai], and the service [the temple ritual], and the promises." The article reads as if it might have served as a classroom lecture to ministerial students. At any rate, it unquestionably indicates the trend of the Old Testament teaching given by this professor—a teaching obviously opposed at a vital point to the teaching of Paul, and obviously irreconcilable with belief in Paul's right to rule, as representative of Christ, in the realm of Christian doctrine. Such teaching belongs therefore to the literature of revolt against Paul.

A third member of the editorial staff of " The American Journal of Theology " teaches, as professor in the Divinity School, the subject of " Dogmatic Theology." This editor contributes an article to the " Biblical World," July, 1912, in which—evidently with the purpose (apparently with the purpose, perhaps I should more carefully say) of laying, quite incidentally, one more ground for the acceptance of that revolutionary critico-historical view which makes Leviticus and Deuteronomy the product of a later age than the Mosaic—he speaks, with easy confidence, of " that intense longing for holiness on the part of the later Israelites which led to the elaboration of the Levitical cult." Here we have two extraordinary assumptions—pure assumptions they both are, without even so much as a shadow of evidence tending to establish either their truth or their probability—one, the assumption that there existed among the Jews generally of later times an " intense longing for holiness," another, the assumption that such supposed national longing for holiness had the effect of giving rise to the elaborate " Levitical cult."

As if it could be truly affirmed of *any* people, at *any*

period of its history, that it was possessed with an " intense longing for holiness "! And then as if such a high spiritual " longing," supposed existent, and supposed risen to the pitch of intensity, could with any probability be imagined giving birth to a system of outward observances in bloody sacrificial rites! How averse teaching like this is from the teaching of Paul hardly needs to be pointed out.

But more outspokenly, though not at all more unmistakably, as holding the attitude of revolt against Paul, this professor appears, in a book of his to which his publishers give the date 1913. " Social Idealism and the Changing Theology " is the title the author chooses for his book. The book may fairly be described as a sustained and elaborate attempt to undermine and overthrow " traditionalism " in theology. ' No,' I seem to hear the author demurring, ' the task of undermining and overthrowing has for all time already been effectively accomplished by modern science and the modern world-view. My book simply recognizes and welcomes the fact, and seeks to save the cause of true—that is, scientific—religion by frankly giving up traditionalism in theology as a worn-out, discredited thing of the past. It did a splendid work [" splendid " is with him a favorite word of generous ascription] ; it did a splendid work for the church and the world in its time, but its time has gone by.'

" Traditionalism in theology "—there need be no mistake—that means " Paulinism," and Paulinism means Paul as the man whom Christ miraculously met on his way to Damascus, and as the man to whom Christ miraculously revealed the gospel he was to preach and to teach. The writer leaves the discerning reader in no doubt of his, the writer's, " scientific " belief that Paul was under a delusion as to any supernatural character in what befell him in his conversion. Paul " had come into the Christian life through a tremendous crisis, in which he saw [that is, thought he saw] a direct divine interposi-

tion." " In the Pauline doctrine, moral character is bestowed upon one by the grace of God. It is essentially
a miraculous donation."

Such language as this last might be used in a good
orthodox evangelical sense. But that it is not so used
by this writer becomes evident when, in the next sentence
but one, he brings himself to advance a truly revolting idea, the idea that " this Pauline conception of redemption " had some genetic, or at least germane and
kindly, relation to " Greek and Oriental mystery cults "!
" Some interpreters of Paul," he says, " believe that he
shared this conception of magical initiation into possession of occult divine power. Be that as it may," he
lightly adds—and so forth. And this, with that characteristic, instinctive, passionate " *Procul! procul!* " of
Paul, standing in the Epistle to the Ephesians, to cry
shame on the suggestion: " Have no fellowship with the
unfruitful works of darkness, but rather reprove them.
For it is a shame even to speak of the things done by
them in secret "—language that might well be applied, if
indeed it was not meant by Paul to be specifically applied, to the infamous lewd orgies practised in those
mysteries which it is here hinted might be closely related
to the " Pauline conception of redemption "! To such
extremity is modern scientifico-historical criticism reduced in the effort to get rid of God in accounting for
Paul and for Paul's gospel of human salvation!

Now this book, which whistles " traditional theology "
down the wind, is, notwithstanding traits appearing here
and there (not infrequently) of crude thought and careless expression, in the main well written—plausibly written I might justly, in closer characterization, say—and
written with manifest sincere intention on the writer's
part to do good. But it tends to vacate religion of supernaturalism, that is, of divine creative grace in regeneration, and to fill the empty place with critico-historical
scholarship, and evolutionary science. " Content," that

is, truth accepted as ascertained—divinely revealed and attested truth—is gone, and only " method," humanly invented, is left us. As if we could get what we need of redemption by means of a scientifically conducted process of induction from scientifically ascertained and scientifically verified facts!

By the way, the author in his preface pays a graceful, gracious tribute to his fellows in " both the theological and the philosophical faculties of the University of Chicago," " as they have helped me," he says, " through published works and through the more intimate means of personal conversation." These brethren thus seem to constitute among themselves a sodality of fine sanguine young spirits (young, I look down upon them as being, from the height of my superior age!) enlisted together, and animating one another, in the joint enterprise of doing away with the domination of Paul and thus promoting the cause of " modern," " scientific " religion.

It would be an oversight not to make brief allusion to one important point at which this third associate editor may be said to revolt *from,* rather perhaps than *against,* the apostle Paul, and that is Paul's profound doctrine of sin—a doctrine which the kindred spirit of Augustine so impressed, and so permanently impressed, upon the accepted theology of the Christian church. In a published book written by our professor in collaboration with two of his fellow professors (each of the three signs his name to his contribution) under the general title, " Atonement," he holds this language : " The older presentations of the doctrine of the atonement presuppose a poignant conviction of sin [imperfect expression of thought]. . . But the conditions which made such a conviction of sin natural in former days have passed away [was ever such a conviction of sin *natural?*]. . . Under the influence of the doctrine of evolution, our age is left in doubt whether any such man as Adam ever existed. . . We have learned from biology that death is not due to sin. . . Thus the Pauline basis of appeal to Adam's sin and its fatal consequences fails to affect us. . . But it is misleading to say that the consciousness of sin is not present to-day. . . We are gradually coming to feel the force of certain facts which call forth a new sense of sin." The professor then devotes a few eloquent sentences to denouncing, as it is the present fashion to do in the ears of a popular audience ready to listen and to applaud, the outrages inflicted, through current business methods, upon the laboring classes in our society. " Strong words," he says, " seem appropriate here. The damnable cruelty of it all makes our blood boil. Here, in the mighty ethical revival of our day is to be found the *real* [italics the professor's] sense of sin." Then, by way of bringing home to the individual conscience a wholesome sense of individual responsibility, and not allowing us to content ourselves with simply setting our blood indignantly aboil at other men's transgressions, he asks a series of searching questions, and at length exclaims: " The moment I ask these questions, I find that I am perhaps no whit better than those upon whom I have been calling down maledictions. We are all involved in the social and industrial system which makes these things possible. We are all sharers in the guilt of our age. . . When we face this situation, we leave behind the finished phrases of our theology and talk in naked terms. If we do not use the word sin, it is because it is too conventional to express our deepest convictions. . . In the social consciousness of our age there is latent a sense of moral obliquity which despairs of a *laissez-faire* policy, and which cries out for deliverance. If Christianity can link its doctrine of atonement to this *real* [italics again the professor's] sense of sin, it will not have to devise arguments to persuade men to accept it. . . Democracy demands conversion—a change of heart —as the supreme atonement for the sins of the past." Observe, it is " democracy " that makes the demand,

and the " conversion " demanded constitutes " atonement,"
nay, but " *the* supreme atonement " for past sins. How
different such doctrine as this is from the doctrine of
Paul, how in effect contrary and antagonistic it is, will be
at once obvious to every reader. " The guilt of our
age "! No mention made, no hint apparently present to
the writer's mind, of that plague of every human heart
which Paul felt and taught so passionately in his doctrine of sin! The guilt of Paul's age was not less, perhaps it was greater, than is the guilt of ours, but Paul
was concerned with the guilt of the individual soul. I
must not allow the necessity I feel of compression to
shut out a further exhibit of teaching on the part of this
professor which every reader will recognize as something profoundly abhorrent from Paul: " When the doctrine of evolution discarded the special creation of man,
it made inevitable a changed conception of God. Man
owes his origin not to a transcendent creative act, but to
the slow working out of a world process." It is to be
borne in mind that I am not criticizing this professor's
teaching as false teaching, but only as teaching which,
whether false or true, is in open revolt from Paul, in
virtual revolt against Paul.

I revert for a moment to that latest book of our professor already remarked upon, to find a passage similar
in tenor to what has just been shown—fundamentally
similar, but with a very singular difference in form of
expression. " The conception [Paul's, derived from Jesus
Christ] of ' natural ' man as corrupt and unworthy, the
belief in the necessity of a miraculous transformation
through regeneration, the representation of Christian
goodness as something bestowed upon one from a higher
realm rather than as something worked out from within "—this language, which accurately enough describes
" Paulinism," describes also a doctrine which our professor rejects. He says it formulates theology " in terms
of *aristocratic* privilege." The word " aristocratic "

recurs again and again, e. g.: " So long as men did their thinking in terms of *aristocratic* distinctions "; " a theology [Paul's] which represented the relation between God and man in *aristocratic* terms "; " *aristocratic* ethics "; with the advance of " democracy " " the ethics of *aristocracy* will be challenged "; " in so far as theology embodies *aristocratic* principles, it too meets with adverse criticism "; " the biblical writers [in the view of this democratic age] take their place among their fellow men claiming no *aristocratic* immunity from the common temptations and weaknesses of humanity "; " the pathway to citizenship in the kingdom of heaven must not [" democracy " demands] be barred by *aristocratic* conditions." This rhetoric is vague perhaps, but the drift of meaning is plain enough, namely, that present-day dominant " democracy " makes Paul an impossible anachronism. And, with Paul, Jesus perhaps? For did not Jesus impose an " *aristocratic* condition " when he told Nicodemus, " Ye must be born again "; also when, in answer to his disciples' " Are there few that be saved? " he said: " Strive to enter in through the *strait* gate; for many, I say to you, will seek to enter in and will not be able." But " democracy " says: " The pathway to citizenship in the kingdom of heaven must not be barred by *aristocratic* conditions." " Aristocratic "! Spurgeon, for example, preached Paul's theology; Spurgeon's preaching " aristocratic "! The common people that heard him gladly never dreamed it. Was Paul the founder of an aristocracy? If so, it was an aristocracy of a very peculiar order. Paul's own words may be quoted to describe it: " For see your calling, brethren, that not many are wise after the flesh, not many mighty, not many noble; but God chose the foolish things of the world . . and the weak things of the world . . . and the base things of the world." But these were " chosen " by God, and they thus did undoubtedly constitute a class of persons who, by a violent (quasi-demagogical?) application of language, could be called an "aristocracy." They were the "saved," out of the general mass of the unsaved. Does the "democracy" of the age, in the opinion of our professor of dogmatic theology, demand that *this* "aristocratic" distinction be obliterated? Paul's theology would gladly obliterate it; how? Not by removing Christ's "strait gate" of entrance into his kingdom; nay, by transferring (*through* Christ's "strait gate") all the unsaved into the ranks of the saved! But the immediate purpose here is simply to show the revolt against Paul flagrant in the University of Chicago at the innermost citadel of his doctrine concerning the human need of redemption.

A fourth editor is an honorably outspoken man, who, with characteristic manly unreserve, conversing with me, confessed himself outright a Unitarian in belief.

A fifth editor is that professor who, not very long ago, intrepidly ventured forth by himself into the open, as a kind of solitary advance-guard, to draw the fire of the opposing force, if such force there should prove to be, and to learn by experiment how much might wisely be risked by a Baptist professor in a Baptist School of Divinity in the way of untrammeled free thought and free expression. Horne Tooke, I believe it was, who was once asked how much treason a man might write in England and not hang for it. 'I don't know yet,' he replied, 'but I am trying to find out by experiment.' The advance-guard's experience has thus far seemed to indicate that the body behind him may advance safely on his path as far and as fast as they please.

And he had put himself on record, in a printed book published by the University of Chicago Press, as holding and teaching the view that Paul's heavenly Christ is a "myth"!

It is at least interesting and curious, perhaps also significant, as showing how little seriously, with what light-hearted *insouciance,* these editorial professors take their responsibility, in inviting and publishing such an article as that by Weiss, and I accordingly mention the fact, which I learned directly from a considerable proportion of their number that they have not read the article. One of these was a leading man among the " Managing Editors." I asked him whether Weiss's article was about what he expected it would be. " I have not read it," he said; this was several months after it appeared. Most of the other members of the editorial corps to whom I addressed an inquiry on the subject returned the same answer.

Now let me repeat that I do not doubt the perfect sincerity of all those of whom I have thus been speaking. They unquestionably think that they hold the truth. If they do hold the truth, they are rendering a valuable service to the church and to the world, and they are to be praised, not blamed. I do not blame them. I think they are wrong, but whether they are wrong or right, *they certainly are in revolt against Paul.* This I cannot help believing to be an attitude and an activity on their part to be deeply deplored. For, at this moment of crisis, I am firmly convinced, belief in Paul as the accredited and authoritative organ of the Lord Christ in the heavens is by eminence an article, not to say *the* article, of the standing or falling church.

Q

CHAPTER IX

FACE TO FACE WITH PAUL THE MAN

"THE end of a production should always call to mind its beginning."

I have thus quoted a wise saying of Joubert, a celebrated, but not sufficiently celebrated, French maxim-maker. The principle announced is sound and sagacious, applied anywhere in literature. It may certainly be well applied here. After the interlude, I will not say digression, that has immediately preceded, one feels the need of a frank and open return to Paul the man. This return is accomplished in a manner that will no doubt strike the reader as unusual, in the following verses, which in effect resume in a dramatico-lyrical form, the apologetic of the book. No reader who has felt the fervor of conviction that throbs throughout the preceding pages, will wonder that the author of such a work, he being supposed a poet, should be conscious of an impulse, and should yield to it, to essay rising from the levels of prose into the higher realm of poetic expression, in treating his subject.

I made a venture of this sort once before, in a different book, published several years ago, " Modern Masters of Pulpit Discourse," and I was chagrined to learn, from the frank acknowledgment of two of my most valued readers, that though they had read everything between the covers *except* the verse, they had not read that! One of these readers was a brilliant and accomplished university professor who testified that he had read the book throughout *three times*. And *three times* he had made that important omission! I make this humiliating disclosure about these two discriminating readers, in the way of leading up to an earnest deprecation of the serving of such treatment by any one upon the poem that follows.

I am becoming more confidential than it is prudent for me to be before the public, but I beg the privilege of adding that of still another book of mine, " The Epic of Paul," a very long narrative poem, a gentleman told me, " I read it all at a sitting "; and then, observing perhaps—who knows?—too expansive a smile of pleasure on my face, he went on mischievously, " It was not for the poetry, it was for the story." I dare assure any reader of this book that, whether or not he finds the poem following good as a poem, he cannot fail to find it good as an argument, and therefore appropriately enough included here. Let me hope then that *all* my readers will do their author the kindness faithfully to read the verses following— with which he completes and closes the present volume.

I

O Thou, the most victorious soul
    That ever quickened human clay—
Eyes always fastened to the goal,
    Feet always instant on the way—

Tell me the secret of thy power
    To do, to suffer, and prevail;
Whence hadst thou thine exhaustless dower
    Of force incapable to fail?

How didst thou overcome the world?
    Why was it that not all the weight
Of all those woes upon thee hurled
    Could thy high heart of hope abate?

Why was it that not all the shame
    That evil-minded men might hiss
From tongues of scorn upon thy name
    Could taint the fountains of thy bliss?

Why, that disease indeed could break
   Thy body toward the dust of death,
But could not thy firm spirit shake
   To make thee draw one halting breath?

Why, that no trouble of the mind,
   No flutter in the anxious breast,
Could ever the fast bond unbind
   That bound thee safe in perfect rest?

II

But didst thou always thus indeed
   Inviolate keep the peace of Christ?
O brother of my soul, I need
   To know, Has thus one man sufficed?

When thousand little things perplexed,
   When waywardnesses, whims perverse,
Obstructive, in thy fellows, vexed—
   Small trials oft than great ones worse—

Say, didst thou then bide ever calm,
   Ever thy soul in peace possess,
As to the music of a psalm
   Moving amid life's daily stress?

Would those who saw thee hourly nigh,
   Who with thee dwelt in mutual touch—
Challenged for witness—testify
   That the great Paul was always such,

In mien, in port, in deed, in word,
   Through all the least assays of life,
As when to write those letters stirred,
   So with high calls to virtue rife?

III

Which will Paul answer? Yea? Or Nay?
   I hardly know which better were.
If he should roundly answer, Yea,
   It might more damp my spirit than spur—

To feel how far the mark I miss;
   Yet heartening were it but to know
That some one had attained to this,
   Had touched the goal toward which I go.

But should Paul answer thus instead:
   Nay, I attained not what I taught;
That goal I sighted far ahead,
   And only thither wrought and sought,

Winning some distance day by day
   Toward the perfection that I saw
Recede before me on the way,
   And fairer, nearer Christ, withdraw—

Seems that a solace it would be;
   For I should think, Perhaps my Lord
Will patience have and pity me,
   Nor mete me out too strict award.

If he, even he, victorious Paul,
   Strove only, and did not attain,
Then I, even I, need never fall
   Desponding as to strive were vain.

IV

And this, O Paul, indeed was thine,
   To struggle and not count thine aim
To have been apprehended. Mine,
   Let it be mine, to do the same!

Yet tell me, thou crowned conqueror,
　　How was it thou hadst heart to strive—
Not one misgiving, one demur—
　　And naught to keep good hope alive?

" Nay, but thou much mistakest now,
　　O brother striver, after me,"
I hear Paul say; " remember thou,
　　I knew that I should conqueror be,

" At last, and rich results should reap,
　　If but I did not cease to strive;
That knowledge well availed to keep
　　My courage and my hope alive."

V

My thought had been not to postpone
　　Paul's victory to after time;
To strive as he strove, that alone,
　　Had seemed a victory sublime.

Was there sublimer victory his
　　In prospect? Was he to achieve?
A glorious crown of victory is
　　Achieving, yea; and to believe

That such a crown awaited him,
　　Invisible as yet, but sure,
With faith no failure here could dim—
　　That well might help him so endure.

But thou, O Paul, tell me once more—
　　That faith of future victory thine,
Which thus thy spirit still upbore,
　　As with a buoyancy divine—

Whence came it? Or how won'st it thou?
    Was it sheer confidence of strength
Thine, made thee, spite of failure now,
    Secure of triumphing at length?

Reliance on one's own resource,
    The presage of achievement, prize
Of effort, and one's native force
    Ever in joyous exercise—

That is last proof of nature high,
    Of spirit to be victor born;
It is itself a victory
    That laughs discomfiture to scorn.

Twice victor then, O Paul, wert thou;
    First, by firm fortitude to strive,
Defying failure thee to cow,
    Next, by brave hope kept still alive.

VI

Alas, it was Paul's greatness then
    Him that illustrious conqueror made;
" Alas," for all we lesser men
    See in this light our prospects fade.

O Paul! O Paul! I am cast down,
    Not lifted up, because of thee!
I never shall obtain thy crown,
    Victory like thine is not for me!

But Paul makes answer to my sigh:
    " No strength, nay, only weakness mine,
I won because it was not I,
    But Christ in me. A gift divine

" To me my victory was, and is,
　　No trophy to be worn in pride,
But purchase of his agonies
　　Who once to win it for me died.

" Now unto God our Father be
　　Eternal thanks and glory given,
Who unto us the victory
　　Gives, through his Son; by whom were riven,

" Once and for all, the gates of death,
　　When he in triumph from the grave
Rose, and above the land of breath
　　Ascended, girt with power to save!"

VII

Raptures like these of laud from Paul,
　　Ascriptions high, doxologies,
As on resistless pinions all
　　Upbear me into ecstasies—

And still I ask, How did he know,
　　Or did Paul know, that Christ arose,
And, beyond height exalted so,
　　Has might to vanquish all our foes?

Our foes, not Paul's alone, but ours,
　　For of the victory as to " us "
Given he speaks.   Are heavenly powers
　　Then for us too embattled thus?

VIII

Had Paul my hidden doubt divined?
　　He answered and abolished it;
I felt as might the finite mind
　　In contact with the infinite.

Paul spoke of that stupendous hour
    When, to raise Jesus from the dead,
God put forth his almighty power,
    And—death and hell discomfited—

Enthroned him at his own right hand,
    Amid the heavenlies, far above
All hierarchies of command,
    Executors of wrath or love,

And far above whatever name
    Of lordship or authority—
In this world or the next, the same—
    The Prince supreme of princes, he!

Paul's words themselves declaring this
    Heaved with a mighty swell and surge,
As when the sea in its abyss
    Feels earthquake underneath it urge.

IX

With passion and with power he spoke;
    A certain indignation sweet,
Sweet but intense, within him woke,
    As thus he made his answer meet:

" How did I know that Christ arose?
    I felt his resurrection power,
In great regenerative throes,
    Renewing me from hour to hour.

" How did I know that Christ arose?
    Did he not meet me on my way
Damascusward, in quest of those
    Whom thence I might bring bound, to slay,

" Only for that they loved my Lord!
   Alas, not known by me as mine,
Him against whom I madly warred!
   He met me, and, oh, love divine!

" Did not at once destroy me quite,
   But only smote me to the ground
With a hailstorm of heavenly light,
   And thunder-burst of heavenly sound,

" Awful and heavenly sound, which said,
   Why dost thou persecute me, Saul?
And when I, less alive than dead—
   So did that light, that sound, appal!—

" Asked, Who art thou? to me replied,
   I Jesus am of Nazareth—
Then, then, I knew that he who died
   On Calvary was Lord of death,

" And that all power on earth, in heaven,
   As in the invaded underworld,
To Christ, the Crucified, was given,
   Who had that light upon me hurled!

" Nor has he since then ever ceased—
   But, since, his voice sounds heavenly soft,
(Each hour the softness seems increased!)—
   To tell me, many a time and oft,

" The things I need to know, that I
   His will may truly, only, teach.
His will is He—my calling high
   Christ as the Lord of all to preach.

X

" Deem'st thou I could have counted so
    As nothing, less than nothing, all
I once had valued here below,
    Have been from Saul transformed to Paul,

" Had I not known that Christ was risen,
    And was ascended up on high?
Could have sung triumph-songs in prison,
    Explored the earth from sky to sky,

" Still journeying, at uncounted cost—
    Sickness, and weariness, and pain,
Faintness from fasting, shipwreck; tost
    With tempest naked in the main;

" In perils ever, every form,
    Rivers and robbers; wilderness
And city; buffeted with storm;
    Worse buffeted with sore distress

" From plots among my countrymen
    Against me, yea, from traitorhood
Nourished among my brethren; then,
    By whom I most would serve, withstood,

" The Gentiles; oft in hunger, thirst,
    Cold, nakedness, denials of sleep,
Travail, imprisonment, and—worst
    Anguish imprisonment can keep

" For the quick spirit—enforced arrest
    Of travail; thrice, the Roman rod;
The scourge, five times, at Jewish hest;
    Stoned, and for dead left on the sod·

" All these things, and besides them all,
    The ceaseless care I could but feel
For what the churches might befall,
    My heart atremble to appeal,

" If any suffered, or was glad—
    Who was there weak, but he in me
A fellow in his weakness had?—
    Charged with vicarious sympathy,

" Which made me toward my brethren yearn
    In costly quivers of the heart;
If any stumbled, I would burn
    Fervid to take the stumbler's part—

" Thus lived I, thus I daily died,
    Say rather, for so many deaths
I suffered for the Crucified
    As were the tally of my breaths.

XI

" Say, O stout-hearted to believe,
    Believ'st thou Paul indeed did thus
Of free-will choice his lot receive,
    Fought with wild beasts at Ephesus,

" All for a Christ he did not know
    Had risen in glory from the dead,
And had, ascending, made a show
    Of subject powers in triumph led?

" Nay, nay, my brother, slow of heart
    Thou, to believe the grace of God,
While swift, too swift, to choose thy part
    Believing downward toward the clod,

" I knew, I knew, whom I believed,
  I trusted him with perfect trust;
He would not let me be deceived,
  I should rise with him from the dust!"

XII

Abashed, ashamed, I rallied yet
  To say: O Paul, forgive once more,
Nor, though I show my folly, let
  My folly vex thee, I implore.

If thou hadst but believed, not known,
  That Christ was quickened from the dead,
And sat on an almighty throne,
  Of principalities the head—

Thy faith alone, without the fact,
  Would not that nobly have sufficed?
What force to fire thy zeal had lacked
  A dead, believed a living, Christ?

" Oh, faithless, thou, to dream that faith
  Could work the miracle of me!
Faith too not faith, but fancy-wraith
  Without pretense of right to be."

But granted faith were such a force,
  Yet whence were such a faith to me?
A reason there must have been, a source,
  To faith like that, or fantasy!

" Something once brought me to receive
  For true that which, before, my whole
Being revolted to believe—
  What was it so subdued my soul?

XIII

" Not argument; I could oppose
　　Their argument with argument;
It was not witness borne by those
　　Who followed Jesus where he went

" While living, and who testified,
　　Never so stoutly, they had seen
Their Master after that he died;
　　Had forty days long with him been,

" At intervals; had with him talked;
　　Had seen him eat and drink; had heard
His, Peace be unto you; had walked
　　With him, their hearts within them stirred

" To burning, as, upon the way,
　　He spake and opened unto them
The Scriptures, insomuch that they
　　Felt they had touched the garment's hem

" Of some one heavenly—afterward,
　　Clear, in the breaking of the bread,
Revealed to them as Christ the Lord,
　　Indeed, then, risen from the dead!

" Witness so strong could not avail
　　To shame my froward unbelief;
I listened often to the tale,
　　Only each time with deeper grief,

" More burning scorn, to hear it told—
　　With strange additions thereunto
In repetition manifold,
　　As would each teller fain outdo

" His fellow, and make marvel more:
 How once, they, being in secret met,
Their Lord had entered through the door
 Fast shut, and shut remaining yet;

" And how, at length, before their eyes
 Their Master, after forty days
Of tarrying with them, they saw rise
 Till heaven received him from their gaze.

" And when he thus to view was lost,
 They tarrying in Jerusalem
Until the day of Pentecost,
 And waiting what would happen them,

" How then their Lord, arrived in heaven,
 There welcomed by the heavenly host,
Had thence sent down upon the Eleven
 The promise of the Holy Ghost,

" In sound as of a rushing blast
 Of mighty wind with solemn boom;
And there were tongues like fire that fas
 Clung to each one within the room.

XIV

" Strange that all this I could resist!
 But so I did, perversely blind;
My eyes were holden, and I missed
 To let the light into my mind—

" Because my heart, which held the key,
 Had locked it shut; I do not know
What lesser proof had mastered me
 Than that great light which laid me low.

" Oh, the exceeding grace of God
　　Toward me, such ill-deserving one,
To lay me level with the clod—
　　Lowly enough to know his Son!

" Thus, and not otherwise, was I
　　Bond-servant of Christ Jesus made;
Less than Lord throned in power on high
　　Had never such as Paul obeyed.

XV

" Or did I haply a chance flash
　　Of lightning in a cloudless sky,
With, after that, a muttering crash
　　Of thunder breaking from on high,

" Mistake for a supernal flame
　　Of glory drowning out the sun,
And for words uttered, with my name,
　　Distinctly dropping one by one,

" Like gentle thunderbolts of sound,
　　That framed a question dread to hear—
But, lying prostrate on the ground,
　　My body all was as one ear!—

" Was this, forsooth, illusion pure,
　　Which, nathless, through long years of strife
Helped me a thousand deaths endure,
　　And made a triumph of my life?

" Did Paul behave like one distraught?
　　Read thee his letters once again,
Think of the homely things he taught,
　　And wholesome, to plain common men.

" What am I saying? Wilt thou hence
   Ask, Is not Paul once more become
A fool in this his confidence
   Of boasting? Were I wiser dumb,

" Than speaking thus? Perhaps; but I
   Gladly am fool for Christ. And thou,
Let me, with even my folly, try
   If I may meet thy folly now.

XVI

" Was Paul a mystic? Yea, and, Nay.
   With high transcendences he dealt,
Doubtless, but with them mixed alway
   Things the most sanely thought and felt.

" This ever to the utter end,
   The earthly utter end of all;
Thy quest through history extend,
   And find no saner soul than Paul.

" God kept me such, against the stress
   Of strong temptation to aspire
Above just measure through excess
   Of revelations more and higher.

" Vouchsafed to me beyond my peers.
   Effectual means his wisdom found
To let me breathe in other spheres,
   With yet my feet firm on the ground.

" A thorn he planted in my flesh,
   Sharp plague and torment to my pride,
Reminding me at need afresh
   That self must still be crucified.

" Concerning this, I thrice besought
  My Lord that it might be removed;
His grace would make my suffering naught,
  But leave my patience to be proved!"

XVII

O Paul, O Paul, enough, enough!
  With all these doubts and questions mine,
Well had I earned a round rebuff,
  Rather than gentleness like thine.

XVIII

Greatheart, all blessings on his name!
  But for his faith my faith had failed;
I, if at last not put to shame,
  To him shall owe it I prevailed.

But nay, oh, nay! I do him wrong,
  And miss his spirit, speaking thus;
Loudest amid the ransomed throng
  His voice I hear, " Not unto us!"

To him then not, yet *for* him, yea,
  Let me forever thanks accord;
'Mid gifts received and many they,
  Still the chief place to Paul award!